The Divine Nature

Copyright © 2014 Derick Moody
rights reserved.

ISBN: 978-1-7340906-2-8

For my dear Emma,

*A sweet, celestial star
unsuppressed by the dark blanket of space.*

*As a star's sparkle
displays a distant dance of past lights,
I gaze upon shimmering glows of a vanished brightness
and am warmed thereby.*

*Time impedes our embrace,
yet your sweetness twinkles across eternity
and keeps my steps straight through the lonely twilight;
and shall until the Son rises.*

*I love you.
I will love you past all veils,
time and darkness.*

*May this proof of my love
penetrate the night
which parts us.*

CONTENTS

1	Godliness	1
2	Love	13
3	Charity	24
4	Compassion	36
5	Mercy	52
6	Kindness	63
7	Selflessness	72
8	Humility	84
9	Faith	104
10	Courage	115
11	Hope	126
12	Joy	138
13	Longsuffering	151
14	Justice	165
15	Wisdom	179
16	Honor	189
17	The Gifts of the Spirit	205

Godliness

"*Arise, shine; for thy light is come, and the glory of the* LORD *is risen upon thee.*"[1] Even "*the glory which* [you] *had with* [God] *before the world was.*"[2] Have you seen it? The hidden gem; that immortal star shrouded by the seemingly boundless void of space and time.

"*For, behold, darkness shall cover the earth, and gross darkness the people: but the* LORD *shall arise upon thee, and his glory shall be seen upon thee.*"[3] Can you see it? This divine light, "*Which light proceedeth forth from the presence of God to fill the immensity of space.*"[4] "*The light which is in all things, which giveth life to all things, … the light which shineth, which giveth you light.*"[5] Truly, this light is in all things. It is everywhere. He is everywhere, here and now. The Almighty is in you. Search your soul; there you will find that pulsing power planted inside you. This light will illuminate your vision and reveal to you, your divine nature. Look closely and you will see its secret glow shining in you and all those who surround you. "*God is in you of a truth.*"[6]

The monotonous machine of mortal life masks mankind's magnificent sublimity. Day by busy day, we carry on with life's repetitive projects hardly noticing one of Heaven's most remarkable revelations. It is there hiding behind the backdrop of hum drum routines. Whether due to routine or ignorance, far too many of us are sleepwalking through life. Hours and opportunities pass us by like cars on a highway, and though we are trapped in the heavy traffic of God's fortune, so many are stuck senselessly staring at their surroundings.

Every minute, masses of people miss out on some of God's most resplendent sermons. Wherever you go and whatever you may be doing – talking on a phone, driving to work, walking down a hall, or even looking in

---

[1] Isaiah 60:1
[2] John 17:5 – "… O Father, glorify thou me with thine own self with the glory which I had with thee before the world was."
[3] Isaiah 60:2
[4] D&C 88:12
[5] D&C 88:13,11
[6] 1 Cor 14:25

the mirror – a celestial secret is sounding in every direction. It would seem inappropriate to label something with such widespread exposure a secret, were it not receiving such pandemic disregard.

It's time to awaken from predictable daily droning and start listening to the testimonies that accompany every second of life. *"Day unto day uttereth speech, and night unto night sheweth knowledge. There is no speech nor language, where their voice is not heard. Their line is gone out through all the earth, and their words to the end of the world."*[7]

Have you heard the testimony of the stars or listened to the voice of knowledge spoken by the very earth upon which you stand? The earth, stars and space constantly resonate a record of God's work. However, there still remains a more powerful and pervasive proclamation than that which comes from the beautiful background of life. It is in life's foreground that we find this ever-flowing, yet untapped stream of insight.

More persuasive than our unconscious surroundings are the convincing declarations coming from life's basic building blocks. Were not the heavens, the earth, and all that is contained therein created as subsidiaries to the Lord's greatest work? Concluding the formation of the earth with its scenery and animal life, God said, *"Let us make man in our image, after our likeness."*[8] Surely, those impressed by the testimonies spoken by the earth and skies should fall down in stunning wonder over God's most prominent creation.

You are that creation! Your life, including your expressions, talents and behaviors are a continual proclamation of your Creator. You are a walking testament, together with each brother and sister under *"the Father of our Lord Jesus Christ, of whom the whole family in Heaven and earth is named."*[9] In faces we see every day is a most glorious display of God's grandeur. Their personalities allow us to peek at portions of perfection.

But what is the content of these testimonies? What message or principle is disclosed in mankind? Are the revelations acquired from mankind, tiny droplets lost in the vast ocean of 'all things denoting there is a God?'[10] No doubt, your life and existence is evidence of God's own existence; however, God intends us to glean greater knowledge from our interactions with man – His most precious creation.

The Apostle Paul touched on this topic in a letter to the

---

[7] Psalms 19:2-4
[8] Genesis 1:27 – "God created man in his own image, in the image of God created he him; male and female created he them."
[9] Ephesians 3:14,15
[10] See Alma 30:44 – "all things denote there is a God"

Corinthians stating, *"God, that comforteth those that are cast down, comforted us by the coming of Titus."*[11] The essence here, though simple, is savory – God comforted these people specifically through the instrumentality of a mortal man. Titus, an imperfect person acted as an extension of God's flawless expressions of comfort. Thus the recipients of Titus's consoling gestures, if attentive, could see a shadow of God's supreme expressions of comfort.

Similarly, every person on earth is sent at times to stand in behalf of God to manifest His majesty. In multiple ways God may *"reveal his Son in* [you],"[12] that *"the life also of Jesus might be made manifest in* [your] *mortal flesh."*[13] For this reason God has commanded, *"Hold up your light that it may shine unto the world."*[14] Nevertheless, the great miracle is that the light we see in others is not their own. Instead we glimpse God's light, for 'He is the light which we hold up.'[15] God, who has *"wrought all our works in us,"*[16] exhibits His personality through the behaviors of people we ignore every day. Reflections of Deity can be seen in everyone; for man is created *"in the image of God."*[17]

Pay attention! For even an average, ordinary person can be a special pulpit from which God will speak some of His sweetest sermons. These spiritual lessons can be accessed in casual conversations, in business, play or any human interaction. Consider how much godliness pours out of some people's personalities. Have you not seen portions of God's compassion as others offered you a helping hand? Can you spot imprints of God's patience in examples of people you know? Perceptive children may detect the charity of God by observing the selfless care of their parents. Even something as simple as a smile from a stranger can send a gleam of God's own cheery temperament.

The most remarkable things are revealed within our relationships! Insight into God's personality can be acquired in any association. Yet, remember this is most intentionally true in our closest associations – friends and family. Considering such a substantial amount of one's mortal life is

---

[11] 2 Corinthians 7:6
[12] Galatians 1:16 – See vs.15: "But when it pleased God, who separated me from my mother's womb ... To reveal his son in me"
[13] 2 Corinthians 4:11 – Brackets added: see vs.10) "that the life also of Jesus might be made manifest in our body."
[14] 3 Nephi 18:24
[15] 3 Nephi 18:24 – "Behold I am the light which ye shall hold up – that which ye have seen me do."
[16] Isaiah 26:12 – "LORD, thou wilt ordain peace for us: for thou also hast wrought all our works in us."
[17] Genesis 1: 27 – "God created man in his own image, in the image of God created he him; male and female created he them."

spent within a small circle of relationships, it is fair to assume that our Omnipotent God, who "*hath determined the times before appointed, and the bounds of* [our] *habitation,*"[18] labors heavily over the detail of such circles of influence. Through the prepared instrumentality of friends and family, God gives each of us targeted teachings on His divine traits.

    Make no mistake, there is plentiful purpose in the close relationships God arranged for you. Is not your understanding of the depth of God's love developed from the love shown by your parents? Have you seen flashes of Heavenly Father's forgiveness in friendships? Can you discern signs of God's commitment to you in the covenants made between husband and wife? It is not by studying scripture or even the school of suffering that God most commonly unveils His character. This epiphany is mostly learned in living. It is most readily accessed in our everyday encounters with common people. Man is a canvas whereon the Spirit paints a portraiture of God. With an inspired eye we can catch these persistent portrayals of the Sublime taking place in all of our interactions.

    The beauties of the earth cannot compete with the beautiful glow of godliness residing in human beings. Through the blessing of the Divine Spirit, we comprehend the inherent glories in God's creations. In man we see many of God's greatest marvels, and may discover profound and eternal doctrines. On this matter the scriptures say, "**He hath made everything beautiful in his time**: *also he hath set the eternal in their heart without which man cannot find out the work that God hath done.*"[19] Heavenly Father makes things beautiful. He is behind all beauty – this is His work and His glory.

    Regarding God's work, we recall the familiar verse, "*For behold, this is my work and my glory – to bring to pass the immortality and eternal life of man.*"[20] Yet, these processes of immortality and eternal life can also be described in a context of beautification. As God sanctifies our character, life and light is infused into our soul; we are made beautiful, and our countenances begin to shine with a celestial sparkle. In this way the Father extends His glory to men and fills everything He touches with His beautiful light.

    Nevertheless, it is not enough for us to enjoy the warmth of this principle from a distance. No, this truth must be felt at the heat of the hearth. Therefore know that God's work is to make you beautiful, to glorify you, to build you, and fill you with light. With the 'Eternal' Spirit in your heart, the process of beautification can be seen all around you – within

---

[18] Acts 17:26 – Brackets added
[19] Ecclesiastes 3:11 – Emphasis added – Original verse is replaced with the Hebrew translation found in footnote b
[20] Moses 1:39

yourself and the lives of others. Once aware of God's patient process of beautification, we can better comprehend 'His work and His glory.' But this is not all. If our eyes are keen, we may perceive the very thoughts and intents of God's heart which move His hands.

Over the ages philosophers have puzzled over humanity's unique collection of qualities. Observing the interplay of these qualities, they pondered the enigmatic meanings of this mortal life. Such philosophical inquiries are not so unlike that of the psalmist who wondered, *"What is man, that thou art mindful of him? and the son of man, that thou visitest him?"*[21] Knowing the significance of such questions, it is not coincidental that the scriptural canon begins with this unveiling about the cryptic capacities of mankind – *"And God said, Let us make man in our image, after our likeness."*[22]

What does it mean to be made in God's image? In what ways are mortal men made in the likeness of the Immortal God? Aiding our interpretation of the word *likeness*, we learn in a later verse, *"Seest thou that ye are created after mine own image? Yea, even all men were created in the beginning after mine own image. Behold, this body, which ye now behold, is the body of my spirit: and man have I created after the body of my spirit."*[23]

Now the notion that our physical structure resembles the appearance of Deity should not be devalued. We know well that Satan's timely temptations can be deflected by using a shield of understood doctrines. Such was true for Moses when he confronted the master of darkness face to face. Here Moses utilized this same truth to parry the adversary's attacks. With faith in his identity, *"Moses looked upon Satan and said: Who art thou? For behold,* **I am a son of God, in the similitude of his Only Begotten;** *and where is thy glory, that I should worship thee?"*[24] Moses's maneuver to counter Satan has not lost any practical relevance or efficacy in our own situations. However, man's similitude to God reaches far beyond comparatively frivolous physical features.

Though aware of the physical similitude between man and God, the Prophet Alma still posed the questions, *"can you look up, having the image of God engraven upon your countenances?"* and *"Have ye received his image in your countenances?"* [25] If man by birth is naturally fashioned after the image of God, why raise these questions? It is therefore apparent that man reflects God's image in ways that are different from the physical. In fact, Alma

---

[21] Psalms 8:4
[22] Genesis 1:26
[23] Ether 3:15,16
[24] Moses 1:13 – Emphasis added
[25] Alma 5:14 and Alma 5:19

gives this alternative "image of God" priority in terms of life and salvation.

Our shared physical characteristics with God will not grant us automatic entry into the Celestial world. As we ponder the possible meanings of this 'image in our countenance,' we should recall the teachings of Peter, who coined the term, *"the divine nature."* We read, *"According as his divine power hath given unto all things that pertain unto life and godliness, through the knowledge of him that hath called us to glory and virtue: Whereby are given unto us exceeding great and precious promises: that by these ye might be partakers of the divine nature."*[26]

God has given us the *"precious promises"* of being able to partake of the things pertaining to *"life and godliness."* By answering God's call to *"glory and virtue,"* we partake of His *"divine power"* that rests within us, even our *"divine nature."* Mankind, the pinnacle of God's creations can cultivate this divine nature. The sacred countenance of God can be carved into our character.

Further insight into Peter's rich conceptual couplet is obtained by analyzing the Greek words for divine and nature. The divine nature or Greek *theios phusis*, contains the connotation of godly growths. *Theios* derives from the word *theos* meaning *God*, it is a straight forward translation literally meaning *divine, godly or god-like*. The same root word *theos* is recognizable in our word theology, the study of God. On the other hand, the word *phusis*, translated as *nature* carries an additional informative image. *Phusis* means *disposition, constitution or the nature of a person*.[27] *Phusis* contains the root word *phuo*, meaning *to puff or swell up* in the sense of sprouting, germinating and growths. Thus by virtue of humanity's Eternal heritage, we have an inherent endowment of Celestial seeds residing in our souls.

God has planted in every person spiritual capacities that partially depict His own holiness. These spiritual seeds are seen in qualities such as *"faith, virtue, knowledge, temperance, patience, brotherly kindness,* [devotion,][28] *charity, humility, and diligence."*[29] Ironically the uniqueness we find in ourselves and label our humanity is not a substance coded in our mortal genetics; rather, these magnificent traits in man are evidences of the godliness residing in our souls. The *"beauty of holiness"* [30] shines in man's

---

[26] 2 Peter 1:3,4
[27] Greek Strong's Dictionary #5453 pronounced (foo'-o) and 5449 (foo'– Sis)
[28] Greek Strong's Dictionary #2150 – Godliness – eusebeia – (yoo-seb-i-ah-) built with two parts: eu meaning well and sebomai (seb'-om-ahee) which is piety or to be devout. Sebomai is a disposition or desire to please God.
[29] See 2 Peter1:4-7 and D&C 4:6
[30] Psalms 96:9 – "O worship the LORD in the beauty of holiness: fear before him, all the earth."

countenances. If we will 'partake of this divine nature,' it will grow brighter and brighter till the 'shew of our countenance will witness **for** us'[31] that we are *"heirs of God, and joint-heirs with Christ."*[32]

The doctrine of the divine nature offers clues not only to our identity, but to our potential. Mankind's divine seeds show merely a shadow[33] of our Sovereign Father; yet when in full bloom, these seeds grow into a countenance of confidence allowing us to *"wax strong in the presence of God."*[34] As the Psalmist wrote, *"I will behold thy face in righteousness: I shall be satisfied, when I awake, with thy likeness."*[35] This likeness comes only by traveling the straight and narrow *"way of holiness."*[36] – a path wherein God sanctifies His children, till they *"shall be holy "*[37] after the image of the *"Man of Holiness."*[38]

Pay close attention to those around you. Observe their behaviors both subtle and large. Search for the rooted principles in their hearts which consequently motivate their movements. Through this practice you will see how man's noble qualities are outgrowths of God's divine characteristics. All people have within them at least some degree of courage, honesty, mercy, kindness, love, humility and justice. Are not these the very virtues of the Almighty God? Consider the wonder in it all, part of God is in you! Images of God's nature and conduct are being revealed in the lives of mere mortal men.

Every person is a miraculous revelation! From the dull, ugly and deformed to the unpopular, unintelligent and undistinguished, even including the prideful, brutish and vain – no man is an exception to their spiritual genetics. Since godliness is seeded in our souls, any person can cultivate their noble birthright, if properly nourished. Of necessity such a

---

[31] See Isaiah 3:9 – Original: "The shew of their countenance doth witness against them"
[32] Romans 8:17 – vs 16"The Spirit itself beareth witness with our spirit, that we are the children of God: 17) And if children, then heirs; heirs of God, and joint-heirs with Christ; if so be that we suffer with him"
[33] Hebrew Strong's Dictionary #6754 – tselem (tseh' – lem) – Tselem means a statue, as in a replica or representation of an original, tselem similarly means, shade, illusion or shadow: in the sense that a thing is merely a shadow, or shade of the original. Same word is found in Genesis 1:26, 27, 5:3 and 9:6.
[34] D&C 121:45 – "let virtue garnish thy thoughts unceasingly; then shall thy confidence wax strong in the presence of God"
[35] Psalms 17:15
[36] Isaiah 35:8 – "And an highway shall be there, and a way, and it shall be called The way of holiness; the unclean shall not pass over it; but it shall be for those: the wayfaring men, though fools, shall not err therein."
[37] Leviticus 11:44 – " … sanctify yourselves, and ye shall be holy: for I am holy."
[38] Moses 7:35 – "Behold I am God; Man of Holiness is my name; Man of Counsel is my name;" See also Moses 6:57 – "for, in the language of Adam, Man of Holiness is his name."

truth should influence all our interactions; it should have an active behavioral role in all forms of our sociality.

A comparable precept was taught by C.S Lewis who said, "It is a serious thing ... to live in a society of possible gods and goddesses ... It is in the light of these overwhelming possibilities, it is with the awe and the circumspection proper to them, that we should conduct all our dealings with one another, all friendships, all loves, all play, all politics. There are no ordinary people. You have never talked to a mere mortal. Nations, cultures, arts, civilizations–these are mortal, and their life is to ours as the life of a gnat. But it is immortals whom we joke with, work with, marry, snub, and exploit."[39]

Whatever or whoever you are now fades into irrelevance in the context of your extraordinary possibilities. Just as *"all is as one day with God, and time only is measured unto men,"*[40] you should see yourself, and all people, within this new perspective – a perspective defined by potential. Man's identity is best understood in the brightness of what he can become. *"For now we see through a glass, darkly; but then face to face: now I know in part; but then shall I know even as also I am known."*[41] Through the dark glass of carnal concerns we only comprehend ourselves and the universe in part, but as we come closer to Christ our perceptions will begin to pierce eternity.

Your divine nature is not automatically endowed through death. It is not a grave which will 'engraven God's image upon your countenance.' Even while we are held captive beneath the gravity of the flesh, the height to which man can climb is astounding. Due to your divine birthright, you have the potential to cause *"the very power of hell* [to be] *shaken forever."* It is within your capacity to cause 'the devil to never have power over your heart.'[42] This miracle is recorded in the scriptures for all to see. Here we read how the holy city Zion was composed of men who were formerly cruel and unruly. Among Zion's citizens were those *"snatched"*[43] from the vilest sinners on the earth.

Though the mud of mortality dulls our spirit's full splendor, it does not have the power to prevent us from becoming saints in the *"city of our*

---

[39] C.S. Lewis. *The Weight of Glory*. 1942. p.18,19
[40] Alma 40:8
[41] 1 Corinthians 13:12
[42] Alma 48:17 – "if all men had been, and were, an ever would be, like unto Moroni, behold, the very powers of hell would have been shaken forever; yea, the devil would never have power over the hearts of the children of men."
[43] See Mosiah 27:29 – "I was in the darkest abyss ... but I am snatched, and my soul is pained no more."

God."[44] This human potential is not some whimsical fairy tale told to inspire naïve minds. Our capability to copy behaviors of the Lord of the entire Universe is a reality, for we are *"the sons of God, and it doth not yet appear what we shall be: but we know that, when he shall appear,* **we shall be like him***; for we shall see him as he is."*[45]

Never lose sight of how essential developing the Christian character is in the Creator's plan. Too many think of salvation as a product and not as a process. Others describe it as a destination instead of a development. When religion is belittled to a simple game of mastering pious choreography the *"weightier matters of the law, judgment, mercy, and faith"* are left undone.[46] Soul shaping, not sightseeing should be the priority, especially since telestial tourism was never the secret to a provident life.

Heaven is not about getting. Heaven is about becoming something godly so that you are more capable of giving. The Apostle James emphasized this vital but often forgotten truth stating, *"Pure religion and undefiled before God and the Father is this, To visit the fatherless and widows in their affliction, and to keep himself unspotted from the world."*[47] This verse challenges our definition of religion. It even causes us to ponder: How we would describe the religion of the Eternal Father?

The pivoting point of James's message is the interpretation of the word *religion*. Though our current culture has largely left the competitive coliseum of church evangelism typical of the early centuries in American history, we are still regularly asked to identify and explain our beliefs. These opportunities come to us as questions such as – what do you believe or what is your religion?

When responding to these questions, one may pause for a second, fumbling for an idea in the mind's messy attic of memories. After this desperately speedy search, they emerge victorious holding tight to an organizational title – Buddhist, Catholic, Muslim, Mormon, Jew. Stuck in these situations where there may only be seconds to respond, it is not completely unacceptable to spit out a similarly short response. Nevertheless, if the extent of our religion is nothing more than a club name, we err.

Today, too many regard their religion with similar esteem as a

---

[44] See D&C 97:19 – "And all nations of the earth shall honor her, and shall say: Surely Zion is the city of our God"
[45] 1 John 3:2 – Emphasis added
[46] Matthew 23:23 – "Woe unto you, scribes and Pharisees, hypocrites! For pay ye tithe of mint and anise and cumin, and have omitted the weightier matters of the law, judgment, mercy, and faith: these ought ye to have done, and not to leave the other undone."
[47] James 1:27

Costco membership – as if the benefit of faith was some silly card granting exclusive deals on spiritual produce. It is this same unhealthy mindset that has people focusing on trivia instead of truth. What is your religion? Is it an organizational label or is it principles of love and obedience as James suggests? The meaning contained in the word *religion* can be inclusive of every belief, practice, teaching and doctrine. Communicating ideas this large inherently creates many difficulties. As we manage concepts of this size, we are forced to make judgments. We must sift through many possible descriptions in order to select an optimal way of portraying our thoughts. Logically one's final choice of words represents the most pertinent or valuable aspects of our message. If we are correct in making this assumption, then *"pure religion"* according to James is all the more surprising.

Though James's description of religion is astonishing, there are further implications found in the stunning semantics of the word translated into English as *religion*. The Greek word here for religion is – *threskeia*;[48] this word expresses the ceremonial aspects of religious worship, namely its rituals, including temple ordinances. With this expanded definition of religion in mind, reconsider James's words, *"Pure **religion** and undefiled before God and the Father is this, To visit the fatherless and widows in their affliction, and to keep himself unspotted from the world."* Considering the critical and sacred role temple worship has in Christian theology, the consequences of omitting pure religion is terribly severe. However, we should not suppose James's intent is to minimize Christianity's ceremonial rites. Perhaps instead, James is trying to restore the significance of Christian living to its proper place.

When was the last time you participated in the ceremony of service, or sacrificed by offering comforting companionship or conversation? Is living a life of love a daily ritual? Do you pass the bread of brotherly kindness and offer the waters of encouragement? Do you clothe yourselves with chaste and virtuous thoughts? Do you practice the rites of forgiveness and prudence? Just as the ordinances are necessary components of God's plan of redemption, one must not forget that living a godly lifestyle is equally essential. 'Talking of Christ, rejoicing in Christ, preaching of Christ, and prophesying of Christ'[49] may not be enough; we must receive His image

---

[48] Greek Strong's Dictionary #2356 – threskeia (thrace-ki'-ah) derived from 2357 – Threskos (thrace-kos) meaning ceremonious in worship or pious. Threskos has the base of 2360 – Throeo (thro-eh'o) which means to make an outcry, to wail, clamor or cry aloud. Such suggests that ceremony is used as a way of magnifying our cries to the Heaven.

[49] 2 Nephi 25:26 – "And we talk of Christ, we rejoice in Christ, we preach of Christ, we prophesy of Christ"

in our countenances. This is pure religion. Anything less is 'straining at gnats.'[50]

The gospel of Jesus Christ is not about theoretical musings; it is about action. The objective of the gospel is to create changes in our physical world. In order for one's faith to become real, it must pass from the invisible into the tangible. Though a speaker may be successful in conveying some degree of intellectual understanding, know that academic reasoning, no matter how thorough, means nothing if unapplied.

Gospel genius does not excuse sinfulness, neither will scriptural intellect compensate for wickedness. Neal A. Maxwell echoes this principle saying, "Brilliance, by itself, is not wholeness nor happiness. Knowledge, if possessed for its own sake and unapplied, leaves one's life unadorned. ... God possesses perfect knowledge, but He also possesses perfect love, purity, mercy, and so on. What a contrast He is with those mortals who are bright but bad and who are clever but carnal."[51]

Admonitions to apply religious principles are not new. Prophets in every age have urged their listeners to turn academia into desire. Their objective was never just to instruct, but to cause "*a mighty change*"[52] in the hearts of their audience. The Prophets knew that others would "*know of their surety and truth,*" by the Spirit speaking through the mighty change that occurred in them, or in their hearts. [53]

This mighty change of heart can be man's loudest witness that God is working in them. A transformation of character is tactile evidence of the truths responsible for causing those changes. Christ reinforces this principle saying, "*If any man will do his will, he shall know of the doctrine, whether it be of God, or whether I speak of myself.*"[54] Therefore, give heed to the principles of the gospel. Allow them to be written in your heart that they may be born into your behaviors to be "*known and read of all men.*"[55] From time to time, you must also read from the book of your own behaviors to discover the doctrines which determine your daily deeds. In living the precepts of God, "*the record of Heaven ... which quickeneth all things,*"[56] will 'make alive' the truth of your journey. Then, while sojourning the straight and narrow "*thine

---

[50] Matthew 23:24 – "Ye blind guides, which strain at a gnat and swallow a camel."
[51] Neal A. Maxwell. *The Inexhaustible Gospel*. Adapted from a speech given 8/18/1992
[52] Alma 5:12 – (Also see vs. 12-14)
[53] See Mosiah 5:2 – "we know of their surety and truth, because of the Spirit of the Lord Omnipotent, which has wrought a might change in us, or in our hearts, that we have no more disposition to do evil but to do good continually."
[54] John 7:17
[55] 2 Corinthians 3:2 – "Ye are our epistle written in our hearts, known and read of all men:"
[56] Moses 6:61 – "Therefore it is given to abide in you; the record of Heaven; the Comforter...which quickeneth all things, which maketh alive all things"

ears shall hear a word behind thee, saying, This is the way, walk ye in it."[57]

"What is man, that thou shouldest magnify him? and that thou shouldest set thine heart upon him?"[58] "I have said, Ye are gods; and all of you are children of the most High."[59] "Forasmuch then as we are the offspring of God,"[60] we have His divine nature in us. Therefore, "the Lord make you to increase and abound in love one toward another, and toward all men."[61] "For this is the message that ye heard from the beginning, that we should love one another."[62] "Love ye therefore the stranger,"[63] "love thy neighbor,"[64] and "he who loveth God, love his brother also."[65]

"If a man say, I love God, and hateth his brother, he is a liar: for he that loveth not his brother whom he hath seen, how can he love God whom he hath not seen."[66] It should not be hard to "love one another,"[67] because "virtue loveth virtue" and "light cleaveth to light."[68] When we know and love God, His traits become recognizable in others, making it easy to love them. Since our primary objective in life is to learn to love God, we should naturally develop a love for all the people around us – for God is in them. Human love is **the** revelation from and of the Eternal Father, for "we have known and believed the love that God hath to us. God is love; and he that dwelleth in love dwelleth in God, and God in him."[69] Beloved, let us love one another: for love is of God; and every one that loveth is born of God, and knoweth God."[70]

Mankind's divine nature produces partial but parallel representations of God's sacred countenance. Reflections of His glory are mirrored even in common acquaintances; they are modeled in our loved ones. Everyday experiences spectacularly exhibit divine qualities. The brilliant glimmer of godliness radiating from man illuminates our entire earth, and testifies to the world – that man is an image of God.

---

[57] Isaiah 30:21
[58] Job 7:17
[59] Psalms 82:6
[60] Acts 17:29
[61] 1 Thessalonians 3:12
[62] 1 John 3:11
[63] Deuteronomy 10:19
[64] Leviticus 19:18 – "love thy neighbour as thyself."
[65] See 1 John 4:21 – "he who loveth God love his brother also."
[66] 1 John 4:20
[67] John 15:12 – "This is my commandment, That ye love one another, as I loved you."
[68] D&C 88:40
[69] 1 John 4:16
[70] 1 John 4:7

Love

Life isn't a multiple-choice test. No, you will actually need to activate your mind and draw from your memory everything you know and believe. Imagine a sheet of paper landing on a desk in front of you. At the top of the paper in bold letters is one question – **Who is God? Using your own words describe The Divine/Deity.**

How well do you know the being you call God or Father? To what degree can you articulate the characteristics of the being you worship? Could you detect Him without sight or recognize Him purely from His personality? We know these are significant and relevant questions insomuch as, "*this is life eternal, that they might know thee the only true God, and Jesus Christ, whom thou hast sent.*"[1]

Do not suppose that my purpose in posing these questions is solely some Twinkie fluff, rhetorical challenge. Perhaps for a change, take road less traveled; literally grab a paper and start writing. Since we are talking about your God this should be a breeze, shouldn't it?

It would be a shame if one could ramble on for hours about politics, sports teams or a school subject and hardly be capable of carrying on a conversation about the essential qualities of God. Know also that a composition of Sunday school clichés and vague catch phrases may not be sufficient. So, if it was your intention to scribble down a bunch of diluted descriptions and still receive a gold star, you may be disappointed.

Now the purpose of this test is not to harvesting your responses; instead, it is to actually engage in the process itself. For obvious reasons this assignment will not be graded, however there is a lot more at stake here than an alphabetic badge to stick on a future resume. Awarding such a silly trophy would only trivialize the topic. Can you see how serious this issue is? We are talking about your God. We are talking about Eternal life, salvation, and your soul.

Joseph Smith once taught, your "first object is to find out the character of the only wise and true God, and what kind of a being He is."[2] Take a moment and honestly orient where understanding God's character lands on your list of priorities. Since Eternal life is related to your

---

[1] John 17:3
[2] Joseph Smith (1805-1844). The King Follett Sermon

knowledge of God, this simple question is one of the most important topics in all existence. This matter must not be treated lightly, cast aside or ridiculed.

How nice it would be to bury this subject underneath frivolities and tomorrows, but this is one issue we cannot afford to massage comfortably into our unconscious minds. Also, don't think that you can avoid the question by just calling it cliché. This is not some collegiate class that can be forgotten upon completion. If this subject is without exaggeration the most important, no other activity should take precedence.

Borrowing the words of Joseph Smith, I want to revisit the question, "I want to ask this congregation, every man, woman and child, to answer the question in their own hearts, what kind of a being God is? Ask yourselves; turn your thoughts into your hearts, and say if any of you have seen, heard, or communed with Him? This is a question that may occupy your attention for a long time. I again repeat the question – **What kind of a being is God?**"[3]

Even deciding where to start in answering this question is insightful. Would it be best to begin by describing the Father's physical features? Maybe you feel it wise to detail God's interactions with man in terms of His roles and functions. Those electing this course will discover the relationship between God's many names and the way he influences our lives. This list might include the following: Father, Creator, God, Deliverer, Friend, Lord, Messiah, and Redeemer.

Each of these titles offers some level of understanding about God; but unfortunately, the final product here is not so different from our mortal job applications. Like our own résumés, this list only gives us a simplified snapshot of a person's true character. Such superficial inquiry is insufficient for "I want you all to know Him, and to be familiar with Him."[4]

When considering God and His works, we need to focus on the question – Why? Why is God our Father, why is He our Creator, our Friend and our Deliverer? What motivates Him to do all that He does, and what makes Him who He is? What is "***the nature of that righteousness which is in our great and Eternal Head***"?[5] The scriptures state, "*as he thinketh in his heart, so is he;*"[6] should we not then explore the very thoughts, feelings and beliefs that persuade the actions of our Deity?

Though it is a common human trait to conceal our deepest desires,

---

[3] Joseph Smith (1805-1844). The King Follett Sermon – Emphasis added
[4] Joseph Smith (1805-1844). The King Follett Sermon
[5] Helaman 13:38 – Emphasis added
[6] Proverbs 23:7

the scriptures are not timid in telling us about God's innermost motivations. Herein we find the remarkable revelation, *"He doeth not anything save it be for the benefit of the world; for he loveth the world."*[7] There it is. Hiding in a modest eighteen words is the most essential doctrine of the universe. From this simple verse we learn that everything God has done, from the beginning of time to the present, from *"yesterday, to-day and forever,"*[8] has all been motivated by love. Everything passes through one central context – Love.

But there are those who would debate this idea. They would ask whether God works to benefit mankind globally or intimately. Are we the recipients of God's love? Is everything done for our benefit? Do you doubt whether God's genius can manage all circumstances, settings and scenarios so as to simultaneously benefit all of mankind without ignoring the individual? Where does God weigh the concerns of kingdoms amidst the complaints of a single soul? Where among His duties of governing galaxies, worlds and cultures do you, His child, fit in? Can we say God doeth not anything save it be for 'your' benefit, just as the scriptures say He works for the benefit of the world?

Do not suppose that God is some unsympathetic, sovereign sentinel, so swallowed up in the affairs of space and time that he has lost touch with solitary souls. It is written that *"the very hairs of your head are all numbered."*[9] The purpose of this scripture is not to show us that God is caught up in calculating hair follicles; instead, the message is that God concerns Himself with the minutiae of our lives. *"The hireling fleeth, because he is an hireling, and careth not for the sheep."*[10] God is not some Heavenly *"hireling"* who is preoccupied with the percentages of His occupation. He is not content to leave behind a few straying sheep for the sake of the flock.

We know that God doeth not anything save it be for **your benefit**, for God *"having an hundred sheep, if he lose one of them* [will] *leave the ninety and nine in the wilderness, and go after that which is lost, until he find it."*[11] *"For ye were as sheep going astray,"* but because God 'careth for His sheep and loves them,' He will labor until you are *"returned unto the Shepherd and Bishop of your souls."*[12]

---

[7] 2 Nephi 26:24
[8] 1 Nephi 10:18 – "For he is the same yesterday, today, and forever; and the way is prepared for all men"
[9] Matthew 10:30
[10] John 10:13
[11] Luke 15:4 – Brackets added – Original uses the words 'doth not' in place of the brackets.
[12] 1 Peter 2:25 – "For ye were as sheep going astray; but are now returned unto the Shepherd and Bishop of your souls" – See Bible Dictionary p.625 Bishop – "Bishop. Greek episkopos, meaning 'overseer.'"

But why all the concern? Why is God doing all this work for our benefit? What is God's great motive? The scripture concludes with the simple statement – *"for he loveth the world."* Everything God is and does, His divine nature is fixed on the principle of love. If you are searching the scriptures to learn about 'who God is' outside the context of a lovingly devoted Father, your foundation is as stable as a Jenga tower – build up scholastic or gospel knowledge as high as you can, but sooner or later the tower is going to tumble.

Not only should the study of God's word be undertaken through a lens of love, every experience in life should funnel through the principle of love. *"For all the law is fulfilled in one word, even in this;* **Thou shalt love** *thy neighbour as thyself."*[13] With a principle such as this, we need to move beyond the chicken-soup-for-the-soul- like contemplations. We must come to partake of the fruits planted by practical application. The entire meaning of life is love! The purpose of our existence is to master this singular, sovereign virtue. You are alive here and now to learn **how** to love.

The Savior himself taught this principle to a Pharisee who questioned, *"Master, which is the great commandment in the law?"*[14] Considering, *"the whole duty of man"*[15] is to keep the commandments there could be no better question than this – which commandment deserves most of our attention? Christ answered, *"Thou shalt love the Lord thy God with all thy heart, and with all thy soul, and with all thy mind. This is the first and great commandment. And the second is like unto it, Thou shalt love thy neighbour as thyself. On these two commandments hang all the law and the prophets."*[16]

Logically it follows that the greatest commandment in the law coincides with the most important objective of our lives. You do not have to hunt down a meditating hermit on the top of the Himalayas to find the meaning of your existence. The answer is right before you. The first and second great commandments share this common denominator – love. Love is the pivotal principle!

Christ's concluding statement was, *"On these two commandments hang all the law and the prophets."* Think for a moment about the informative image in the word *"hang."* Just as a painting hangs on a single nail in the wall, the weight of every prophecy, moral teaching, sacred ritual and celestial law is suspended on one central concept – love.

---

[13] Galatians 5:14 – "Emphasis added
[14] Matthew 22:36
[15] Ecclesiastes 12:13 – "Let us hear the conclusion of the whole matter: Fear God, and keep his commandments: for **this is the whole duty of man.**"– Emphasis added
[16] Matthew 22:37-40

Reflect also upon the brutally battered body of the Lamb of God which was tortuously nailed upon the cross. As Christ hung on the cross, His virtue was held up by His love. Truly, every word and principle of God is fixed in its appropriate spot and held in its place by love, "*For there is one God … And to love him with all the heart, and with all the understanding, and with all the soul, and with all the strength, and to love his neighbour as himself, is more than all whole burnt offerings and sacrifices.*"[17]

The scriptures repeatedly, emphatically and conspicuously proclaim that love is the dominant principle of Christianity. Love is not some self-oriented sales scheme to mass market material, nor is it an artistic form of hyperbole, flavor of the week or book club focus. As the greatest virtue of heaven and earth, the value of love is immune to the decay of ever shifting cultural trends and periodic zeitgeists. Let time pass, whether it be years or millennia, rust will not settle. So, we ponder this imperative – what is love and how can we fit it into every tiny aspect of our lives.

Is there any doubt that love is the grandest treasure in the entire universe? Multiple scriptures support this claim; for example, James ennobles the virtue of love referring to it as "*the royal law.*"[18] Paul emphasizes love as Christianity's core directive saying, "*love is the fulfilling of the law.*"[19] Further insight comes from Paul who weighed the celestial scales writing, "*And now abideth faith, hope, charity, these three; but the greatest of these is charity.*"[20]

The Prophet Mormon adds his testimony of divine love (which is charity) exhorting, "*Wherefore, cleave unto charity, which is the greatest of all.*"[21] Moroni joins in giving an affirmation of haunting graveness, "*except men shall have charity they cannot inherit that place which thou hast prepared in the mansions of thy Father.*"[22] Similarly Nephi strictly states, "*Wherefore, the Lord God hath given a commandment that all men should have charity, which charity is love. And except they should have charity they were nothing.*"[23] Truly man is nothing without love. But remember that this message also applies to larger spheres; for without love, churches, communities, countries and worlds are nothing.

---

[17] Mark 12:32,33 – See vs. 34) "And [Jesus] said unto him, Thou art not far from the kingdom of God."
[18] James 2:8 – "fulfill the royal law according to the scripture, Thou shalt love thy neighbour as thyself"
[19] Romans 13:10 – "Love worketh no ill to his neighbour: therefore love is the fulfilling of the law."
[20] 1 Corinthians 13:13
[21] Moroni 7:46,47 – "Wherefore, cleave unto charity, which is the greatest of all, for all things must fail – But charity is the pure love of Christ, and it endureth forever."
[22] Ether 12:33
[23] 2 Nephi 26:30

Another witness of the preeminent role of love comes from a verse divulging God's foremost feature. With simple poetry the Apostle John defines Heavenly Father's nature stating, *"God is love."*[24] Who is God? He is an exalted being who loves perfectly. Father's mind, character, theory and practice is so intensely centered upon love that His entire being is said to be love. Thus, we conclude the better we comprehend love, the better we will comprehend God – for *"God is love!"*

Still, as beautiful as this statement may be, we are trying to avoid giving soft responses to hard questions. Even though John's insight is precious, his comments cycle us back to the original challenge – along with defining God, we must now define love. Any value in John's statement relies on us being able to accurately expound on love.

Our first problem is that the concept of love is too large to trap inside one word. A single, scanty expression cannot adequately transmit every nuance of meaning intended in the idea. We require much more than four letters to supply the exhaustive view we seek. The word love, only provides a one-dimensional slice of a three-dimensional concept.

In order to get a panoramic, multi-dimensional view of God and love, we must gather knowledge from every angle and utilize every perspective. Eventually, our understanding of love must reach every facet and corner till it carves love's shape and texture. Yet all the while, we are not carving an image of an inanimate concept; we carving the very contours of the sacred image of God and the divine nature that resides in man.

Fortunately, the Apostle Paul already made the initial incisions in the dissection of the idea of love. With his teachings on charity, a word denoting divine love, we have a most valuable examination of this concept. Also, ensuring continuity of our topic, know that the Greek word for love, in the scripture *"God is love,"* is the same word Paul translated as charity. Wrote Paul,

> *"Charity suffereth long, and is kind; charity envieth not; charity vaunteth not itself, is not puffed up, Doth not behave itself unseemly, seeketh not her own, is not easily provoked, thinketh no evil; Rejoiceth not in iniquity, but rejoiceth in the truth; Beareth all things, believeth all things, hopeth all things, endureth all things. Charity never faileth"*[25]

With these verses, Paul pulls us out of a pit of clichés to show us a

---

[24] 1 John 4:8 – "He that loveth not knoweth not God; for God is love."
[25] 1 Corinthians 13:4-8

perspective of love that is far beyond an Oprah special or sappy chic flic. With a swift slice, we learn that love is composed of many other virtues, virtues that have their own unique complexity. Our discovery here is similar to that of the biologist, who looking under a microscope saw that organisms are constructed of tiny components called cells. Following this he later found that these cells were made of even smaller pieces named molecules, which themselves are composed by smaller segments – elements and atoms.

By analyzing Paul's teachings on Charity, we see how divine love is composed of the following fragments:

Patience -------------- which is akin to "longsuffering"
Kindness -------------- "is kind"
Contentment --------- which "envieth not"
Humility ------------- which "vaunteth not itself" and is "not puffed up"
Integrity ------------- which does not "behave itself unseemly" and
Selflessness ---------- which "seeketh not her own."
Peacemaking -------- which is not "easily provoked"
Mercy ---------------- which "thinketh no evil" in others.
Joy ------------------ "rejoiceth not in iniquity, but rejoiceth in truth"
Courage ------------- "beareth all things"
Faith ---------------- "believeth all things"
Hope ---------------- "hopeth all things"
Perseverance -------- "endureth all things"
Charity -------------- which is that which "never faileth"

Clearly part of Paul's message is that every Godly attribute is an outgrowth of love. Also, though all Godly attributes relate to one another in some degree, love has a special association with them all. This is why Paul, like every other Prophets places love at the forefront of all principles saying, "*Above all these things put on Charity.*"[26]

Though Paul's analysis of charity is one of the gospel's greatest teachings, is it a comprehensive, conclusive explication of love? Does he include all of love's acts and attributes? True, faith, hope, humility and patience are pieces of love, but how do they fit together? Are there more sides and dimensions of love not included in Paul's writings? Questions like this remain and therefore call us to further investigate each of love's

---

[26] Colossians 3:14 – "Above all these things put on Charity, which is the bond of perfectness."

distinct components, so that we may fully understand love, and therein fully know God.

A key insight on love's position in the pantheon of holy principles is contained in a rebuke made by Christ, "*This people draweth nigh unto me with their mouth, and honoreth me with their lips; but their heart is far from me.*"[27] Using the image of a mouth and lips to represent praise and worship, we are taught that devotion must be correctly connected to the heart in order to be acceptable to God. Yet, it is safe to say that the mouth and lips are not the sole culprits of empty piety. Couldn't we replace the lips with any part of the body and maintain the truth of the statement? Do you suppose one would be better off drawing near to God with their ears, eyes, or head? Perhaps one might occupy Heaven by drawing near to God with their hands or feet?

Moving from the analogy of the body, what if we made things more real by drawing near to God with humility, kindness, courage or faith? Do any of these operating alone bring us to God's dwelling place? No, the point is, without appropriately applying our heart – the symbol of affection and desire – our outward devotions fall short. Without love, offerings of our faith are fake, kindness becomes a scam, courage become empty bravado, humility artificial flagellation, and all other sacrifices and virtues are void. A pure motive of love must back our behaviors or else the outward expressions lose their value.

Mormon taught the same principle saying, "*A man being evil cannot do that which is good; for if he offereth a gift, or prayeth unto God,* **except he shall do it with real intent it profiteth him nothing** *... For behold a bitter fountain cannot bring forth good water; neither can a good fountain bring forth bitter water.*"[28] Without love directing our actions, the fountain of our intent becomes bitter and of no profit. The motive of love must be pumped into every behavioral limb; it must reach all the other godly attributes to thereby supply them with their necessary nourishment.

With Mormon's emphasis on intent fresh in our minds, we are more capable of considering Paul's contributions to this principle. Stressing the importance of our intentions, Paul writes, "*Though I speak with the tongues of men and of angels, and have not charity, I am become as sounding brass, or a tinkling cymbal. And though I have the gift of prophecy, and understand all mysteries, and all knowledge; and though I have all faith, so that I could remove mountains, and have not charity, I am nothing. And though I bestow all my goods to feed the poor, and though I*

---

[27] Matthew 15:8 (also Isaiah 29:13)
[28] Moroni 7:8,11 – Emphasis added

give my body to be burned and have not charity, it profiteth me nothing."[29]

Considering that they most simple symbolism of the heart is to represent intent and motivation, we see that love is most fundamentally manifest as desire. Thus, when someone states a love for something, they are expressing affection, passion and desire. Nevertheless, if love is synonymous with desire some complications still remain. Mark Twain observed, "Life does not consist mainly, or even largely, of facts and happenings. It consists mainly of the storm of thoughts that are forever blowing through one's mind."[30] If Twain considered the "storm of thoughts" to be a mighty whirlwind, he would laugh at that comparatively dainty drizzle after seeing the voracious hurricane of competing desires tormenting men's hearts.

The tempests of the heart are caused by our capability to simultaneously love/desire multiple things in life. The wish that finds expression is the victor in an ever-shifting hierarchical order of our desires. Somewhere in every person, written at the top of this contentious list of cares is a great, guiding, preeminent passion. Though different intensities of love can be found at every height of the hierarchy, it is the concern at the top of our lists that describes the depth of love demanded in the first and second great commandments.

The feeling we are expected to have towards God and all mankind is greater than civility or friendship. Consecration to God must be more than an occasional craving for kindness. We must have more than a fascination with faith. In order to "*cleave unto Him, with all our heart,*"[31] God must mean more to us than the air we breathe.

The Psalmist captures this level of desire we should feel toward God, saying, "*O God, thou art my God; early will I seek thee: my soul thirsteth for thee, my flesh longeth for thee in a dry and thirsty land, where no water is.*"[32] This real "*hunger and thirst after righteousness*"[33] is largely responsible for repentance; it generates the character changing powers of Heaven. When we truly love God, we are not satisfied to simply snack on the Spirit while a feast of faith is ever before us.

Mankind's mortal malleability enables us to develop our desires. With our power to love, we can "*love God and serve him with all our heart and*

---

[29] 1 Corinthians 13:1-3
[30] Mark Twain (1835-1910)
[31] See D&C 11:19 – "Yea, cleave unto me with all your heart"
[32] Psalms 63:1
[33] Matthew 5:6

with all our soul,"[34] or we can desire as Cain, who "*loved Satan more than God.*"[35] Even so, a desire doesn't need to be inherently demonic in order to distract us from Deity. Christ illustrates this daunting truth saying, "*He that loveth father or mother more than me is not worthy of me: and he that loveth son or daughter more than me is not worthy of me.*"[36]

Nothing should take priority over God. This test of your priorities is the most elementary test of life. God is specifically 'trying you that He might know all that is in your heart.'[37] Yet, the strongest evidence that desires play the prime role in life is that God ultimately "*granteth unto men according to their desire, whether it be unto death or unto life.*"[38] Likewise we are taught that at the end of all things God will "*judge all men ... according to the desire of their hearts.*"[39] None can dispute that this judgment is just, for the reins of desire direct our thoughts and behaviors and best define who we are.

Even so, mankind has proven quite cunning in imitating righteousness without any semblance of saintly intentions. Some give for self-gain; others portray humility to win favor and power. Masquerade meekness can conceal an ulterior motive to manipulate, while others go about pompously publicizing their compassionate acts. Cheap reproductions of love are so rampant that we often feel a need to preface love, saying it is real or genuine.

Although man has successfully found ways to mimic actions without intent, we cannot separate intent from action. That being said, we return to Paul's teaching on charity and begin see additional principles pertaining to charity – divine love.

Incorporated in his original statements are equally valuable counter-theses, namely: if we are not "*longsuffering*" we do not love. If we are not "*kind*" our love is counterfeit. If we "*envy*" or "*seek our own*" then our love is a sham. One cannot "*vaunteth itself*." or be "*puffed up*" and think they are loving. Non-persevering, fatiguing love is better qualified as prolonged infatuation so as not to be associated with that charity which

---

[34] Deuteronomy 10:12 – Brackets added – "what doth the LORD thy God require of thee, but to fear the LORD thy God, to walk in all his ways, and to love him, and to serve the LORD thy God with all thy heart and with all thy soul."
[35] Moses 5:28 – "Cain…loved Satan more than God."
[36] Matthew 10:37
[37] 2 Chronicles 32:31 also Deuteronomy 8:2 – "the LORD thy God led thee these forty years in the wilderness, to humble thee, and to prove thee, to know what was in thine heart"
[38] Alma 29:4 – "he allotteth unto men…according to their wills, whether they be unto salvation or unto destruction."
[39] D&C 137:9 – "For I, the Lord will judge all men according to their works, according to the desire of their hearts."

"*never faileth.*" Those susceptible to provocation are crippled in their capacity for compassion and charity. Does your life display your belief in, hope for, and rejoicing in the God you love? If not, your love is only in "*word, and in tongue; but not in deed and in truth.*"[40]

Divine love manifests both "*in deed and in truth.*" Thus, it is imperative that we learn **how to love**. Our objective is to understand the concept of love in full. Therefore, we need to continue exploring the love of our Eternal Father. Our investigation must continue till we comprehend how love inspires every holy attribute. This can be done by placing each of love's tributary attributes underneath a microscope of reflection. But do not forget that while we are learning about love and each of its specific branches, we are ultimately coming to know the nature and character of God our Father.

As you follow the individual streams of each particular attribute back to its source, know that you are not being led to back to an ethereal principle, but to a person. We are not discovering what love is as a concept, but the source of all love – God. God is Love. It is His dominant desire. Heavenly Father loves you, and 'being affectionately desirous of you, He is willing to have imparted unto you, not the gospel of God only, but also His own soul, because ye are dear unto Him.'[41] Since love is a desire, you must believe that it is God's most basic desire for you "*to be with* [Him,] *that we may be one.*"[42] Father's deepest wish is for you to return to home to Him. We have the undeniable evidence of Father's love in the sacrifice of His Son; "*For God so love the world, that he gave his only begotten Son, that whosoever believeth in him should not perish, but have everlasting life.*"[43]

---

[40] See 1 John 3:18 – "let us not love in word, neither in tongue, but in deed and in truth."
[41] 1 Thessalonians 2:8 – Brackets added "being affectionately desirous of you, we were willing to have imparted unto you, not the gospel of God only, but also our own souls, because ye were dear unto us."
[42] D&C 29:13 – "to receive a crown of righteousness, and to be clothed upon, even as I am, to be with me"
[43] John 3:16

Charity

It is not possible to overstate the vital role love has in life. Discussion about *love* saturates the religious world. It overflows into secular fields, spilling into much of our social and cultural subject matter. Because love has ubiquity and preeminence in the story of man, we must consider if we comprehend the *"great love"* wherewith God loves us?[1] Love is something far greater than our cultural catchphrases or the calligraphy of a hallmark card. Our conception of love must be better than that of our politics, the domain of immature masses swooning and swaying over seductive slogans.

If love is a desire and these desires come in myriads of magnitudes, how do we distinguish one degree of love from another? Unfortunately, the English language only provides one word to represent love's enormous span of sentiments. For example, "I love you" is the expression used by adolescents in their juvenile flirtations. The same words are used to describe feelings toward earthly possessions. "I love you" is the phrase tenderly spoken between husband and wife, just as it is the cheer of over-excited fans applauding an athlete's performance. Ironically, we say "I love you" to convey affection to our children, and echo these same words to keepsakes and pets.

Love is the centerpiece of Christianity. All virtues grow from the motivating desire of love; therefore, it is unsuitable to simply define this most majestic principle as a desire, albeit a profound and intense desire. Your mortal and eternal quest is to acquire the attributes of Heavenly Father's divine nature. Thus, our examination rightfully begins with the most cherished celestial attribute – charity.

In order to distinguish charity from other concepts, we need to sort out the linguistic problems in the word love. Some relief from these problems comes by studying the Hebrew and Greek words which are translated as *love* in the scriptures. When we read the word love in the scriptures, it actually could be one of a whole variety of words which speaks of a specific shade of this concept. For example, in the Old Testament love

---

[1] Ephesians 2:4 – "But God, who is rich in mercy, for his great love wherewith he loved us"

is translated from multiple Hebrew-Aramaic words: *'ahabah* and *'ahab*, *chashaq* and *chesheq*, *chashuwq*, *chishshuq*, and *chishshur*.

> **'Ahabah** and **'ahab**[2] – These words cover a similar spectrum to our own word love. 'Ahabah and 'ahab can imply a strong emotional attachment, friendship, affection as well as the love between a husband and wife.
> **Chashaq**[3] – To cling, join, love or delight
> **Chesheq**[4] – Desire and delight
> **Chashuwq**[5] – Attached, "i.e. a fence-rail or or rod connecting the posts or pillars"
> **Chishshuq**[6] – "Conjoined, i.e. a wheel-spoke or rod connecting the hub of the rim"
> **Chishshur**[7] – To bind together or combine, as in a hub of a wheel that holds the spokes together.

This list illustrates how a single word can potentially communicate distinctly different messages; potent evidence to the value of refining the language we choose to represent our thoughts. From this abbreviated list of words we derive two main ideas: the first, associates love with desire, the second evokes a powerful and specific image of love – union, being joined, attached and bound.

Examining the Greek language of the New Testament provides us even more breadth to the word love. From this culture we are given the following three words:

> **Agapao, agape**[8] – Godly love, the attitude of affection and benevolence that God has toward Christ and all His children.
> **Phileo**[9] – Brotherly love, to be fond of, or to be a friend.
> **Thelo**[10] – to delight in, choose, prefer, inclined toward, would, will and desire.

---

[2] Hebrew Strong's Dictionary #157,160 – Pronounced (aw – habe) and (a – hab – aw)
[3] Hebrew Strong's Dictionary #2836 – Pronounced (khaw – shak)
[4] Hebrew Strong's Dictionary #2837 – Pronounced (khay – shek)
[5] Hebrew Strong's Dictionary #2838 – Pronounced (khaw – shook)
[6] Hebrew Strong's Dictionary #2839 – Pronounced (khish – shook)
[7] Hebrew Strong's Dictionary #2839 – Pronounced (khish – shook)
[8] Greek Strong's Dictionary #25,26 – Pronounced –(ag-ap-ah'-o) and (ag-ah'-pay)
[9] Greek Strong's Dictionary #5368 – Pronounced –(fil-eh'-o)
[10] Greek Strong's Dictionary #2309 – Pronounced –(thel'-o)

For the most part *thelo* operates similar to our contemporary use of the word love, whereas *phileo* and *agape* add intriguing implications. It is noteworthy that in all scripture *phileo* is not used in commandments to love God. Of all the words translated as love, *agape* stands out with a particularly compelling definition – the attitude of the Father toward His children, divine or sacrificial love. Considering the notion contained in a*gape* leads us to the question – what is Godly love?

In the New Testament the word *charity* is a translation of the Greek word – *agape*. For this reason, many religions have assigned charity the role of representing the ideals asserted in *agape,* namely God-like love. The notion that charity (*agape*) reflects divine love is likewise established in the scriptures which state, *"charity is the pure love of Christ."*[11] Similarly the Bible Dictionary adds charity is, "The highest, noblest, strongest kind of love, not merely affection; the pure love of Christ."[12] Though the imagery here is correct and beautiful, we must push our understanding further in order to articulate the specifically unique qualities of charity. So we ponder, what manner of love is possessed by God? What is the highest, noblest and most godly aspect of love?

Ether described Christ's love saying, *"I remember that thou hast said that* **thou hast loved the world, even unto the laying down of thy life** *for the world … And I know that this love which thou hast had for the children of men is charity."*[13] Yet is charity merely a fleeting moment of magnanimity? Surely divine love consists of something more than a single, special act? Was the 'laying down of Christ's life' a sacrifice limited to Gethsemane and Calvary, or did His sacrifice include other actions of His life? Christ's consecration included not only the laying down of His life through death, but also the laying down of His whole livelihood. In laying down His life, He laid down his whole self. Christ's consecration called for a surrender of personality as well as His person. However, this should not lessen the special tribute we respectfully pay to the *"infinite atonement*;"[14] the day when Jesus manifested *"greater love"* by 'laying down His life for us, His friends.'[15]

Preferring a friend's welfare above our own, even and especially unto death is certainly a grandiose degree of love; but there is still a higher

---

[11] Moroni 7:47 – "But charity is the pure love of Christ, and it endureth forever; and who is found possessed of it at the last day, it shall be well with him"
[12] Bible Dictionary Charity p. 632
[13] Ether 12:32 – Emphasis added
[14] Alma 34:12 – "there can be nothing which is short of an infinite atonement which will suffice for the sins of the world."
[15] John 15:13 – "Greater love hath no man than this, that a man lay down his life for his friends."

order possessed by Christ and the Father. Of all merits and expressions, the greatest quality of love is to love those who we feel are undeserving of our love. Charity is a continuation of love amid little or no reciprocation. Loving those who do not love us is the most heavenly form of love in the universe; it is Divine, it is Charity, it is the pure love of Christ. No loftier level of love exists, than that which sustains concern and good feeling towards those who refuse to return the same. It is this love which *"maketh [the] sun to rise on the evil and on the good, and sendeth rain on the just and on the unjust."*[16]

For this reason and perhaps more than we may ever know, charity is *"acquainted with grief."*[17] But charity is not selfish sorrow; rather it is a sadness born of sympathy. God is liberal with His love, and 'even after our betrayals and backsliding, He still loves us freely.'[18] Because God is charitable, He gives without reservation.

However, this liberal love leaves Him vulnerable to the painful consequences of mankind's unkind and abusive choices. Consider then the agony of soul God experiences because of His great love. As a loving parent of prodigal sons and daughters, Heavenly Father is keenly acquainted with grief, and for this reason He *"sheds forth [His] tears as the rain upon the mountains."*[19] Because He is all-knowing, the Lord is perfectly aware of all our actions. From Heaven He watches His children play out their lives with indifference and even resentment toward Him. But in the face of such coldness and heartless hatred we discover the greatest miracle of it all; namely the Infinite Atonement was not just made for saints, but that *"Christ died for the ungodly!"* [20]

"And when I passed by thee, and saw thee polluted in thine own blood, I said unto thee, when thou wast in thy blood, Live; yea I said unto thee when thou wast in thy blood, Live. ... Now when I passed by thee, and looked upon thee, behold, thy time was the time of love; and I spread my skirt over thee, and covered thy nakedness: yea, I sware unto thee, and entered into a covenant with thee, saith the Lord GOD, and thou becamest mine."[21] God loves the very men who despise Him, He loves them even after all their betrayals and abuse. Though God is *"despised and rejected*

---

[16] Matt 5:45
[17] Isaiah 53:3 – "He is despised and rejected of men; a man of sorrows, an acquainted with grief"
[18] Hosea 14:4 – "I will heal their backsliding, I will love them freely: for mine anger is turned away from him."
[19] Moses 7:28 – And it came to pass that the God of Heaven looked upon the residue of the people, and he wept"
[20] Romans 5:6
[21] Ezekiel 16:6,8

of men,"[22] He does not *"cry unto any, saying: Depart from me ... but he saith: Come unto me all ye ends of the earth."*[23] Though *"we hid as it were our faces from him,"*[24] He does not hide in indifference toward us. Some act as though there is nothing sinister in luke-warmness. Surely it would be easier for God to distance himself from us when we make ourselves enemies to Him. But 'even to our old age and grey hairs God carries us,'[25] for charity continues to esteem others when others esteem us as naught.

Father calls after us even when there is *"none to answer."*[26] Throughout humanity's darkest ages, there has never been a time when God has not provided an escape for His children. In every case Father steadily offered the remedy of repentance: *"For he did cry from the morning, even until the going down of the sun, exhorting the people to believe in God unto repentance."*[27] These constant invitations to repent, which have been spoken in all generations will stand through eternity as a monument of God's *"everlasting love."*[28]

Twisted countenances warped by wickedness surrounded Him. Fellow members of the family of God spit upon the very image from which they were formed. Loud, scathing voices raised toward the heavens yelling, *"Crucify him, crucify him."*[29] The omniscient eyes of the Eternal Father were fully aware of the malicious men who desired the death and torture of His Only Begotten son. God knew all of their evil plans; yet, He continued and *"clave the wood for the burnt offering."*[30]

His *"all-searching eye"*[31] must surely have probed past scenes where corrupt civilizations, seduced by hatred showered the earth with the blood of the innocent. Chiding chants echoing throughout history rose up with Christ's contemporaries criticizing the Father, cursing His kingdom, and blaspheming His teachings. In the midst of these menacing mockeries God marched up Moriah's mount and *"built an altar there."*[32]

Knowing all things that would come upon the earth, the past and

---

[22] Isaiah 53:3
[23] 2 Nephi 26:25
[24] Isaiah 53:3
[25] Isaiah 46:4 – "And even to your old age I am he; and even to hoar hairs will I carry you: I have made, and I will bear; even I will carry, and will deliver you."
[26] Isaiah 50:2 – "when I came, was there no man? When I called, was there none to answer"
[27] Ether 12:3
[28] Jeremiah 31:3 – "I have loved thee with an everlasting love: therefore with lovingkindness have I drawn thee."
[29] John 19:10
[30] Genesis 22:3
[31] 2 Nephi 9:44
[32] Genesis 22:9

present cries of the railing crowds fused with the future. Perversely proud preaching spread across every place on the earth, and atop their Babel hearts they "*laughed* [God] *to scorn.*"[33] As their Father, He knew all their faces; they were "*the workmanship of* [His] *own hands,*"[34] who once "*shouted for joy*" [35] at the laying of the foundations of the earth. Their shouts were different now. Souls distorted by hatred, and hearts consumed with malevolence joined the malicious mob in the chant, "*Crucify Him, Crucify Him.*"

Yet while these men derailed Him, God "*laid the wood in order, and bound*" His son. Then the Father "*laid him on the altar upon the wood … and took the knife.*"[36] With knife in hand, and no "*lamb for a burnt offering,*"[37] God and His Son "*went both of them together*" [38] to teach the world the measure of Charity.

Even after mankind's corruption and recalcitrance, "*God commendeth his love toward us … **while we were yet sinners.***"[39] God pleas for the perjurer, He blesses His betrayers, and restores trust to the traitor. Father is faithful through our failures, He is forgiving of our faults, "*he is kind unto the unthankful and to the evil.*"[40] God tirelessly reaches out to those who have deserted Him.

Without any hesitancy, He willingly receives those who did not receive Him.[41] There is no specific celestial alignment required for us to be restored to His favor. No, the preparations have already been made, and with all the charity in His heart, Father anxiously awaits for the very moment He can intervene and rescue us. As King Hezekiah proclaimed, "*The LORD was ready to save me,*"[42] we too must believe that 'God is ever ready to save us!'

---

[33] Psalms 22:7 – "All they that see me laugh me to scorn: they shoot out the lip, they shake the head,"
[34] Moses 7:32 – "Behold these thy brethren; they are the workmanship of mine own hands"
[35] Job 38:7 – (vs. 4) "Where wast thou when I laid the foundations of the earth? … (vs.7) When the morning stars sang together, and all the sons of God shouted for joy?"
[36] See Genesis 22:9,10 – "And Abraham built an altar there, and laid the wood in order, and bound Isaac his son, and laid him on the altar upon the wood. And Abraham stretch forth his hand, and took the knife to slay his son."
[37] Genesis 22:7 – "Isaac spake unto Abraham….where is the lamb for a burnt offering?"
[38] Genesis 22:8 – "And Abraham said, My son, God will provide himself a lamb for a burnt offering: so they went both of them together."
[39] Romans 5:7,8 – Greek word for love – Agape – Emphasis added
[40] Luke 6:35
[41] D&C 6:20,21 – "I will encircle thee in the arms of my Love. Behold, I am Jesus Christ, the Son of God. I am the same that came unto mine own, and mine own received me not."
[42] Isaiah 38:20 – "The LORD was ready to save me: therefore we will sing…all the days of our life"

In all His gift giving and abundance of blessings, He is *"not grieved"* when He gives[43] for *"it is his good will to give you the kingdom."*[44] There is no inner conflict in His courtesy. He does not spend time calculating the costs of compensation. God 'does good, and lends, hoping for nothing again.'[45] Such is the charitable heart, it does not 'give grudgingly or of necessity.' Also, not only does *"God loveth a cheerful giver,"*[46] God is a cheerful giver. When we have charity, service is a bliss and not a sacrifice; it is a joy not a job, a delight, not a duty.[47]

As we ponder God's ability to love against man's abuses of autonomy, we have the proper context for assessing God's level of commitment to us. The subtle undertones of charity paint a picture of God's unwavering, consistent love. With this in mind, recall the Hebrew words mentioned earlier: *chashuw*, *chishshuq*, and *chishshur* which collectively express images of being bound together, attached and union. Charity binds the human family together. Charity creates a bond between all men and is the only power that can permanently unite the people of the earth. Truly we are *"knit together in love,"*[48] and can only be eternally connected by *"charity, which is the bond of perfectness."*[49]

Reminiscing about the imagery of union, thoughts naturally turn to the sacred union of marriage. Under the marriage covenant, man and woman consecrate their lives to one another and are sealed to God and to each other in oneness. The connection contained in the marriage covenant reflects God's commitment. Thus, we tread reverently as we contemplate the magnitude of the marriage covenant, especially since it has been said, *"Husbands, love your wives, even as Christ loved the church and gave himself for it."*[50]

Paul challenges our professions of charity saying, *"Wherefore shew ye to them, and before the churches,* **the proof of your love***, and of our boasting on your behalf."*[51] Though unreciprocated love captures the theoretical idea of charity, it is the image of union that best captures charity's practical manifestations. In the end, when our lives are in review, the enduring

---

[43] Deuteronomy 15:10 – "Thou shalt surely give him, and thine heart shall not be grieved when thou givest unto him."
[44] D&C 29:5
[45] Luke 6:35 – "love ye your enemies, and do good, and lend, hoping for nothing again"
[46] 2 Corinthians 9:7 – "Every man according as he purposeth in his heart, so let him give; not grudgingly, or of necessity: for God loveth a cheerful giver."
[47] See D&C 41:1 – "Hearken…O ye my people…ye whom I delight to bless with the greatest of blessings,"
[48] Colossians 2:2 – Greek word for love – Agape
[49] Colossians 3:14
[50] Ephesians 5:25 – Greek word for love – Agape
[51] 2 Corinthians 8:24 – Emphasis added

connection of charity will determine the 'proof of our love.' Revelations of this enduring connection can be seen in elderly couples walking down the streets holding hands. In them we see a love that was inseparable in life – a love that in Christ cannot be severed by death. These open displays of proven, refined fidelity divulge God's divine devotion. If we are intuitive and contemplate the lives of these aged and weathered lovers, the Holy Spirit will teach us how 'God too will love us unto the end.'[52]

Reflecting on God's characteristics the Prophet Jacob exclaimed, *"O how great the holiness of our God! ... he cometh into the world that he may save all men if they will hearken unto his voice; for behold, he suffereth the pains of all men, yea, the pains of every living creature, both men, women, and children, who belong to the family of Adam."*[53] Rather unique to this verse is a footnote containing a Hebrew equivalent to the English word *holiness*. The note provides the word *"qodesh"* meaning "committed" and "consecrated."[54] Thus, Jacob's exultant praise could also be read – O how great the commitment of our God! O how great the consecration of our God! O how great the charity of our God!

Charity is consecration – the immovable and unwavering commitment. Divine love is infinite, it is inseparable and eternal. *"For the mountains shall depart, and the hills be removed; but* [God's] *kindness shall not depart from thee."*[55] Charity endures because those possessing this virtue consecrate themselves to God in a way that forms a celestial seal. Mutual consecration creates an eternal connection, a connection that is the indivisible, committed love of charity. A connection that *"never faileth!"* [56]

If God's love was like man's, His wrath would not remain restrained after humanity's persistent onslaught of provocation and displeasure. Perhaps the greatest of men might patiently resist a few waves of insult, profanity or rebellion, but none are like unto our God who has *"spread out* [His] *hands all the day unto a rebellious people."*[57] Nevertheless, charity is more than tolerating insults; it is loving the insulter. Charity is not merely restraint; it is reciprocating ill with love. Charity is not a flight into apathy. Charity is running to *"succor"*[58] the sinner. Oh with such remarkable haste

---

[52] John 13:1 – "Jesus … having loved his own … the word, he loved them unto the end."
[53] 2 Nephi 9:20,21
[54] 2 Nephi 9:20 footnote a
[55] Isaiah 54:10 – Brackets added
[56] 1 Corinthians 13:8 – "Charity never faileth …"
[57] See Isaiah 65:2 – "I have spread out my hands all the day unto a rebellious people."
[58] Hebrews 2:18 – "For in that he himself hath suffered being tempted, he is able to succor them that are tempted." Greek Strong's Dictionary # 997, 998, 995 – Succour – Greek – **Boetheo** –(bo-ay-theh-o)– Boethoe means to run to the aid and help of another. It is built from to words boe (a call or cry for help) and theo (to run).

does our Father rush to respond to our grievances! Because God is unhindered by the slowing sludge of grudges, He *"will order all things for your good as fast as ye are able to receive them."*[59]

Would you suppose that God requires anything less of His followers? He has said, *"I have decreed in my heart … I will prove you in all things, whether you will abide in my covenant, even unto death, that you may be found worthy."*[60] Practicing charity is the ultimate challenge of Christian discipleship. Jesus warned, *"ye shall be hated of all men for my name's sake."*[61] When your love is cast aside, mocked or hated, somehow true disciples must continue to feel and express love towards their offenders. Also, this concern must be legitimate, including a retention of good will and good treatment to their antagonist.

Your love must persist through indifference, cold shoulders, biting words and every form of blatant, out-right hatred. *"Ye have heard that it hath been said, Thou shalt love thy neighbour, and hate thine enemy. But I say unto you,* **Love your enemies,** *bless them that curse you, do good to them that hate you, and pray for them which despitefully use you, and persecute you."*[62] In order for us to complete the Christian curriculum, we will have to pass the course on "loving your enemies." These classes eventually will test whether we can maintain charity amidst hatred. *"For if ye love them which love you, what reward have ye? do not even the publicans the same? And if ye salute your brethren only, what do ye more than others? do not even the publicans so?"* [63]

Do your good feelings fight through fury and offence? Our Father's kindness continues when it is met with coldness. God's sweetness sustains icy insults and sinister sarcasm. Could you embrace someone who has manipulated you? God's charity returns cursing with compliments. He serves not shuns the sinner. Because He is charitable, Father responds to rudeness with mercy, provocation with patience, cruelty with compassion, and sedition with kindness?

Have you ever honestly prayed for your persecutors? How did you pray? Was it full of pride and insult? Did your heart whisper under a verbal façade – bless them to realize how stupid their position is, how flawed they are, please Lord reveal to them all their vanity and wrong. Remember, *"Be not partial towards them in love above many others, but let thy love be for them as for thyself; and let thy love abound unto all men, and unto all who love*

---

[59] D&C 111:11
[60] D&C 98:14
[61] Matthew 10:22 – "but he that endureth to the end shall be saved."
[62] Matthew 5:43, 44 – Emphasis added
[63] Matthew 5:46,47

[God's] *name."*[64]

The day will come when you will be called to stand before God to give an account of your mortal life. We cannot describe in detail what will transpire on that day. However, knowing that *"the end of the commandment is charity out of a pure heart,"*[65] you can be sure that the development of charity will be meticulously weighed and measured.

Stirring what may be a foreshadowed feeling for the Day of Judgment, we read a piercing dialogue between Peter and Jesus. But before studying this conversation recall that there were three different Greek words for love – *thelo* (desire and affection), *phileo* (brotherly love), and *agape* (divine love). Know that each time you read the word *love*, it is possible that any one of these three significantly distinct connotations could have been intended. Hoping to bridge the significant translation gap in these verses, the original corresponding Greek words have been placed in parenthesis. We read,

> *"15. So when they had dined, Jesus saith to Simon Peter, Simon, son of Jonas, lovest (agape) thou me more than these? He saith unto him, Yea, Lord; thou knowest that I love (phileo) thee. He saith unto him, Feed my lambs.*
> *16. He saith to him again the second time, Simon, son of Jonas, lovest (agape) thou me? He saith unto him, Yea, Lord; thou knowest that I love (phileo) thee. He saith unto him, Feed my sheep.*
> *17. He saith unto him the third time, Simon, son of Jonas, lovest (phileo) thou thou me? Peter was grieved because he said unto him the third time, Lovest (phileo) thou me? And he said unto him, Lord, thou knowest all things; thou knowest all things; thou knowest that I love (phileo) thee. Jesus saith unto him, Feed my sheep."*[66]

Do not be surprised when you are brought to face your Maker, if you are posed similar questions; after all charity *is "the great commandment in the law,"* and we are to 'love *(agape)* the Father with all of our heart and with all our soul and with all our mind.' So someday, like Peter, we may be asked, *"Lovest thou me?"*

Will you be able to look into the all-seeing eyes of the Eternal God and say 'Lord thou knowest that I love (agape) thee.' Or will you shrink, will you admit before the holy assembly that your love had been lacking, that your desire to obey God was influential in making life decisions but

---

[64] D&C 112:11 – Brackets added – Originally: my
[65] 1 Timothy 1:5
[66] John 21:15-17

was subject to veto from vainer things? Can you say that your commitment to God was nonperishable, non-negotiable and unconditional? Or had you made pageantry promises – vows bendable to the next wave of trends, tweets and texts? Can you say to your Heavenly Father with a pure heart, Lord thou knowest that I love (agape) thee?

Considering the majority of what we know about God is presented to us in the form of words, it is difficult to step outside the vocabulary and see the concepts for what they really are. So we try to apply these ideas into our real life circumstances hoping that this will give us a clearer vision of the principles. Through this process we gradually understand righteousness in a more relevant level of reality. However, the luxury of personal experience is limited in its tale of the Lord's atoning love.

Teaching on the meaning of the Atonement, Russell M. Nelson commented, "In Hebrew, the basic word for atonement is *kaphar*, a verb that means 'to cover' or 'to forgive.' … Closely related is the Aramaic and Arabic word *kafat*, meaning 'a close embrace.'"[67] Can the extent of man's arts, dreams or imagination do justice to what is suggested in the word embrace? No poetry can properly portray what it means to be, "*encircled about eternally in the arms of* [God's] *love.*"[68] Recalling that charity is an inseparable bond, the scene of an eternal unbreakable embrace is the essential picture of charity.

Do not forget that God is a real being, He is a real person. Heavenly Father has a personality. He has characteristics, feelings and demeanor. God has a face. "*When the Savior shall appear we shall see him as he is. We shall see that he is a man like ourselves. And that same sociality which exists among us here will exist among us there.*"[69] Therefore, when we read the finale of the Lord's Atonement as being "*clasped in the arms of Jesus,*"[70] we must read it in the context that God is real.

These tender scenes of reunion are not commercialized propaganda, nor do they depict choreographed formalities. No! These are the deepest desires, emotions, and wishes of the God of the whole Universe. With the same sociality that exists among us here and now, there as we are immersed in that fresh and tangible scenery, we will realize that the final chapter of man is real.

---

[67] Russell M. Nelson. "The Atonement." *Ensign*. Nov. 1996 p.34
[68] 2 Nephi 1:15 – "the Lord hath redeemed my soul…and I am encircled about eternally in the arms of his love."
[69] D&C 130:1,2
[70] Mormon 5:11 – "yea, they will sorrow for the destruction of this people; they will sorrow that this people had not repented that they might have been clasped in the arms of Jesus"

Know that this embrace will mean as much to Him who has watched and prayed for you from on high as it will mean to you; for *"Herein is love, not that we loved God, but that he loved us."*[71] Then with Celestial glory, the arms of His charity will eternally encircle you; an enduring bond of perfection, re-uniting you forever in the family of God, where *"neither death, nor life, nor angels, nor principalities, nor powers, nor things present, Nor height, nor depth, nor any other creature, shall be able to separate us from the love of God."*[72]

---

[71] 1 John 4:10
[72] Romans 8:34

Compassion

Compassion is the great motivator of magnanimity. Within compassion we discover a universal love for all human beings; a connecting concern for all souls. So much of the tangible substance of love is sourced in compassion. Feelings of compassion move us in meaningful and momentous ways. Compassion comforts; it cares, listens, feels, weeps, succors, embraces and heals. *"Thou, O Lord, art a God full of compassion, and gracious, longsuffering, and plenteous in mercy and truth."*[1]

The sharp sympathetic swellings of compassion do not allow an awareness of another's afflictions to go un-acted upon. Whether the compassionate respond in conversation, an outstretched hand or a timely embrace, because of their compassion charity is never a chore; it is authentically instinctual. So it is with God who reflexively responds to man's misery. No time is wasted worrying whether or not He should intervene. God's speed to succor is not interrupted by piles of paperwork, for compassion sets the pace of His help and provision.

Compassion is the quality of love that activates an awareness of others. It is the actuation of sympathy and empathy. Compassion redirects attention from one's self to others. It scans visage and senses sufferings. Its most simple manifestation is the question of – how are you doing? It is then manifested in its most important of ways – through the art of real and attentive listening. The compassionate ever search the status of others, trying to truly understand their feelings, thoughts and perceptions.

Compassion is more than concern. It is a concern that compels one to action. This principle is illustrated in Jesus's words, *"Behold, my bowels are filled with compassion towards you. Have ye any that are sick among you? Bring them hither. Have ye any that are lame, or blind, or halt, or maimed, or leprous, or that are withered, or that are deaf, or that are afflicted in any manner? Bring them hither and I will heal them, for I have compassion upon you."*[2]

The word *compassion* is built from two Latin roots: *com* – with or together, and *pati* – to suffer. Thus, compassion literally means to suffer

---

[1] Psalms 86:15
[2] 3 Nephi 17:6,7

with or together. The same family of phrases includes the words *sympathy* and *empathy*. Sympathy comes from the Greek word *sympatheia*, a word composed of *syn* – together, and *pathos* – feeling. Similarly, empathy is of Greek origin, it comes from the word *empatheia*, which is built from *en* – in and *pathos* – feeling. Paul illustrates this image of empathy in an epistle to the Hebrews; writing, "*Remember them that are in bonds,* **as bound with them;** *and them which suffer adversity,* **as being yourselves also in the body.**"[3]

By uniting the above definitions together into a overarching concept, our picture of compassion becomes more complete. Compassion is to suffer together, or to suffer with; it is to feel something inside and to feel together. In this light we see how Christ's atonement was a perfect display of compassion, for "*O how marvelous are the works of the Lord, and* **how long doth he suffer with his people.**"[4] Christ who suffered "*pains and afflictions and temptations of every kind*" by taking "*upon him the pains and the sickness of his people,*"[5] has suffered with us in a most intimate way.

Seeing the extent that God suffers with us should make us reevaluate our willingness to share other's suffering. Sure, we may have progressed past the point of malicious imps who mock those that mourn, but avoiding abuse is not enough. In fact, the very problem we are trying to eradicate is avoidance itself. We cannot be content to simply cut out criticism, callousness and cruelty. When we emulate Christ's conduct, we never abandon those in need to endure sorrows in solitude.

How do you express your empathy? Surely compassion is something more than a call to "cowboy up." It should also be more than longing leers or lengthy lectures. How often do we ignorantly shove doctrine down the throats of distressed souls who cry as Job, "*Have pity on me, have pity upon me, O ye my friends; for the hand of God hath touched me.*"[6] Truth is not always the needed antidote. "*To him that is afflicted pity should be shewed from his friend.*"[7] There is a time for therapeutic teaching, but more often the balm of listening is the best prescribed medication. Treating an afflicted soul with tutorials and rebuke is rarely as effective as an empathetic embrace. Compassion remedies heartache more reliably than reproof.

Another significant shape of compassion is sketched by the companion term commiserate. Like compassion, commiserate shares the Latin prefix *com*, meaning with or together. The second piece of

---

[3] Hebrews 13:3 – Emphasis added
[4] Mosiah 8:20 – Emphasis added
[5] Alma 7:11
[6] Job 19:21
[7] Job 6:14

commiserate is *miserari,* a root word meaning to bewail or lament. This aspect of commiseration shows us how to suffer with others, namely by grieving and lamenting with them. This only happens as we allow ourselves to be vulnerable enough to stay connected to others; which includes staying connected to their pain and grief. Compassion is the attribute which forms and maintains that connection despite hardship and anguish. How many tears have you shed for the travail of the innocent? Have you learned to weep with the wretched and cry for the wicked? How long have you lamented over the misery felt by the human family?

Some men snub sinners and the destitute, others sorrow for them, but it is the godly who will sorrow **with** them. Heavenly Father, who knows the full intensity of our adversity truly does *"Weep with them that weep."*[8] In His compassion, God shares every tear that falls from our eyes, and knowing more about mourning than all men, He rightfully is the one who *"will wipe away tears from off all faces."*[9]

Our planar perception of compassion takes a more spherical shape as we fuse additional cultural perspectives to our understanding. In the Old Testament two main words represent compassion:

> [10]**Chamal**: To commiserate, have compassion or to pity and spare.
> [11]**Racham**: Compassion, *racham* evokes an image of a pregnant mother who cherishes her unborn child. It is also translated in the scriptures as tender love, mercy, womb, bowels and pity.

From the Greek's vantage point, we are given the following words:

> [12]**Splagchnon**: *Splagchnon* contains a root word *splen* which is translated as bowels or intestines. Consistent with the Hebrew culture the bowels represented the innermost tender affections. *Splagchnon* represents compassion, inward affection and tender mercy.
> [13]**Splagchnizomai**: Also contains the root *splen* and means to be moved from inside, to be moved with compassion or to yearn with compassion. It is to feel sympathy and to pity.

---

[8] Romans 12:15 – "Rejoice with them that do rejoice, and weep with them that weep."
[9] Isaiah 25:8 – "He will swallow up death in victory; and the Lord GOD will wipe away tears from off all faces"
[10] Hebrew Strong's Dictionary #2550 – Pronounced (khaw-mal')
[11] Hebrew Strong's Dictionary #7356 – Pronounced (rakh'-am)
[12] Greek Strong's Dictionary #4698 – Pronounced (splangkh'-non)
[13] Greek Strong's Dictionary #4697 – Pronounced (splangkh-nid'-zom-ahee)

[14]**Eleeo** and **eleos**: Defined as compassion. It is to feel misery with another, to pity and to show mercy, it represents sympathy and is most typically used when referring to acts of sympathy.
[15]**Oikteiro**: From the Greek word *oiktos* meaning pity. *Oikteiro* means to express pity and have compassion, it is a distressed feeling brought on by observing the pains of another.

Fusing these words together paints a panoramic picture of God's great compassion. God's (*chamal*) compassion spares instead of scorns the sinner, for "*It is of the LORD's mercies that we are not consumed, because his compassions fail not.*"[16] God (*racham*) cherishes and nurtures the weak and the frail; including those with weaknesses of will and frailties of faith. Can you comprehend the (*oikteiro*) dramatic degree of distress God endures because of compassion? From the inner core of God's character, He yearns to be near us, He aches to console us in our discomfort. Heavenly Father is so (*splagchnizomai*) deeply moved towards us in our pains that He visits those suffering with tender affections. The (*eleeo*) interceding strength of God's sympathies moves His tender heart to acts of commiseration, consolation and encouragement.

Nevertheless, do not let definitions detour you from real compassion. Articulate descriptions can never substitute for the rich lessons we obtain by observing sequences of life. The definition of compassion is better displayed in the sympathy shown between siblings, the constant concern of parents and the empathy in marriage. Providing evidence that our mortal relationships illustrate God's sentiments, we read a comparison made by God Himself, saying, "*As one whom his mother comforteth, so will I comfort you.*"[17]

Could mastery of linguistics replace the clinical schooling that comes from of observing the tireless sacrifices of a mother? Is there any academic degree that could compete with the educating experiences of nurturing your own children? It is through experiences, not books that one will truly come to see "*how that the LORD thy God bare thee, as a man doth bear his son.*"[18]

Whether by scripture or life experience, the power of the Holy

---

[14] Greek Strong's Dictionary #1653,1656 – Pronounced (el-eh-eh'o) and (el'-eh-os)
[15] Greek Strong's Dictionary #3627 – pronounced (oyk-ti'-ro)
[16] Lamentations 3:22
[17] Isaiah 66:13
[18] Deuteronomy 1:31 – "the LORD thy God bare thee, as a man doth bear his son, in all the way that ye went"

Ghost, *"which maketh alive all things,"*[19] sketches a most compelling picture of compassion. By this power you may receive a partial partition of the veil as it illuminates meaning in your daily experiences. By searching the scriptures, the Holy Spirit will catalyze sacred revelations so that they become applicable and meaningful to you. Among the revelations which may be 'made alive' in you, is to see how God *"shall weep in secret places for your pride; and [His] eye shall weep sore, and rundown with tears, because the LORD's flock is carried away captive."*[20] Upon sensing God's sentiments, you will wonder as did the ancient Prophets, *"How is it that the heavens weep and shed forth their tears as the rain upon the mountains?"*[21] What could possibly injure the Omnipotent Creator of the Universe so as to bring tears to His holy eyes? *"How is it that [God can] weep, seeing [He is] holy, and from all eternity to all eternity?"*[22]

Watching from celestial skies no thought, action or feeling escapes God's omniscience. But is God's omniscience responsible for the 'heaviness'[23] in Heaven? Knowledge alone cannot account for the tears that fall from Father's eyes. God's intellect is responsible for the anguished observation of an ancient people, *"Behold, they are without affection, and they hate their own blood;*[24] however, it is Father's compassion that brings Him the agonizing awareness which evokes the cry, *"Should not **the heavens weep, seeing these shall suffer?"*** [25] God's genius can quantify the world's wickedness, but it is His compassion which carries the burden of it. There is no doubt that our sins weigh upon His thoughts; yet, it is the consequences of our sins that concerns Him the most.

Seeing sin so tortures His heart because He knows the sufferers; He loves the sufferers. The Father's all loving heart causes Him to share the sorrows of men, not just merely calculate their discomfort. As it was said in a time past when *"Jesus wept," "Behold how he loved him,"*[26] someday you too will witness the depths of God's love and watch as He is pained by your suffering – a pain which is morbidly multiplied by the misery of all

---

[19] Moses 6:61 – "Therefore it is given to abide in you ... the Comforter... which quicketh all things, which maketh alive all things; that which knoweth all things, and hath all power according to wisdom, mercy, truth, justice"
[20] Jeremiah 13:17 – Brackets added
[21] Moses 7:28
[22] Moses 7:29 – Brackets added
[23] Greek Strong's Dictionary #3077 – The Greek word for sorrow is lupe: meaning sadness, grief, sorrow & heaviness.
[24] Moses 7:33
[25] Moses 7: 37 – Emphasis added
[26] John 11:35,36 – According to Strong's Dictionary this Greek word for wept is used only once in the scriptures. It comes from the word – Dakruo (#1145): which has the root dakru or tear, thus dakruo means to shed tears.

mankind.

Of all desecrations, sacrilege and perversions of principle that could possibly enter into the mind of man, none is so detestable then to suppose that Heavenly Father does not comprehend or care about your circumstances. We must never forget that these descriptions portray attributes of the Father – your Heavenly Father. It may sound harsh, but no word seems more suitable than to say that it is absolute blasphemy to imagine a God bereft of concern for humanity. It is blasphemy to forget or minimize the exhaustive efforts the Eternal father who spends *"every moment"*[27] tending to the needs of His children. It is a blasphemy to depict God as some obligatory servant in a wild and corrupt vineyard whose heart was never in the pruning.

Perhaps you think that God is going through some mid-Eternity crisis, maybe you think He is tired of all the pressure and has decided to start exploring other options. Maybe you feel that He is fed up with the antics of His rebellious, juvenile children or that His attention is occasionally stolen by a seductive taste for heavenly hoagies at the celestial Subway. When the soul of the Sovereign Father sighed, *"What could have been done more to my vineyard, that I have not done in it?"* You must never doubt that God exhausts His omnipotent capacity to restore you to His presence. Or would you suggest that God 'sits upon His throne in a state of thoughtless stupor while His enemies are spreading the work of death around the world.'[28]

It is blasphemy to suggest that if only the Father could really understand you or feel what you are feeling, that He might be a more sympathetic servant. Have you forgotten who God is? Men are quick to acknowledge that the Father is omniscient and omnipotent. They also readily recognize that He has all wisdom and justice. But if we fail to admit or remember that the Father is *omnipathos* just as he is omnipotent, we imagine a horrifically disfigured deity. Few forget Christ's depth of understanding who *"suffereth according to the flesh … that his bowels may be filled with mercy, according to the flesh, that he may know according to the flesh how to succor his people according to their infirmities."*[29]

Never question the depth of the Holy Father's understanding who

---

[27] Isaiah 27:3 – "I the LORD do keep it; I will water it every moment lest any hurt it, I will keep it night and day."
[28] Alma 60:7 – "Can you think to sit upon your thrones in a state of thoughtless stupor, while your enemies are spreading the work of death around you?
[29] Alma 7:13

taught *"whether one member suffer, all the members suffer with it."*[30] Our Father suffers with us! His comprehension of your pain, sorrow, and struggle is perfectly thorough. After all the tears that have fallen from eyes of the Eternal Father, to diminish His sympathy, empathy and compassion toward you or any child is sacrilege.

We who worship a weeping God also bear the name of the *"man of sorrows."*[31] Thus, in order to be acquainted with God we will have to be *"acquainted with grief."* Understanding the pains of genuine discipleship, Christ prophetically prepares His followers saying, *"Blessed are they that mourn."*[32] The Apostle Paul reveals in a later verse the volume of these laments, writing, *"Now I rejoice, not that ye were made sorry, but that ye sorrowed to repentance: for* **ye were made sorry after a godly manner…For godly sorrow worketh repentance** *to salvation not to be repented of: but the sorrow of the world worketh death."*[33] What is the sorrow of the Gods? Is it even possible for immature man to sorrow *"after a godly sort?"*[34]

"Godly sorrow worketh repentance." If this is so, if experiencing this celestial sadness is requisite for repentance, this matter deserves our serious contemplation. Throughout history the topic of change has teased the curiosity of our world's greatest minds. Many have committed their intellect to explore practical techniques capable of kindling the process of change. For centuries men have hoped to discover some substance which could be able to create enduring conversion.

From intrinsic and extrinsic perspectives, great men have questioned what can be done to assist changes in others and how can we facilitate changes within our-self. Like us, they pondered, how does one generate changes in thoughts or in thought processes? How do we change behaviors, habits or personalities? What steps must a person take on the path of repentance; what roads must be traveled on the trail of change? Since man has a *"power to become"*[35] we know that change is possible, but still we wonder what procedures appropriately precede becoming *"a new creature."*[36]

---

[30] 1 Corinthians 12:26
[31] Mosiah 14:3
[32] Matthew 5:4 – "Blessed are they that mourn: for they shall be comforted."
[33] 2 Corinthians 7:9,10 – Emphasis added
[34] 2 Corinthians 7:11 – "ye sorrowed after a godly sort, what carefulness it wrought in you, yea, what clearing of yourselves, yea, what indignation, yea, what fear, yea, what vehement desire, yea what zeal, yea, what revenge!"
[35] D&C 39:4 – "But as many as received me, gave I power to become my sons; and even so will I give unto as many as will receive me, power to become my sons."
[36] 2 Corinthians 5:17 – "if any man be in Christ, he is a new creature: old things are passed away; all things are become new."

Though Paul qualifies godly sorrow as being necessary for penitent change, little explanation is given about what *"godly sorrow"* actually is. In the struggle to define godly sorrow, one might recall the scenarios where God sorrowed over the distress of His children. From a literal stand point it would not be remiss to label such scenes as *"godly sorrow."*

The question is, is it acceptable to connect God's literal sorrow to the godly sorrow Paul speaks of? If God suffers on account of His compassion, the assumption would be that compassion holds a key to experiencing godly sorrow. Remember also, Paul's emphasis of godly sorrow is that it *"worketh repentance."* So, how could a godly sorrow brought about by compassion lead to repentance?

Compassion facilitates repentance through selflessness. Compassionate motives markedly differ from the conceited *"sorrow of the damned"* which *"sorrowing* [is] *not unto repentance."* Like a toddler's tantrum, unrepentant sorrowers grieve *"because the Lord* [will] *not always suffer them to take happiness in sin."*[37] What a contrast to our Heavenly Father, whose source of sorrow is never self-pity, who never sheds a shred of selfishness in His tears. Everything in God's sorrow is generated by His compassion for others. Selfish fear only manufactures brief shifts in behavior, whereas compassion is capable of causing a replete, remorseful repentance.

If sorrowers only see how consequences affect one's self, change is far less efficient and effective. Every action, large and small, has consequences that branch far beyond our self. The compassionate consider the rippling effects of their choices. Their awareness extends to see how their choices affect others. To avoid the self-centered *"sorrow of the damned,"* our lamentations must expand to contemplate the pain we produce in others.

No moral action exists with effects secluded to one's self! Because the *"bond of charity"*[38] is an empathetic link, unrighteous decisions directly impact those who love us. Thus, bad behaviors cannot be excused by the flawed philosophy – my actions are okay because I am not harming anyone. Our sin always brings sorrow to those who love us; therefore sin especially affects God, whose love for us is perfect. Since the 'great commandments of the law' are to love God and our neighbor, it shouldn't be surprising to suppose that lasting repentance is an accessory to loving God and others.

Could compulsion ever be sharp enough to cut away thick habits of wickedness from hardened hearts? Cheap, coerced and obligatory

---

[37] Mormon 2:13 – Brackets added
[38] See D&C 88:125 – "clothe yourself with the bond of charity, as with a mantle, which is the bond of perfectness and peace."

offerings last as long as their worth. We must examine the motivations behind our offerings, for God has asked, *"To what purpose is the multitude of your sacrifices unto me?"*[39] A sacrifice prepared with compassion is always acceptable to God; for compassion has a way of altering our desires so that we are willing to place our desires upon the altar. When sympathy stirs the soul, desires change and our love for God and man becomes greater than our love for self and sin.

Why are you trying to live a righteous life? What resides within a soul that dares challenge to change everything in the carnal nature? Since empathy, sympathy and commiseration move us in such an enormously profound way, compassion can transform the way we act. For this reason, we need to expand the perceptual provinces. How wide does our awareness reach?

To what extent will we allow compassion transfigure our thought and actions? Why do you weep over wickedness? Is it solely because of regret's tortuous sting, or have you discovered what it means to *"sorrow after a godly manner?"* Have you yet sorrowed, not for yourself but for the pain and suffering you have brought others? Have you sorrowed for the pain you have caused God? How will you let this love and concern you feel toward God and others change you? It is touching this last question that we find compassion's most infringing aspect – a magnificent mindfulness of God's level of involvement in our lives.

God is present in all of our interactions. Whether we are dealing with a lunatic or a king, a parent or a child, a stranger or a spouse, God has woven himself into the fabric of our relations. We cannot wish Him away from our dealings with co-workers, nor can we expect exceptions in our exchanges with an enemy. God is an inseparable recipient of everything our actions send out. This is the grand secret implied in Mosiah's teaching, *"And behold, I tell you these things that ye may learn wisdom; that ye may learn that* **when ye are in the service of your fellow beings ye are only in the service of your God.**"[40] This precept is not partial to service, whether service or suffering is rendered to a fellow being, the act is received by God.

Could there be a more compelling incentive to maintain charitable composure in every social interaction? Despite the directness of Christ's doctrine, we still repeatedly fail to grasp the overwhelming implication of this scripture. True, as James reminds us, we should respect all men

---

[39] Isaiah 1:1 – "To what purpose is the multitude of your sacrifices unto me? saith the LORD: I am full of the burnt offerings"
[40] Mosiah 2:17 – Emphasis added

because they *"are made after the similitude of God,"*[41] but our reverence and esteem towards man should be as our reverence and esteem towards God. This is the climactic mystery contained in compassion. Compassion is to fully comprehend the meaning of Christ's words, **"Inasmuch as ye have done it unto one of the least of these my brethren, ye have done it unto me."**[42] These words plainly and accurately place Christ in the center of our interactions.

It is impossible to escape God's presence in any social exchange. The Holy Messiah, who paid the price of the incalculable Atonement, took upon Himself the sensations of suffering in all people. Christ felt the touch and pang of physical discomfort, the awful force of fear, the daunting distress of doubt. He experienced the twists of mental torments and the contact of every tear. *"For we have not an high priest which cannot be touched with the feeling of our infirmities; but was in all points tempted like as we are, yet without sin."*[43] When we add to another human being's misery, we are also responsible for increasing the agony the Son of God endured in Gethsemane and Calvary.

Therefore, let all of your communications be handled with the utmost care. For if you extort others, demean others, yell, injure, mock or shun any human being – your actions are done as if to Christ Himself. If you trample others under your feet, or make yourself superior to another 'you have done it unto Christ.' Ignorance and apathy are not safeguards from this truth, for omissions are part of the equation as well. Christ expounds on this principle with his teaching, **"Inasmuch as ye did it not to one of the least of these, ye did it not to me."**[44] In this light, Paul's rebuke is given added weight, *"But when ye sin so against the brethren, and wound their weak conscience, ye sin against Christ."*[45] No justifications can disconnect Deity from the ills one inflicts upon another – it cannot be done!

Can we comprehend how intrusive this teaching is? This principle should dramatically influence our perceptions of everyday activities. Are we truly to say, "If I sit down on a bus with strangers, am I supposed treat the person next to me as I would the Christ? Am I really to serve in my occupation as if my service is to God?" The answer is a resounding yes, for *"whatsoever ye do, do it heartily, as to the Lord, and not unto men."*[46]

---

[41] James 3:9
[42] Matthew 25:40 – Emphasis added
[43] Hebrews 4:15
[44] Matthew 25:45 – Emphasis added
[45] 1 Corinthians 8:12
[46] Colossians 3:23

Nevertheless, this principle is not entirely condemning. True, compassion is at times an aching awareness, but it is not limited to painful pathos. Compassion can also allow you to access happiness as well as suffering. Just as we say the bad inflicted to others is inflicted upon Christ, we are also compelled to say that service, goodness and kindness is likewise directed to Him who will *"Rejoice with them that do rejoice."*[47] Compassion is not just a fear of causing pain, it is a desire to create joy in others and share in their successes. The faithful disciple 'feeds the hungry, gives drink to them that thirst, they clothe the naked and shelter the stranger, they visit the sick'[48] and tend to the desperate because their compassion brings the joy of Christ's redemption to those who suffer. Therefore, *"Ponder the path of thy feet,"*[49] and keep a constant vigil in all sociality that you may remember Christ in every exchange.

Unsurprisingly, those who care for Christ are willing to enter into a covenant of compassion with Him, through baptism. Faithful followers who have suffered a godly sorrow have no difficulty *"mourn*[ing] *with those that mourn."*[50] Also, because they desire to receive the sacred gift of the Holy Ghost, the comforter, disciples naturally *"comfort those that stand in need of comfort."*[51] Being empowered by the Holy Spirit, disciples are granted a greater measure of strength so that *"We then that are strong* [can] *bear the infirmities of the weak."*[52]

Therefore, it is little wonder that those who bear the name of Christ will *"bear one another's burdens."*[53] As disciples of Christ striving to *"do the things which* [we] *have seen* [Christ] *do,"*[54] we will testify through our compassion to all people *"at all times and in all things, and in all places that ye may be in, even until death."*[55]

One cannot wait for providence to present a perfectly pruned path, one with optimally placed stepping stones to steer us toward those that struggle. In order for us to *"to comfort all that mourn;"*[56] we must be the initiators of good. We must take the initiative to seek and create opportunities to intervene.

---

[47] Roman 12:15
[48] Matthew 25:34-45 – See the entire passage.
[49] Proverbs 4:26
[50] Mosiah 18:9 – Brackets added
[51] Mosiah 18:9
[52] Romans 15:1 – "We then that our strong ought to bear the infirmities of the weak, and not to please ourselves."
[53] Mosiah 18:8
[54] 2 Nephi 31:12 – Brackets added
[55] Mosiah 18:8
[56] Isaiah 61:2

The saints could reach the gates to Zion, if we put as much effort into finding *"the hands that hang down"*[57] as much as some hunt for the ever-elusive TV remote. Oft times one need only enough consideration to initiate a conversation to keep our Christian code of conduct. How can we expect to eliminate loneliness when we continue to build electronic walls around all of our relationships? There is no 'app' to replace the power of the human touch; there is no technology that substitutes for a smile, hand shake or embrace.

Compassion *"is no respecter of persons"*[58] and *"esteemeth all flesh in one."*[59] Being indifferent to one's position, the compassionate do not require special status before serving; compassion is always non-selective in its sympathy. Emulating the example of the Lord, the compassionate reach out to embrace all peoples; for *"The LORD is gracious, and full of compassion; slow to anger, and of great mercy. The LORD is good to all: and his tender mercies are over all his works."*[60] Compassion carries a love for all class, kindred, creed and race: it responds impartially to friends, acquaintances, outcasts and enemies. It does not discriminate against outsiders. Since the compassionate comprehend how they too *"were strangers,"*[61] they 'love the stranger as themselves.'[62]

Because compassion is not 'partial in itself,' the compassionate will not set the man of 'goodly apparel in a good place while putting the poor under a footstool.'[63] Compassion equalizes one's eyes with empathy allowing them to discern that *"one being is as precious in* [God's] *sight as the other."*[64] The compassionate change their perception of others from 'foreigners to fellow citizens,'[65] they respect all men as fellow sufferers for the sake of Christ.

When you look at others, do you see them as strangers or brothers? Look at the people next to you; regardless of rough appearance or awkward apparel, this does not change the fact that they are family. Every action

---

[57] D&C 81:5 – "Wherefore, be faithful ... succor the weak, lift up the hands which hang down, and strengthen the feeble knees."
[58] Acts 10:34
[59] 1 Nephi 17:35
[60] Psalms 145:8,9
[61] Deuteronomy 10:19 – "Love ye therefore the stranger: for ye were strangers in the land of Egypt."
[62] Leviticus 19:34 – "But the stranger that dwelleth with you shall be unto you as one born among you, and thou shalt love him as thyself."
[63] See James 2:2-4
[64] Jacob 2:21 – Brackets added
[65] Ephesians 2:19 – "Now, therefore ye are no more strangers and foreigners, but fellowcitizens with the saints, and of the household of God"

involving others must be undertaken with a fixed belief that we are interacting with a child of God. Not only are others an immortal soul of immeasurable potential, they are part of your eternal family bound to you by immeasurable love of God. Such was the seer's sight of Enoch who could behold *"the spirits that God had created."* Because Enoch beheld *"things which were not visible to the natural eye"*[66] he could discern sinners as siblings. To a people 'dull of hearing' seeking 'counsels in the dark' and 'devising murder'[67] he taught, *"The Lord which spake with me, the same is … my God, and your God, and* **ye are my brethren.**"[68]

Whether we cross a rebel or a believer, our hearts should not have to recalculate our care, for all are brethren. In order to avoid the social estrangement desired by the adversary, it will be imperative to see people in this context. Satan has invested so much into severing the ties which hold the human family together. He cunningly divides nations, communities, cultures and families. Do you suppose it is God's prerogative to have us walk down streets and halls with our heads down? Were the veil lifted from your eyes, you would remember the great love we as fellow members of a Heavenly family once shared.

Compassion is tolerant to all types of distress. It does not delight to see suffering even in those who are seemingly deserving of it. There is no need to conceal a secret smile when the *"wicked fall into their own nets."*[69] The compassionate will 'not rejoice when its enemy falleth, and does not let its heart be glad when his enemy stumbleth.'[70] There is nothing innocent about finding pleasure in another person's problems or pain. Is it not the devils who are merry over man's misery and feast over humanity's failures? The very essence of satanic ecstasy is a celebration of the suffering of others. It is the humor of hell that laughs over other's lamentations. Therefore to desire distress in any, even and especially our enemies is a damnable disposition.

To any who have let contempt contaminate a relationship, such should heed the advice given by F. Enzio Buche, "When you cannot love someone, look into that person's eyes long enough to find the hidden rudiments of the child of God in him."[71] And if you fail to find the familial

---

[66] Moses 6:36 – "And he beheld the spirits that God had created; and he beheld also things which were not visible to the natural eye; … A seer hath the Lord raised up"
[67] See Moses 6: 27,28
[68] Moses 6:43-Emphasis added
[69] Psalms 141:10 – "Let the wicked fall into their own nets, whilst that I withal escape."
[70] Proverbs 24:17 – "Rejoice not when thine enemy falleth, and let not thine heart be glad when he stumbleth"
[71] Elder F. Enzio Busche. Remarks were made during a BYU Devotional May 14, 1996.

bond you share with your offenders, love them nonetheless, for God has repeatedly said, "*Inasmuch as ye do it unto the least of these, ye do it unto me.*"[72] Allow your heart to be filled with compassion. Search the eyes of all God's children until you can see that shared sadness kept secret in their soul, "*we being a lonesome and a solemn people, wanderers, cast out from*" our heavenly home, "*born in tribulation, in a wilderness.*"[73] Trouble is stitched into every man's story for "*man is born unto trouble, as the sparks fly upward.*"[74]

Suffering is the school of the saints, and there is a massive amount of course work required to complete the Christian curriculum. Most of us are familiar with the prerequisite courses of life; for example, we commonly talk about how afflictions educate us in matters of spiritual arithmetic, wherein we calculate the costs of consecration. We know that adversity assesses our fluency in celestial literature whether we, like Christ, can call upon the word of God to defend against the devil's doctrines.[75] Similar to scientific inquiry, we, "*not knowing beforehand*"[76] will test various hypothesis through faith, then prayerfully draw conclusions from "*an experiment upon [God's] words.*"[77]

Through these means, the struggles of mortality are a medium for receiving Heaven's greatest treasures. Pains produce patience. Faith is fashioned in fiery afflictions, and love can be learned in loneliness. Yet, there are other reasons why we may be asked to pass through certain calamities. The academics of discipleship are more than math, science and English. God would have us get a passing grade in communications as well. God is intent to educate His servants in a special type of multilinguality. God, through affliction, teaches us the tongues of tribulation – dialects that are spoken through compassion.

Our cognitive instincts are trained to filter life experiences by how they shape our own soul. But suffering is not explicitly sent to build strength in the sufferer. There is more to life's hardships than sharpening our own spirit's mind and muscles. There are tribulations "*that we are appointed thereunto;*"[78] which God will have us pass through for the express

---

[72] D&C 42:38
[73] Jacob 2:27 – Originally: "cast out from Jerusalem, born in tribulation in a wilderness, and hated of our brethren"
[74] Job 5:7
[75] See Luke 4:4,8,10 – Jesus responds to the devil 3 times: "Jesus answered ... it is written."
[76] 1 Nephi 4:6 – "And I was led by the Spirit, not knowing beforehand the things which I should do."
[77] Alma 32:27 – "arouse your faculties, even to an experiment upon my words, and exercise a particle of faith"
[78] 1 Thessalonians 3:3 – "no man should be moved by these afflictions: for yourselves know that we are appointed thereunto."

purpose of benefitting other people.

True, every affliction has the possibility of refining our faculties, but we must realize that we are not always the sole or even the primary benefactors of these experiences. Sometimes we sojourn a specific set of pains and problems for the purpose of preparing us to rescue others who may falter along similar paths. Paul taught, *"Blessed be God ... who comforteth us in all our tribulation,* **that we may be able to comfort them** *which are in any trouble."*[79] Tribulation broadens our reach. It grants us an articulation of speech capable of speaking to another's comparable difficulties. With this blessing we are able to more accurately communicate *"the comfort wherewith we ourselves are comforted of God."*[80]

Therefore, let your afflictions enlarge your language of consolation, for 'As ye are partakers of the sufferings so shall ye be emissaries of the consolation.'[81] So it was for Christ, who learned the prose of pain by paying the price of our sins. Isaiah records, *"The Lord God hath given me* **the tongue of the learned***, that* **I should know how to speak a word in season to him that is weary***: he wakeneth morning by morning, he wakeneth mine ear to hear as the learned."*[82] What is the tongue of the learned? How was Christ taught to speak a word to us in season? The scripture states, the Messiah is learned and knows how to speak to them that are weary. But is this message constrained to a singular season of weariness, or are there other seasons which the Lord can speak to and hear as the learned?

In every season of circumstance God communicates to our cries as one who is learned, for it is written, *"And he shall go forth, suffering pains and afflictions, and temptations of every kind ... he will take upon him death ... and he will take upon him their infirmities, that his bowels may be filled with mercy, according to the flesh, that he may know according to the flesh how to succor his people according to their infirmities."*[83] *"For in that he himself hath suffered being tempted, he is able to succor them that are tempted."*[84]

God knows how to speak to us, *"For the Lord God giveth light unto the understanding; for* **he speaketh unto men according to their language, unto their understanding***."*[85] He knows every subtle aspect of your perception. He knows all the thoughts and intents of your heart; therefore,

---

[79] 2 Corinthians 1:3,4 – Emphasis added
[80] 2 Corinthians 1:4
[81] See 2 Corinthians 1:7 – "as ye are partakers of the sufferings, so shall ye be also of the consolation."
[82] Isaiah 50:4 – Emphasis added
[83] Alma 7:11,12
[84] Hebrews 2:18
[85] 2 Nephi 31:3 – Emphasis added

He knows how to speak to your heart and will approach you in a way that is ideal to your understanding. Are there any cries that Father and Christ do not comprehend? *"Blessed be God, even the Father of our Lord Jesus Christ, the Father of mercies, and the God of all comfort,"*[86] who is fluent in all forms of affliction, who speaks perfectly the language of loneliness and knows all too well the dialects of the distressed.

God has intensely and profoundly felt inside Himself the complete collection of humanity's feelings for *"In all their affliction he was afflicted."* These are not the feelings of a passive spectator at a sporting event. God responds to succor sending *"the angel of his presence,"* therewith He will 'save you, and in His pity He will redeem you and carry you all the days of old.'[87] Heavenly Father who 'lays His hands upon us by the hands of His servants'[88] may similarly disclose the 'angel of His presence' in the eyes of His servants. Just as distress can easily be caught in a person's countenance, desperation has a unique way of unveiling empathy in the eyes of others. In such moments as eyes meet, a miraculous sympathetic glow seems to suck part of the suffering out of our souls.

Can you imagine then, that if we are so awestruck over such small mortal glances, what emotion will attend when we are brought face to face with the Holy Father! Then you will look upon Him and be re-introduced to the countenance of compassion which shines in His eyes, and Father, who is no stranger to tears, will most tenderly *"wipe away all tears from* [your] *eyes."*[89]

---

[86] 2 Corinthians 1:3
[87] Isaiah 63:9 – "and the angel of his presence saved them, in his love and in his pity he redeemed the; and carried them all the days of old."
[88] See- D&C 36:2 – "And I will lay my hand upon you by the hand of my servant"
[89] Revelation 7:17 – Brackets Added – "… and God shall wipe away all tears from their eyes."

Mercy

Of all love's expressions, none is so sublime as mercy. Without mercy love is brittle, capable of crumbling over slight irritations; thus, mercy is largely responsible for love's longevity. When cutting words slice our affections and separate us from one other, it is mercy that regenerates warm feelings, trust and friendship. When circumstances strain out love, mercy revives charity. Were it not for mercy, how many of our relationships would be stuck in an eternal winter and never know the refreshing of spring? Worlds rotate and seasons spin allowing the "*course of the Lord* [to be] *one eternal round*,"[1] only because mercy restores balance to this cycle.

Mercy and forgiveness share a special bond. We primarily come into contact with mercy through forgiveness. Forgiveness is the grasping arm of grace. It is the caress of charity. Forgiveness has the power to resurrect kindness, revive relationships, and re-establish harmony to every variety of tumultuous situations. Forgiveness purifies poisonous spite; it decontaminates discord and detoxifies contempt. Mercy is the vaccine to the virus of vengeance and the urgent treatment for infectious anger. With mercy we reduce the rub of colliding cultures and decrease the friction of contention.

Mercy and compassion share many fibers in the fabric of Christian love. It is a very subtle distinction that separates the two. Compassion is an unprejudiced response, operating in every shade of social association. Compassion focuses on the feelings of the sufferer more than its affiliation with the sufferer. In contrast, mercy operates at more of an interpersonal level. Implied in mercy is a relationship between two parties. In fact, one of the assumptions we make is that turmoil has struck between the two parties and severed their connection.

Compassion doesn't have these precursors; whereas in mercy, relationships precede a problem, and the problem comes prior to mercy. This is why the economical analogies concerning mercy are so fitting. The story begins with a loan. Circumstances or poor decisions make the loan un-payable, and because the full payment is not made the relationship itself

---

[1] 1 Nephi 10:19 – Brackets added – Originally: "wherefore, the course of the Lord is one eternal round."

is damaged.² Once this point is reached mercy is required to restore peace. Mercy and compassion are distinguished by that to which they respond to. Compassion responds to sorrows as mercy responds to crimes. Compassion responds to suffering as mercy responds to infractions. Compassion responds to tribulation as mercy responds to transgressions. Compassion responds to fears as mercy responds to offenses.

The monetary examples used by the Savior show us that in the economics of mercy there is high hypocrisy in withholding forgiveness. How often do we penalize unpaid payments of pennies while carrying large mortgages of maleficence? How common it is to see people imprison others over paltry sums even after Christ ransomed us at such an incalculable cost.

Because we 'are not our own' and have been *"bought with a price,"*³ false and fake forms of forgiveness are not isolated insults between opposing sides of a fractured relationship. Unwillingness to forgive mocks the very mercies of the Messiah. Such is why when it comes to forgiveness, we are not allowed leniency. When it comes to mercy, there is no room for exceptions or excuses, for it is written, *"I, the Lord, will forgive whom I will forgive,* **but of you it is required to forgive all men**.*"*⁴

Mercy cannot rekindle relationships until all resentment is released. Despite the clarity of God's commandment to forgive all men, there are those who still struggle to express the simple statement – I forgive you. Some can only swallow these words by covering their contempt with counterfeit coats of cordial conduct. Others offer façade forgiveness and dress up their resentments, waiting for an opening to release the rude rudiments of their bitterness. Such are they that sit at the table and exchange pleasantries and congenial conversation, but beneath their contrived courtesies they have buried both bitterness and scorn. These are they who will politely pardon the person so long as they are present, but rapidly jump back into gossiping as soon as they have departed.

Forgiveness has to be more than good manners. It needs to include good feelings and good will. Such defined the mercy of Nephi who *"did frankly forgive"*⁵ his brothers who had it in their heart to kill him. Frank forgiveness doesn't drag its feet waiting for a moment of vindication to pass

---

² See Matthew 18:21-35 – Parable of the unforgiving servant
³ 1 Corinthians 6:19,20 – "know ye not that … ye are not your own? For ye are bought with a price"
⁴ D&C 64:10 – Emphasis added
⁵ 1 Nephi 7:21 – "I did frankly forgive them all that they had done, and I did exhort them that they would pray unto the Lord their God for forgiveness."

before it offers a hand of fellowship. Neither will it barter mercy, demanding a steep price of servitude to pay for an apology.

Some shrink their mercy by adding qualifying restrictions. Such is not necessary for the divine grace which has been exemplified by Christ who allows us "*to be redeemed without money.*"[6] Christ shows us the way, and to those who thirst for forgiveness He says, "*come ye to the waters, and he that hath no money; come ye, buy, and eat; yea, come, buy wine and milk without money and without price.*"[7] Just as God is "*ready to pardon, gracious and merciful,*"[8] we should not hesitate to overlook other's offenses. "*Therefore if thou bring thy gift to the altar, and there rememberest that thy brother hath ought against thee; Leave there thy gift before the altar, and go thy way; first be reconciled to thy brother, and then come and offer thy gift.*"[9]

Sadly, even among Jesus's followers, forgiveness is becoming a forgotten art. It is as if the most meaningful forms of forgiveness have been forsaken, and the noble virtue of mercy has been denigrated to nothing more than a frivolous phrase. Forgiveness is not solely found in the exchange of words; rather true forgiveness takes place after apologies have made. Bumper sticker benevolence makes mercy an empty motto. Mercy's substance is not contained in words; its essential purpose is restoring a person back to full fellowship. This fundamental finale cannot not be omitted any longer, and our primary focus needs to shift to the events that take place after we say the words, "I forgive you?"

What is the full implication of forgiveness? Mercy's totality can best be seen by examining the way which God forgives us. Man knows no greater power than that which turns transgressors into gods. Among the most supernal expressions of God's power are the powers of redemption, resurrection, reconciliation, and atonement – all of which are tightly connected to themes of mercy. According to the scriptures, these most holy powers can be observed in the ordinances of the gospel, as it is written, "*in the ordinances thereof, the power of godliness is manifested.*"[10] If the power of godliness is revealed in sacred ordinances, we should ponder – how do the ordinances reveal the full power of God?

Ordinances re-enact and display God's desire to perfectly redeem us. By observing the ordinances, we see specific stages of divine

---

[6] Isaiah 52:3
[7] Isaiah 55:1
[8] Nehemiah 9:17 – "Thou art a God ready to pardon, gracious and merciful, slow to anger, and of great kindness"
[9] Matthew 5:24,25
[10] D&C 84:20 – "Therefore, in the ordinances thereof, the power of godliness is manifested."

forgiveness and the sacred narrative of redemption unfold. We see that in the waters of baptism God washes away our sins[11] and afterwards sanctifies us "*by the reception of the Holy Ghost.*"[12] Next, God entrusts us to be His "*appointed messengers*" with sacred callings conformed from the Order of the Priesthood. Hereby we are "*clothed with power and authority.*"[13] God then showers us with blessing from head to toe till we are welcomed back home to Him – to be in His presence once again.

Lastly, in the grand finale of God's forgiveness we are sealed to Him for all Eternity and receive the fullness of His Charity; we become as one, connected in a way wherein we will never again to be separated from His presence. The stages of forgiveness manifested in ordinances include: cleansing, sanctification, a bestowal of power and authority, a showering of blessings, a return to fellowship and union or sealing. Considering the full measure of mercy emulated by Heavenly Father, we see why it is somewhat insulting to forgiveness reduced to a few fickle words.

Additional insight into our Father's forgiveness is seen in the ancient Mosaic sacrificial ordinances. As stated in the Bible Dictionary, "It is noteworthy that when the three offerings [sin, burnt, and peace] were offered together, the sin always preceded the burnt, and the burnt the peace offerings. Thus the order of the symbolizing sacrifices was the order of **atonement, sanctification, and fellowship with the Lord.**"[14] This precept causes us to contemplate the following: does our forgiveness consider the sinner sanctified? Does it amend misgivings and facilitate camaraderie? Can you include a recalcitrant as kindred and grant him a place at the table? Will your mercy offer brotherhood to a betrayer? In order for us to restore forgiveness to its fullness we must begin to reincorporate principles of atonement, sanctification and fellowship back into our acts of mercy.

One of the greatest miracles of mercy is that it mends misdeeds without leaving behind memorable scars. We should not overlook how fundamental forgetting is to forgiveness. The forgetfulness of forgiveness does not literally imply that mercy induces episodic bouts of amnesia. Rather it is as the Prophet Ezekiel taught, "*If the wicked restore the pledge, give again that he had robbed, walk in the statutes of life, without committing iniquity; he shall surely live, he shall not die.* **None of his sins that he hath committed**

---

[11] See Acts 22:16 – "arise, and be baptized, and wash away thy sins"
[12] 3 Nephi 27:20 – "be sanctified by the reception of the Holy Ghost, that ye may stand spotless before me"
[13] D&C 138:30
[14] Bible Dictionary page 767 – Emphasis and brackets added

shall be mentioned unto him: *he hath done that which is lawful and right; he shall surely live.*"[15] Far too many people's forgiveness comes spring loaded like a jack-in-the-box; patiently waiting for that pristine moment to pop out and say ... I told you so. It is a fake forgiveness that hastily retracts its trust even after tiny infractions. True mercy will come to see a penitent perpetrator as pure.

God does not purchase stock in our mistakes. There are those who say, "I forgive you," but continue to chart and collect every injustice like a mother meticulously documenting her children's lives. Unsurprisingly, after these people have "forgiven you" they remain overly eager to share the scrapbooks of your past mistakes. We do not need to photograph every offense, nor should we feel it necessary to pen every privation as a journal entry. Some people figuratively go so far as to catalog their complaints like a librarian. Inventorying your dissatisfactions will not benefit you. Such behaviors resemble the habits of Satan and his devils who safely store all of our sins in their memories. We must not be like those hellish fiends who go into battle wielding the past as a weapon against the present.

Forgiveness means that we release all resentments. True forgiveness never needs to exhume the graves of past grudges, nor does it keep a backup hard-drive storing a history of past hardships. Just as mercy is associated with regenerative effects, we see a similar but opposite effect in the vice of vengeance.

Vengeance is never benign. Its pathology is astonishingly similar to the progression of a malignant tumor. Both cancer and vengeance grow by feeding on life giving resources. They corrupt wholesome structures, and as they expand, they put pressure on and weaken organs around them. This process continues to pollute the entire body until it devours the last remaining strands of life. Seeing that the threat which vengeance poses is in every way as harmful as a terminal disease, we should heed the warning, *"Thou shalt not avenge, nor bear any grudge against the children of thy people, but thou shalt love thy neighbour as thy self: I am the* LORD.*"*[16] Though the natural man would fume with furious indignation; we must find the divine light within ourselves that urges us to let go, and forgive.

Carrying the weight of vengeance generates a disturbing dissonance in our spirits. Over time bearing this burden sucks out every ounce of serenity from the soul. The vengeful, who tailgate after every tiny transgression, rarely consider that those who choose to hold a grudge are

---

[15] Ezekiel 33:15,16 – Emphasis added
[16] Leviticus 19:18

the ones who must tote its weight. In order to maintain a firm grip on the "iron rod," we will have to let go of all our grudges, for venturing the straight and narrow will require both hands when the *"mists of darkness"*[17] arise.

There are other dangers in recycling resentments. By holding the past hostage, we prevent a person's present progression. Perhaps George Bernard Shaw put it best when he said, "The only man who behaved sensibly was my tailor; he took my measurement anew every time he saw me, while all the rest went on with their old measurements and expected them to fit me."[18] We should remember that God does not only expect us to re-fit our friends, He also desires us to re-measure our enemies. No one deserves to be kept trapped inside a prison of a past perspective. Forgiveness must be allowed to free each individual's future. This is done by reconnecting the principle of sanctification back to forgiveness. For if we are to 'forgive one another even as God for Christ's sake hath forgiven us,'[19] we need to be able to give others a clean slate and a fresh start.

Reinstantiating trust to forgiveness is the grimmest climb of reconciliation. Trusting those who have wronged us previously is necessary to finalizing forgiveness and mercy. Our Christian commission calls us to focus on how we will treat persons we claim to have forgiven. You may ask, "if I am expected to forgive all men, does this mean that I must trust these same men as well?" Judge this matter for yourself. For if you suppose to omit trust in the 'measure you mete,'[20] be prepared to accept that same measurement to be restored to you again.

To what degree do you trust your transgressors? Forgiveness is more than a renewed agreement to participate in ritualistic reciprocities. Even the most commendable saints have been caught imagining, "I can tolerate my enemy and display genuine generosity as I exchange pleasantries. I could even see myself putting on an elegant pageantry of love toward my enemy. It shouldn't be too hard to speak kindly to him, give him gifts, feast or joke with him, but do not ask me to depend on this man … here I draw the line."

Under this narrow version of mercy, Peter would have been

---

[17] See 1 Nephi 12:17 – "And the mists of darkness are the temptations of the devil, which blindeth the eyes, and hardeneth the hearts of the children of men, and leadeth them away into broad roads, that they perish and are lost."

[18] George Bernard Shaw. *Man and Superman.* Act 1 pg.37

[19] Ephesians 4:32 – "forgiving one another, even as God for Christ's sake hath forgiven you."

[20] Matthew 7:2 – "For with what judgment ye judge, ye shall be judged: and with what measure ye mete, it shall be measured to you again."

excluded from further service in the Apostleship, for how could Jesus depend on one who had previously denied him. Since you could no longer call on someone who has carelessly broken covenants, Corianton too would have forever been banned from further missionary service. Because former rebels could not be relied upon, prominent preachers such as Alma and Paul would have remained outlawed from sharing the gospel.

These are not the ways of our Father and therefore are not permissible to His disciples. Remember that *"God is merciful,"* and if you will *"repent of that which thou hast done which is contrary to the commandment which I gave you …* **thou art still chosen, and art again called** *to the work."*[21] How extraordinary it is that God calls us rather than condemns us; that He would chose us when He otherwise might have banished us. It is beyond comprehension that 'God would count us worthy of His calling'[22] even when our past has been spotted with wickedness. "For the law maketh men high priests which have infirmity."[23]

Are you capable of having faith in repentant thieves, whores or brawlers? How long will you funnel human beings through a label? Forgiveness is not complete until the relationship itself is restored to full grace. This is a 'weightier matter of the law'[24] that should not be left 'undone' any longer.

What an unfathomable miracle it is that God's *"chosen generation"*[25] could be found among 'a wild and a hardened and a ferocious people.' That 'a people who delighted in murdering'[26] could become *"a royal priesthood, an holy nation … Which in time past were not a people, but are now the people of God: which had not obtained mercy, but now have obtained mercy."*[27] From life experiences, we understand the complex inner turmoil that accompanies trying to trust someone who has broken confidence. For this reason, we should have the utmost appreciation for Heavenly Father's complete mercy.

Even with The Father's foreknowledge He gives responsibilities to children who will revolt against Him, He gives honor to the same men who may mock Him. Because of mercy, God's greatest opponents have

---

[21] D&C 3:10 – Emphasis added
[22] See 2 Thessalonians 1:11 – "Wherefore also we pray always for you, that our God would count you worthy of this calling, and fulfill all the good pleasure of his goodness, and the work of faith with power."
[23] Hebrews 7:28
[24] See Matthew 23:23 – "Woe unto you, scribes and Pharisees, hypocrites! … ye … have omitted the weightier matters of the law, judgment, mercy, faith: these ought ye to have done, and not to leave the other undone."
[25] 1 Peter 2:9
[26] Alma 17:14
[27] 1 Peter 2:9.10

transformed into some of His most noble servants. These scenarios are not uncommon. For 'to whom much is forgiven, the same loveth much.'[28] When such a tremendous debt is pardoned, our feelings of love and gratitude make us eager to serve our Forgiver.

Mercy expunges enmity, and turns distaste into esteem. It changes evasion into union and ultimately converts foes into friends. After returning an offender to full faith, the next and final task is to climb the peak of proximity. Renewing broken associations should not be thought of as a mastery of choreography. Though preferable to barbarous revenge – expertise in facial mannerisms, communicative quirks and congenial gestures is not a sufficient substitute for real mercy. God teaches that loving feelings have a significant role in forgiveness saying, "*Thou shalt not hate thy brother in thine heart.*"[29]

One cannot conclude forgiveness by secretly storing malcontent beneath benevolence. Would you suppose it merciful to say, "I forgive you; just don't expect me to want to be around you anymore." For some, forgiveness is a "*whited sepulcher, which indeed are beautiful outward,*" but covers feelings as wholesome as "*dead men's bones.*"[30] Could you imagine God following the words "I forgive you," by saying, "as long as you promise to stay away from me and never come near me again?" Then the gates of heaven open, you are handed a key to a distant mansion where you can no longer bother Him with your antics. Our Father does not begrudgingly open the gates of His kingdom. His friendliness is not simply a façade concealing foul feelings.

Avoidance is not forgiveness. Mono-therapy with time has not been clinically proven to cure callousness. When we forgive, we are not just agreeing to return to reciprocities; instead, we return offenders to our proximity and preference. Forgiveness will not work from afar. It must replenish an actual physical affinity. In order to fully forgive, the traitor must be brought back into our circle of friendship. There are no barriers around real mercy. So, when we read, 'that same sociality that exists among us here will exist among us there,' we are forcibly reminded to repair any bitter relationships we have – for there will be no need for fences in heaven.

Nearness is an essential part of the atonement, as Christ said, "*my Father sent me that I might be lifted up upon the cross; and after I had been lifted up*

---

[28] See Luke 7:47 – "but to whom little is forgiven, the same loveth little."
[29] Leviticus 19:17
[30] Matthew 23:27 – "Woe unto you, scribes and Pharisees, hypocrites! For ye are like unto whited sepulchers, which indeed appear beautiful outward, but are within full of dead men's bones, and of all uncleanness."

upon the cross, **that I might draw all men unto me.**"[31] Even though our hearts cry, *"O wretched man that I am,"*[32] *"Depart from me; for I am a sinful man, O Lord,"*[33] God's mercy draws us back to be near Him again, not with the closeness of a crowd, but with the fellowship of family. Can you imagine how it will feel to hear the Father say these words to you, *"I will accept you;"*[34] *"Wherefore thou art no more a servant, but a son; and if a son, then an heir of God through Christ."*[35]

Regardless of what name you use to represent reconciliation, whether it be mercy, penance or atonement, they all essential mean the same thing – being clean and coming home. This is the predominate plot of man's progression to perfection. Seeing how forgiveness is woven into the process of perfection, it is understandable why Luke's record of the verse, *"Be ye therefore perfect, even as your Father which is in heaven is perfect"*[36] is rendered, *"Be ye therefore merciful, as your Father also is merciful."*[37]

Mercy makes perfection possible! Because mercy is located at the center of God's perfection, our smaller imitations of mercy, however minor, display to discerning eyes a snapshot of God's omnipotent power. *"For whether is easier, Thy sins be forgiven thee; or to say, Arise, and walk?"*[38] When we are merciful, we experience a tiny proportion of Heavenly Father's perfection. By forgiving and being forgiven we become *"eyewitnesses of* [God's] *majesty."*[39] For this reason, we will rarely feel as close to the Father than at the time we are actively forgiving another person.

Some of mortalities most memorable moments are when we are allowed to sample mercy's majesty. Though these smaller life experiences are only a shadow of God's supernal mercy, somehow they still have a way of surpassing our comprehension. By every account we are not deserving of mercy. The logic in justice demands that the debts we incur must be met. However, we need to remember that mercy is not justice.

Forgiveness is hardly fair or rational. Mercy contradicts normal logic; it contradicts justice and seems to reverses natural reason. But this is ultimately why mercy is so marvelous. *"O the greatness of the mercy of our God, the* Holy One of Israel!"[40] *"Who is a God like unto thee, that pardoneth iniquity,*

---

[31] 3 Nephi 27:14 – Emphasis added
[32] 2 Nephi 4:17
[33] Luke 5:8
[34] Ezekiel 43:27
[35] Galatians 4:7
[36] Matthew 5:48
[37] Luke 6:36
[38] Matthew 9:5
[39] 2 Peter 1:16 – Brackets added – Originally: his
[40] 2 Nephi 9:19

and passeth by the transgression of the remnant of his heritage? He retaineth not his anger for ever, because he delighteth in mercy. He will turn again, he will have compassion upon us; he will subdue our iniquities; and [He] *will cast all* [our] *sins into the depths of the sea."*[41]

Of the many testimonies of God's mercy, few strike the soul so sharply as the story of the Prodigal son.

> The stoic statue sits, waiting. Here is the forgotten Father, whose wind chaffed eyes solemnly stare into the distance, hoping for that forlorn figure to form on the horizon. No feast can fill the empty chair where silence now sits – the ghastly void. Though surrounded by kindly company, the smiles exchanged across the table are poisoned by a secret piercing loneliness. Quaint conversations unsuccessfully distract him from the screams of the vacant seat. My Son is Gone! My Son is gone … My Son is gone.
>
> I am the man whose steps creased this pebbled path. I knew this stony trail when youth took my travels to a *"far country."*[42] Then with an insolent strut I pressed my pride into the earth. How the blaze of independence blinded me! and wearing my sins as a trophy, I commenced my journey from my Father's house. I no longer remember what feud I traded my family for, perhaps such is well, for arrogance and resentment have many names. But what am I now? A broken, mortal crumb; some sorry sliver dressed in tattered strings, surrounded by the stench of swine.[43]
>
> As I walk toward my father's house, I would that time had erased my error. But all the earth is a testament to my transgression. The assaulting stares of the trees tempt me to retreat. But where can I turn to, I have no place with man. My only company is the wild beasts of which I am now one. Should I turn back? At least the swine will not rebuke me for the mud which coats my skin. How could he accept me? How could I ever dare to look into his eyes again? Yet, lest *"I perish with hunger,"*[44] *"I will arise and go to my father, and will say unto him, Father, I have sinned against heaven, and before thee,*

---

[41] Micah 7:18,19 – Brackets added
[42] Luke 15:13
[43] See Luke 15:15,16 – "and he sent him into his field to feed swine. And he would fain have filled his belly with the husks that the swine did eat: and no man gave unto him."
[44] Luke 15:17

and am no more worthy to be called thy son: make me as one of thy hired servants."[45]

Now *"when he was yet a great way off, his father saw him, and had compassion and ran, and fell on his neck, and kissed him."*[46] My son, My son ... you have returned at last! I am overcome to hold you again. *"Bring forth the best robe and put it on him,"*[47] let it cover the mud and replace his disheveled dress, for it is not meet that my son be arrayed as such. *"Put a ring on his hand, and shoes on his feet"*[48] that he may serve once more in my name. Let the emblems of my power be seen of men that thereby they shall know you as my son. Come now, let a feast be prepared *"Bring hither the fatted calf, and kill it; and let us eat, and be merry,"*[49] for tonight we dine once more as family. Oh Blessed Day! What Joy! What Light! What Love! *"For this my son was dead, and is alive again; he was lost, and is found."*[50]

---

[45] Luke 15:18
[46] Luke 15:20
[47] Luke 15:22
[48] Luke 15:22
[49] Luke 15:23
[50] Luke 15:24

Kindness

Kindness brings balance to love. It is possible to be so bogged down by the weightier matters of the kingdom that the lighter affairs are omitted. Because something seems less significant does not denote that it is dispensable. "*Nay, much more those members of the body, which seem to be more feeble, are necessary.*"[1] Are not the wise of the world continually confounded by "*small and simple*"[2] acts of kindness?

Recall how difficult days can be turned around by the joy of unexpected gifts. Acts of unanticipated kindness have the power to reverse some of the worst feelings felt in the human heart. Such is why we must be kind to our enemies; for just as kindness softens our hearts, it will turn our foe's fierceness into favor.

After reviewing charity, compassion and mercy it is apparent that these qualities embody tremendously dramatic divisions of love. Lingering in these attributes is a feeling of fatal significance. Charity is intimidatingly intense, compassion is profoundly practical, and mercy is majestic and momentous.

So where does kindness fit in amongst the stabilizing pillars of Christian principles? A hasty, initial impression may mistakenly discount kindness, judging it to be undeserving of its own distinction. However, considering the Apostle Paul deliberately included kindness when listing the attributes of divine love, our study of kindness must be taken seriously. God Himself is of "*great kindness.*"[3] Kindness is part of God's character. It is an aspect of the divine nature; therefore, we must learn as God has learned, to "*be ye kind one to another.*"[4]

---

[1] 1 Corinthians 12:16
[2] See Alma 37:6 – "by small and simple things are great things brought to pass; and small means in many instances doeth confound the wise."
[3] Joel 2:1 – "[God] is gracious and merciful, slow to anger, and of great kindness" – Brackets added
[4] Ephesians 4:32 – "And be ye kind one to another, tenderhearted, forgiving one another, even as God ... hath forgiven you"

We must be cautious so as to not neglect the unassuming forms of love; especially since these smaller forms are far more prevalent and practical in everyday life. By way of definition, kindness can represent these simple expressions of love which are comparatively tiny and oft forgotten.

The symphony of life is not played in a continual climax of earth-shattering significance. The drums of destiny do not constantly call us to complete our consecration, nor do thundering trumpets perpetually harass our agency to enter the frontlines of the battle against Satan. Experience is convincing enough to prove that life unfolds with much more *moderato* than *appassionato*. Neal A. Maxwell observed, "life cannot be made up all of kettle drums and crashing cymbals. There must be some flutes and violins. Living cannot be all crescendo; there must be some counterpoint."[5] Because the sound of some instruments is so soft, we must listen carefully to hear the tone of their contributions. So it is with kindness. We must attune our senses to fully appreciate love's subtler expressions, only then can we catch the chords of kindness that set the key in which love's melody is played.

Seldom is the summon given to *"sell all that thou hast, and distribute unto the poor."*[6] Whereas we commonly receive impressions to *"impart of your substance to the poor, everyman according to that which he hath, such as feeding the hungry, clothing the naked, visiting the sick and administering to their relief, both spiritually and temporally."*[7] God will more regularly *"prove* [us] *herewith, to see if* [we] *will"*[8] take the time to provide modest but meaningful service, than test to see if we will 'lay down our life for His sake.'[9] Truly, more people are looking for someone to sit down and talk with them, than for someone who will give them a loan payment or a kidney. People don't always want someone to die for them; sometimes they just want someone to listen to them. God does not demand a climb up Mount Moriah every day; however, He surely expects daily sacrifices of congeniality, smiles, and service.

Amos saw *"a famine in the land"* not of *"bread, nor a thirst for water, but of hearing the words of the* LORD*."*[10] Though this prophesied pestilence refers

---

[5] Neal A. Maxwell. Patience. *Ensign.* Oct 1980, 28
[6] Luke 18:22 – "Yet lackest thou on thing: sell all that thou hast, and distribute unto the poor"
[7] Mosiah 4:26 – See also vs. 27 – "see that all these things are done in wisdom and order"
[8] Abraham 3:25 – "And we will prove them herewith, to see if they will do all the things whatsoever the Lord their God shall command them"
[9] D&C 103:28 – "And whoso is not willing to lay down his life for my sake is not my disciple."
[10] Amos 8:11 – "Behold, the days come, saith the Lord GOD, that I will send a famine in the land, not a famine of bread, nor a thirst for water but of hearing the word of the Lord."

to a global doctrinal dearth, the inhabitants of the world will never be fully nourished until we start feeding one another with acts of kindness. Have you felt that languishing thirst which leaves one yearning for only a meager drop of kindness? In a desert of struggles and sadness faith can become fatally famished and hope perilously parched. On these days, how desperately do we seek relief from an oasis of another person's goodness and grace?

So often what may only seem like a drop of kindness on our part fills another person's thirsting soul to overflowing. Then, after drinking from the cooling waters of kindness, we learn why "[God's] *loving kindness is better than life.*"[11] Recall how often hard days are healed by a humble hug. Oh how much more is our world in need of kindness than cleverness! Our world needs more congeniality than genius, more friendship than fame, service than scholarship, and honor than eminence. It is so much greater to be cordial than beautiful, for sweetness and sensitivity are profoundly more useful than talent and popularity.

Kindness will not cost us an arm or a leg. Often all we need is the courage to start up a conversation – sometimes even a simple smile will do. Within considerate conversations some of life's richest gifts are exchanged –for example, compliments and encouragement. When we are kind, our compliments are not empty congratulations, rather they are sincere and loving commendations. These commendations are quickly recognizable by their familiar warm, melodic tone. As the substance of a cake is in the batter, similarly the substance of love is compassion, faith, mercy, hope and charity. However, it is not the batter but the icing which makes the cake delicious and sweet. Kindness is the sweetness of charity; it is the icing on the cake of Christian virtues.

Any claim of love without kindness is a mockery of charity. How could love ever be enjoyable if it were not amiable? A resilient relationship is one continually fortified by acts of kindness. Such decency distinguishes disciples from the hostile hosts of hell. Devils dwell in a damnable den of discourtesy. Their discussions are never building, only demeaning. A frosted chill of insults insulates their lairs of lies. In contrast, entering a hospitable house feels as if we have walked back into our heavenly home, a place where praise and respect elevate the spirits of all who enter. Gathering round a gracious, courteous company reminds our souls of the sublime communion with angels we once enjoyed.

Don't discount the power contained in incremental acts of

---

[11] Psalms 63:3 – "Because thy lovingkindness is better than life, my lips shall praise thee."

kindness, just as a *"soft answer turneth away wrath,"*[12] kindness can cure scorn. Altruism has the ability to pierce impenetrable apathy. With grace we can gladden the grumpy, and with thoughtfulness we can sooth the obstinate. Ultimately it is by acts of kindness that we will *"overcome evil with good."*[13]

Our Heavenly Father is no foreigner to friendship. He who knows *"how to give good gifts unto [His] children"* teaches us much about how to *"give good things to them that ask."*[14] *"O how great the goodness of our God,"* for *"the Lord which exercise[s] lovingkindness"*[15] will 'hold your hand, and will keep you'[16] even He *"will carry you, and will deliver you."*[17] When your 'hands hang down and your knees feel feeble'[18] the arms of the Eternal Father will pick you up and carry you to safety. When that day comes you will join in the psalm of praise and sing, *"I will mention the lovingkindnesses of the LORD, and the praises of the LORD, according to all that the LORD hath bestowed on [me], and the great goodness toward [me], which he hath bestowed on [me] according to his mercies, and according to the multitude of his lovingkindnesses."*[19]

True, for Abraham's belief he was called a *"Friend of God,"*[20] however the Father is not exclusive in His friendship. God extends friendship to all His children and by the power of the Holy Spirit, He will confirm His affection in the hearts of those who seek it. Then the *"pleasant voice, as if it had been a whisper,"*[21] will speak these words to you, 'Ye are my friend.'[22] As a true friend, God sharpens our countenance as *"Iron sharpeneth iron."*[23] Isaiah tells of this countenance sharpening kindness saying, *"Thus saith the LORD, thy Redeemer, the Holy One of Israel; I am the LORD, thy God which **teacheth thee to profit**, which **leadeth thee by the way** that*

---

[12] Proverbs 15:1
[13] Romans 12:21 – "Be not overcome of evil, but overcome evil with good."
[14] Matthew 7:11 – "If ye then, being evil know how to give good gifts unto your children, ho much more shall your Father which is in heaven give good things to them that ask him?"
[15] Jeremiah 9:24 – "I am the Lord which exercise loving kindness, judgment, and righteousness ... for in these things I delight, saith the LORD."
[16] Isaiah 42:6 – "I the LORD have called thee in righteousness, and will hold thine hand, and will keep thee,"
[17] Isaiah 46:4 – "And even to you old age, I am he; and even to hoar hairs will I carry you: I have made, and I will bear; even I will carry, and will deliver you."
[18] See Hebrews 12:12 – "Wherefore lift up the hands which hang down, and the feeble knees"
[19] Isaiah 63:7 – Originally written in reference to the House of Israel, not in the subjective.
[20] James 2:23 – "Abraham believed God, and it was imputed unto him for righteousness: and he was called the Friend of God."
[21] Helaman 5:46 – "there came a voice unto them, yea a pleasant voice as if it were a whisper"
[22] John 15:14 – "Ye are my friends, if ye do whatsoever I command you."
[23] Proverbs 27:17 – "Iron sharpeneth iron; so a man sharpeneth the countenance of his friend."

thou shouldest go."[24] Just as it is with any good friend, our God teaches and leads us, and makes us better because of our relationship with Him.

In the latter verse from Isaiah, the word *profit* has an interesting Aramaic origin. *Profit* is a translation from the word *ya'al* [25] which has a connotation – to ascend. Of a truth, God our Heavenly Father teaches us how to ascend. He raises us up over our weaknesses, boosts our spirits, builds us, and makes hope and faith soar. God lifts us day unto day, higher and higher *"till we shall mount up with wings as eagles"*[26] and *"ascend into the hill of the LORD."*[27] No image is more suiting to define kindness than the one we see in Him who *"hath raised us up together, and made us sit together in heavenly places in Christ Jesus: That in the ages to come he might shew* **the exceeding riches of his grace in his kindness** *toward us through Christ Jesus."*[28]

For these reasons and more, kindness is the warmth of love. It gives charity its color and timbre. Commitments and connections without kindness are nothing more than cold closeness. Do we not eagerly gather around pleasant and gracious persons as readily as a frost-covered traveler would gather round a fire? How oft do we warm our hopes and spirits on the hearth of kindness! What a stark contrast this is to the animosity of the adversary. It is the devil's prerogative and that of his minions to tear you down by any means possible. By various vicious methods he toils to make us doubt our divine nature and forfeit our confidence. Most particularly, Satan hatefully attacks us with discouragement and denigrating gossip.

Jesus foresaw that in the last days *"the love of many shall wax cold."*[29] Artic storms of rudeness have certainly swept across many of our social interactions; too many relationships are currently covered with an ice of inconsideration. The love in too many families is frozen over with unfriendliness. How desperately do we all desire the *"garment of praise"*[30] when the blue winters of uncertainty strike our confidence? But with altruism, even the hearts of the cold-blooded can be melted.

In contrast to how kindness *ascends* others, we see that harassing

---

[24] Isaiah 48:17 – Emphasis added
[25] Hebrew Strong's Dictionary #3276 – Pronounced "Yaw-al,' a prim. root; prop, to ascend; figurative to be valuable (objective-useful, subjective-benefited)."
[26] Isaiah 40:31 – "But they that wait upon the Lord shall renew their strength; they shall mount up with wings as eagles; they shall run, and not be weary; and they shall walk, and not faint."
[27] Psalms 24:3 – "Who shall ascend into the hill of the LORD? Or who shall stand in his holy place?"
[28] Ephesians 2:6,7 – Emphasis added
[29] Matthew 24:12 – "And because iniquity shall abound, the love of many shall wax cold."
[30] Isaiah 61:3 – "To appoint unto them that mourn in Zion, to give unto them beauty for ashes, the oil of joy for mourning, the garment of praise for the spirit of heaviness"

harshness can shatter a soul. When the kind speak it is *"always with grace, seasoned with salt,"*[31] whereas the language of the cruel is always uncivil seasoned with sarcasm. The cruel are quick to criticize and chastise, while the kind are quick to encourage and succor. Praise for others is always a word fitly spoken *"like apples of gold in pictures of silver."*[32] It is therefore imperative that we tame our tongue, for a contemptuous taunt is toxic to a person's spirit, and insults are *"an unruly evil, full of deadly poison."*[33] It is no small thing to discredit or dishonor another human being. Great caution must ever be exercised with our words lest we curse *"men, which are made after the similitude of God."*[34]

Because of the danger in disparaging words Paul warned, *"Let no corrupt communication proceed out of your mouth, but that which is good to the use of edifying, that it may minister grace unto the hearers."*[35] In Greek the word for *corrupt* is *sapros*, meaning rotten, worthless and putrid.[36] All of these are fitting images for filthy, belittling language. The little member of the tongue can with unkindness 'kindle a great forest.' Though an act of rudeness may initially seem small and insignificant, these mean expressions can consequently create 'a world of iniquity.' Words are so tiny, so unassuming that it is easy for unkind, negative, or hurtful phrases to slip from our lips. But it is because of this subtlety that *"corrupt communication"* is one of Satan's most preferred weapons.

Wrathful words may wound the hearer, but they are murder to the mouthpiece. Within an inconspicuously short sentence the devil damns the herald and damages the recipient. Any word, language, or expression that is unkind to another scalds the souls of those listening while defiling the whole body of the bearer. Though seemingly insignificant, slander's searing flames are as hot as the very 'fires of hell.'[37] For this reason, we must *"speak evil of no man"* and *"be not quarrelsome, but gentle, shewing meekness unto all men."*[38]

Considering the destruction discourteous dialect causes, it is no wonder that the very name Satan means *slanderer*. The Greek word for

---

[31] Colossians 4:6 – "Let your speech be always with grace, season with salt"
[32] Proverbs 25:11 – "A word fitly spoken is like apples of gold in pictures of silver."
[33] See James 3:8 – "But the tongue can no man tame; it is an unruly evil, full of deadly poison"
[34] James 3:8,9 – "But the tongue can no man tame; it is an unruly evil, full of deadly poison. Therewith bless we God, even the Father; and therewith curse we men, which are made after the similitude of God."
[35] Ephesians 4:29
[36] Greek Strong's Dictionary # 4550 – Pronounced (sap-ros)
[37] See James 3: 2-9
[38] Titus 3:2 – Original: no brawlers – Replaced with footnote b containing the Greek substitution of not quarrelsome.

Satan is *satanas*, "A Greek form derived from the Hebrew Satan" meaning an *adversary* or **an accuser**.[39] The latter meaning of accuser takes on a more diabolical denotation when we consider that the Greek word for *devil*, *diabolos* means a *traducer (accuser)*, a *slanderer*. *Diabolo* comes from the word *diaballo* which literally signifies throwing across, *diaballo* suggests a verbal assault or to throw something across the path of another.[40] What some excuse as an innocent insult may become an inhibiting hedge which impedes the journey of injured disciple. Considering the potential consequences of disrespect, how could one ever dare to deter a disciple from the straight and narrow path?

Whose work is accomplished when we put down our brothers and sisters? When you speak ill of another you are emulating the one who "*became Satan, yea, even the devil, that father of all lies.*"[41] When we are indecent, we take upon ourselves an unspeakable image of darkness. Literally, by gossiping we become devils, servant slaves to Satan – the slanderer of our souls. Satan's gospel preaches men's imperfections. It shouts our weaknesses and publishes our mistakes. Sounding across the entire earth is a devilish cry loudly declaring all the crimes of mankind. But, God will put an end to this condescending chatter, for it is written, "*And I heard a loud voice saying in heaven, Now is come salvation ... for the accuser of our brethren is cast down, which accused them before our God day and night.*"[42]

Do you suppose to excuse derogatory designations, reasoning that your rudeness is based on truth? Hurtful honesty does seem a valid defense for ruining a struggling human soul, doesn't it? Those who justify injurious judgments join the nagging numbers of hellish minions who also truthfully tell the transgressions of man. Insults, name calling, and demeaning murmurs are always lies; there is no truth in them! Are you really so confident in your claims? Would you glue a label to another person after merely isolating a single strand of human behaviors? Know that thereby one ignores the entire context of eternity's infinity and with a pathetic perspective attempts to usurp the Omnipotent's powers of judgment. Would you steal judgment from Jesus, the One to whom Heavenly Father 'committed all judgment' to through the everlasting horrors of an atoning sacrifice?[43] Therefore, bridle your tongue and "*Be not rash with thy mouth, and*

---

[39] Greek Strong's Dictionary # 4567 – Emphasis added – Pronounced (Sat-an-as)
[40] See Greek Strong's Dictionary # 1228 – Pronounced (dee-ab-ol-os) and (dee-ab-al-lo)
[41] Moses 4:4 – "And he became Satan, yea, even the devil, the father of all lies, to deceive and to blind men"
[42] Revelation 12:10
[43] John 5:22 – "For the Father judgeth no man, but hath committed all judgment unto the Son"

let not thine heart be hasty to utter anything before God: for God is in heaven, and thou upon earth: therefore let thy words be few."[44]

  As Satan prowls the earth spreading his despicable slander, he specifically seeks out those who are spiritually struggling. Satan pounces and preaches persecutions upon those persons who need encouragement the most. Far too many people have developed deeply toned reflexes to criticize and mock the unfamiliar. Sadly, this habit can be frequently observed in swaggering, conceited adolescents who prey on those who are physically or socially different. These are they who smirk upon sighting the overweight, shy, unpopular, poor, untalented or even the handicap. To them they have found easy targets for their ridicule. Of course they are just jokes, they say. As if masking maliciousness as some sort of sport exempts them from all penalties. To their surprise, they will one day find that clowns too have consequences, and that even a jester must face judgment.

  Gratefully, we are not left alone to fight against the insatiable hatred and violent contempt in the world. Our kindhearted Heavenly Father has said, "*I will not leave you comfortless: I will come to you.*"[45] Fulfilling His holy word, God has sent us the presence of the Comforter, "*which is the Holy Ghost,*" who "*shall teach you all things, and bring all things to your remembrance, whatsoever* [Christ has] *said.*"[46] No stronger means of emphasis could be made toward the value of consolation, than to recall that a member of the Eternal Godhead is entitled the Comforter. In Greek the word for *Comforter* is *parakletos* meaning: *to call to one's side*,[47] *to call to one's aid* or *to advocate*. *Parakletos* is related to the words *parakaleo* and *paraklesis* which similarly denotes *to call near, beseech* or *to call to one's aid*.[48] Thus in a sense, to comfort is to come near to another; it is to stand closely by their side advocating for them and giving them aid. Such is the kindness of God, Christ, and the Comforter who never leave our side, who never stop advocating our cause.

  When defining comfort, it is much more informative to approach it visually instead of verbally. Picture an afflicted individual, one who in his last ounce of hope pleas for help. Responding to this petition is the comforter, one who physically comes near to his presence to aid, strengthen and rescue him. Because of God's great kindness, He stands with us in our

---

[44] Ecclesiastes 5:2
[45] John 14:18
[46] John 14:26 – Brackets added
[47] Greek Strong's Dictionary #3875 – (par-ak'-lay-tos)
[48] Greek Strong's Dictionary #3870 and #3874 – (par-ak-al-eh'-o) & paraklēsis (par-ak-lay-sis)

troubles! Heavenly Father aids us in adversity and is so very near to us when we beseech Him for comfort. When Paul was placed in prison "***the Lord stood by him***, *and said, Be of good cheer;*"[49] similarly God stands by us, encouraging us during the times we are placed in peril.

Further insight into how God expresses kindness comes by examining our word *comfort*. *Comfort* is of Latin origins; it is constructed from the prefix *com* meaning *with* or *together* and *fortis* meaning *strong* and *strengthen*. *Fortis* is related to the Latin word *fort* which is akin to our modern-day usage of the word *fort;* meaning *a fortified place* or *strong hold*. Thus when God comes near to us, one way He specifically comforts us is by strengthening and fortifying our faith. When the Comforter is near, God's power envelopes us like a stronghold. God's comforting kindness makes us stronger; it reinforces our confidence and supports our hopes.

In our world of chaos and turmoil there is great urgency in the commandment, "*Comfort ye, comfort ye my people, saith your God.*"[50] Therefore, may we express our kindness by standing by others" *faithfully, in whatsoever difficult circumstances* [they] *may be.*"[51] God be praised for His loving kindness, which 'strengthens our weak hands and confirms our feeble knees and says to them that are of a fearful heart, Be strong, fear not.'[52] Never forget that your eternally kind Father ever stands with you, for He has promised, "*I will not leave you comfortless: I will come to you.*"[53]

---

[49] Acts 23:11 – Emphasis added
[50] Isaiah 40:1
[51] See D&C 6:18 – "Therefore be diligent; stand by my servant Joseph, faithfully, in whatsoever difficult circumstances he may be for the word's sake."
[52] See Isaiah 35:3,4
[53] John 14:18

Selflessness

Selflessness is the essence of godliness; it is the grandeur of godliness. Selflessness is the great paradox of the universe – by denying all glory, power, and praise for the sake of another, we gain all glory, honor, and praise from God. Service is the work of the gods and selflessness the love of the gods. Selflessness is love's most dominant characteristic. The selflessness in love sparks a spirit of sacrifice. It generates non-obligatory offerings of one's soul. When we are selfless, our hearts feel to say, "*I will very gladly spend and be spent for you; though the more abundantly I love you, the less I be loved.*"[1]

It is of the utmost importance for the disciple of Christ to learn to selflessly surrender. Paul captured the core of a selfless mindset saying, "*Be kindly affected one to another with brotherly love; in honour* **preferring one another**."[2] Making other people our preference and priority is selflessness. Herein is the spirit of sacrifice. Herein is the spirit of piety, and such is the spirit of God. How often do you regard others before yourself? Do you step aside for others to pass, or do you insist that others make room for the size of your ego? Does your life solely revolve around what you want, or do you put other people's needs before your own? We should resist becoming so preoccupied with our own problems and perspectives that we are unable to respond to the needs of others.

Previously we defined love in its broadest sense as a desire. Selflessness is purest denominator of divine love's desire. Selfless love places the welfare of another above your own. Jesus Christ's entire life is a lesson of selflessness, for "*Hereby perceive we the love of God, because he laid down his life for us: and we ought to lay down our lives for the brethren.*"[3] As we shrink the primal predisposition to be preoccupied with our self, our ability to love grows. God, who loves perfectly, does not emphasize His own welfare, rather He selflessly expends His self for our benefit.

Selflessness is the surface to which the "*bond of charity*"[4] adheres; thus selflessness fastens families together and anchors our relationships. In

---

[1] 2 Corinthians 12:15 – Emphasis added
[2] Romans 12:10
[3] 1 John 3:16
[4] D&C 88:125 – "above all things, clothe yourselves with the bond of charity ... which is the bond of perfectness and peace."

contrast, selfishness severs connections; it is the great cause of loneliness to humanity. In order to be liberated from loneliness, one must unlock pride's prison of solitude by becoming selfless. Having pathos and concern for others alleviates the exhausting attention demanded by the *"natural man."*[5] Feral feelings of the flesh such as vengeance and hatred are decontaminated by a magnanimous mentality.

    Selflessness constrains malice. It annuls anger and defeats conceit. With selflessness we erase ego, purge pride, detoxify tempers, and eliminate contempt. Selflessness also empowers our capacity to endure, for fighting in behalf of others reveals an unknown resilience within us. In like manner, fears fold, doubts bend, and limitations kneel before the power of selflessness. Self-denial is a core piece of the disciple's devotion. Devotion is not one-dimensional. Piety should not be trapped inside the precincts of special places, nor should it be dependent upon precise planetary orbits.[6] We can express adulation to the Most High God in diverse ways. Through selflessness there are countless opportunities to show our devotion each day.

    Paul teaches us how acts of selflessness can be means of praising and worshiping God. He states, *"whatsoever ye do, do it heartily, as to the Lord, and not unto men."*[7] We have the ability to direct the motive behind our actions. Whether we are surrounded by co-workers, friends, family, or strangers, we can pay devotion to God by serving others as if they were the Lord Himself. *"I tell you these things that ye may learn wisdom; that ye may learn that when ye are in the service of your fellow beings ye are only in the service of your God."*[8]

    Because 'whatsoever we do' can be done *"as to the Lord, and not unto men,"* any action can be turned into a tribute to The Father. Even our daily duties may become a medium for reverencing the Lord. Regardless of one's occupation, when our tasks are completed 'as unto the Lord' they are accepted as worthy sacrifices and devotion. Even routine, inconsequential chores can change into offerings for our Heavenly Father so long as they are performed 'heartily as if to Lord and not men.' No job is exempt from this principle; it reaches every errand and conduct.

    In order to discern the finer features of selfless etiquette, we must

---

[5] 1 Corinthians 2:14 – "But the Natural man receiveth not the things of the Spirit of God: for they are foolishness unto him: neither can he know them, because they are spiritually discerned."
[6] See Alma 32:10,11 – "do ye suppose that ye cannot worship God save it be in your synagogues only? ... do ye suppose that ye must not worship God only once in a week?"
[7] Colossians 3:23
[8] Mosiah 2:17

contemplate which aspects of our self we are trying to deny. What is the "self" that mankind must learn to diminish? Man is a complex, twisted mixture of good and evil. His mind is constantly tortured by ripping pulls of oppositely fixed forces. For *"it must needs be, that there is an opposition in all things ... and* [men] *are free to choose liberty and eternal life, through the great Mediator of all men, or to choose captivity and death, according to the captivity and power of the devil."*[9]

Because good and evil simultaneously flow through man's thoughts and emotions, it can be difficult to determine who and what we truly are. Sifting to find one's 'true self' from the paradoxical impressions we receive requires great effort. If we never allow ourselves time for quiet contemplation and silent introspection, we will not discover our divine nature. If we are to discover our true self, we must first separate our spirit from the sway of what is called the *"natural man."* The scriptures warn us about the natural man stating that this froward character is an *"enemy to God."*[10] This natural man is also referred to in the scriptures as the flesh. Together these represent carnality, primitive reflexes, animal impulses, and telestial instincts.

Since the flesh or natural man is an enemy to God, it is likewise the enemy to truth, love, and connection. Ultimately the natural man is the enemy to peace and happiness. The flesh's preferences are those prohibited in the Ten Commandments such as lying, stealing, idolatry, rebellion, murder, adultery and covetousness. Other vices of the natural man's are exposed in the Savior's Sermon on the Mount. These include anger, gainsaying, pride, lust, revenge, and self-aggrandizement.

Further descriptions of the natural man's proclivities are spoken by Paul, *"Now the works of the flesh are manifest, which are these; Adultery, fornication, uncleanness, lasciviousness, Idolatry, witchcraft, hatred, variance, emulations, wrath, strife, seditions, heresies, Envyings, murders, drunkenness, revellings."*[11] Additionally, Paul expounds upon man's *"vile affections,"* and *"reprobate mind "*[12] stating such includes, *"Being filled with all unrighteousness, fornication, wickedness, covetousness, maliciousness, full of envy, murder, debate, deceit, malignity; whisperers, Backbiters, haters of God, despiteful, proud, boasters, inventors of evil things, disobedient to parents, Without understanding, covenantbreakers, without natural affection, implacable, unmerciful."*[13]

---

[9] 2 Nephi 2:27 – Brackets added
[10] Mosiah 3:19 – "For the natural man is an enemy to God"
[11] Galatians 5:19-21
[12] Romans 1:26,27
[13] Romans 1:29-31

From the Ten Commandments, the Sermon on the Mount, and these select teachings of Paul, we cover the majority of a disciple's prohibitions. However, just as godliness is expressed in subtle attitudes, the counterforce of the flesh reveals itself in very fine forms. *"Lest Satan should get an advantage of us,"* we must study the way in which these carnal quirks manifest within ourselves – that we might not be *"ignorant of his devices."*[14]

Selfishness is the foremost philosophy of the flesh; its beliefs are based on anything that benefits itself. Simply, the gospel of the flesh is to *"get gain."*[15] While under the spell of selfishness, the underlying motive "to get gain" can be turned into every type of wickedness. The natural man's desire to get gain manifests in four primary ways: by wealth and substance, fame and glory, authority and power and sensory pleasures. In some way or another, most specific sins feed into one of these four areas of selfishness.

Did not Cain commit murder to get gain? In both the past and present, the prerogative of secret combinations has been get gain. Prideful preachers in every dispensation have traded truth for priestcrafts for the sake of getting gain. One cannot count nor tell the myriad of tiny tactics people use every day in order to get gain, or 'take the advantage over another.' Manipulation, bullying, teasing, gossip, abuse of authority, lying and intimidation are among the most common examples of getting gain. Regardless of the specific way selfishness manifests, getting gain always comes at great cost.

The virtue of selflessness is tested in sociality and most significantly in family relationships. Regarding such relationships, the natural man will refuse to acknowledge others. To the natural man people are nothing more than props – inanimate instruments whose sole purpose is to help tell the story of one's own self. This narcissistic perspective is all about I's and me's. That is of course until something goes wrong, then you will watch it rapidly reverse into you's and they's.

Have you allowed yourself to succumb to the natural man's instinctual inconsideration? Are you more concerned about your own comforts or the condition of those around you? The neurochemical reflexes of the flesh operate differently from our spiritual instincts. Instead of having an intuition planted by physiology, spiritual reflexes arise from the light of truth which is sewn into our souls. This light reveals how our

---

[14] 2 Corinthians 2:11
[15] See Moses 5:31 – "That I may murder and get gain." 2 Ne 27:17 – "because of the glory of the world and to get gain will they say this…" Hel 6:17 – "they began to seek to get gain that they might be lifted up on above another," Hel 7:5 - "to be held in office…to rule and do according to their wills, that they might get gain & glory of the world."

behaviors will affect others.

Do you seek to be above your brother, or push him down for preeminence? Have you chosen to take the role of the stereotypical machismo and become an unyielding, brute-bully who aggressively asserts himself in every situation? Though we may avoid being overtly pushy, great caution should attend our acts of assertiveness, for assertiveness is prone to place itself before others and such is the center of selfishness. However, as we become selfless, we should not suppose that this will absolutely annihilate assertiveness. Rather, the selfless are ever mindful of their motives for being assertive.

For the sake of distinction, we should note that many of the feelings of the flesh are more neutral than nefarious. When unprovoked the natural man's first preference is to be callous, conceited, and lazy, its inclination is indifference to all things not itself. When it pertains to others, the natural man is inconsiderate and uncaring, a serious contrast to the devil who boils in hatred instead of living "*lukewarm*."[16]

There is no passivity in the prince of darkness. His disobedience and wickedness is never apathetically evil. Satan's intents are intensely malicious. The flesh will cause injury because it is looking out for itself, whereas the devil injures for the sake of chaos and enmity. This enmity is the most damnable disposition! Only hateful, hellish fiends find satisfaction in deliberately causing pain to another soul. Only a cursed demon, festering in the infernal pit would ever find happiness in another person's problems or ills. Though Satan is pleased with the self-centered ideology, he is never fully satisfied until conceit turns into a more demonic vice, such as of violence, malice, hatred, or vengeance.

Hatred may not be the first choice of the flesh but it is often its preferred affiliate. Though the carnal nature is indifferent to others, when a trespass or offense is perceived, the natural man has proven to be easily swayed by satanic principles. An overly defensive, anaphylactic temper is a major moral flaw of the flesh. The natural man's raging responses to even slight infringements, tend to turn into tantrums similar to those seen in wild, perturbed beasts. These sorts of reactions stand in direct opposition to the Christian values of peacemaking, patience, and charity.

All the word is an arena to the natural man. He sees the world with a corrupt perspective where others are seen as competitors instead of cohorts. The flesh is never satisfied. It always wants more. It is ever

---

[16] See Revelation 3:16 – "So then because thou are lukewarm, and neither cold not hot, I will spue thee out of my mouth."

hungry to the point of gluttony. This gorging appetite always has to be better, faster, stronger, smarter, nicer, funnier, prettier and more popular.

The selfish man always has to come out on top. He needs the first word and the last laugh. Such is why paying complements is uncomfortable for the carnal man; because he fears that building up others will only make him look smaller. Carnality finds pleasure in preeminence. It has been never comfortable with equality. It is concerned with being heard rather than hearing, it takes rather than gives, insults instead of complements and yields to anger instead of compassion. As our carnal nature vies for preeminence, his vision instinctually hones in on imperfections and mistakes. Unsurprisingly, finding flaws has always been easy for the natural man. It is after all like looking in a mirror. Yet one cannot look down on others and hope to keep Heaven in view.

Being stuck with superficial sight, the flesh fails to consider the feelings and wishes of others, *"for man looketh on the outward appearance, but the Lord looketh on the heart."*[17] Lacking the godly gift of foresight, the natural man's insight is imprisoned in the present. It only looks outward, never inward. Such is why the flesh complains when it should be pondering. The natural man's decision process is chemical, brash, and unprincipled – defects which prevent planning and prudence.

One cannot obtain an 'eye single to the glory of God'[18] so long as their sight is single to the satisfaction of their self. A person viewing life through the funnel of the flesh is not able to see through their selfishness. This egocentric perception creates an unwholesome altitude in the eyes of the natural man. Confidence combined with compassion will meet the gaze of another on equal ground, but the confidence of the carnal nature is skewed by inflating and elevating egotism.

Such is why selflessness is key to communication. Paul advises us to 'speak the truth in love;'[19] a task only possible when we genuinely consider the opinions of others. The selfless will contemplate other people's thoughts, feelings, constraints and capabilities before emphasizing their own agendas. In contrast, the carnal mind has a habit of conversational conceit; a communication that is more focused on contest than connection.

---

[17] 1 Samuel 16:7
[18] See D&C 88:67 – "And if your eye be single to my glory, your whole bodies shall be filled with light, and there shall be no darkness in you; and that body which is filled with light comprehendeth all things."
[19] Ephesians 4:15 – "But speaking the truth in love, may grow up into him in all things, which is the head, even Christ."

When communicating, the narcissistic types prefer the sound of their own voice. For him his own speech is so riveting that he continues to chatter in the back of his mind while others make their more boring comments. Lost in the splendor of his own speech, he is tantalized by the telling of his own tales. Similarly, the selfish man is a stranger to quiet success and passive progress. He feels the need to memorialize, market and advertise each of his accomplishments. He wears his medals proudly on his lips and will retell, rerun and rebroadcast every victory until every soul can recount his accomplishments.

These are they who require accolades for any accomplishment. Such find it hard to celebrate successes silently. Inflated individuals who ride life atop the applause of their entourage are so easily swayed into sin. Nevertheless, like the story book emperor who nearly fainted in astonishment over his 'fruit of the loom' apparel, the carnal will someday struggle to swallow their embarrassment over the vanity they paraded in life.

Though the natural man parades his power, he routinely runs from responsibility. To him honor and rules are far too restrictive. To a carnal mind, commitment, consequence and accountability are seen as constraints to freedom. They are chains that choke choices. Instead of fleeing from sin, the unrighteous reflex of the flesh is to conceal wickedness.

What a peculiar contradiction that Satan, who works so hard to convince us that there is no sin, also compels men to undergo such dramatic lengths to cover up their sins. Did not Satan *"plot with Cain, that if he would murder his brother Abel it should not be known unto the world."*[20] Here we see foremost moral code of the flesh – do not get caught.

Morality has never been a strong enough deterrent for the natural man. Immediate consequences may be able to influence his judgments, but any standard could easily be compromised so long as it fits underneath a cloak of darkness. Because he cannot feel at ease in light's illuminating exposure, the natural man, seeking to sedate his shame, is easily seduced by the mists of darkness. Thus, wickedness seeks out dark places, hoping that the darkness will conceal their sins from themselves, God and the world. Hiding his sins in the shadow, the natural man uses this shade to shield him from pains of responsibility, penalty, and guilt.

The egocentric individual would see the entire earth alter its orbit before redirecting his own course. Negotiating with the natural man's narcissistic needs never works, for compromise requires meekness, a saintly trait that is foreign to the flesh. Trying to gain an inch of ground, he loses

---

[20] Helaman 6:27

mile after mile, and being unwilling to bend he inevitably is broken. In consequence of his inflexible, uncompromising and non-negotiable attitudes, his friendships are feeble and his bonds are brittle.

Do not forget that spirituality is unnatural to the natural man. The natural man feeds only on physical, sensory, tactile evidence. Asking the natural man to comprehend spiritual truth is like asking the eyes to hear. *"The way of the wicked is as darkness: they know not at what they stumble."*[21] Darkness cannot discern the movements of the Spirit. It does not comprehend light. It has no facility to register transcendent and eternal truths. Is it therefore surprising that the natural man cannot comprehend the concept of mercy, that it cannot grasp God's ability to overlook sins? Truly, the *"natural man receiveth not the things of the Spirit of God: for they are foolishness unto him: neither can he know them, because they are spiritually discerned."*[22]

Just as the flesh is confounded by faith, so too is suffering skewed by the natural man. When suffering, the instinct of the natural man is to give in to resentment and self-pity. If we are not careful, the sadness in life can consume us. Greif can be a nagging gravity which draws all of our attention into our self. When unchecked, this force pulls our focus away from others. The natural man lives in a shrunken world, one enclosed by a preoccupation with his own problems. Blinded by his own burdens, he no longer sees that we all carry crosses. In contrast, consider the Son of God, who did not let His consummate suffering distract Him from being compassionate and considerate to another hanging on a cross.

The feel good, fun philosophy of the flesh continues to inconspicuously pacify many unfocused disciples. We must be ever vigilant, for we surely will face scenarios which make us weigh the values of the flesh against those of the spirit. When we encounter these periods, the choice is ours —will we feed the flesh and therein starve the spirit, or will we 'put off the natural man and become a saint through the atonement of Christ, the Lord?'[23] By nourishing our spirit with service, truth and love, we loosen the hold that the flesh has on our feelings and thoughts.

Divine Love, which *"seeketh not her own"*,[24] selflessly sacrifices the four elementary lusts of the flesh – wealth and substance, fame and glory, authority and power, and sensory pleasure. Christianity contradicts the

---

[21] Psalms 4:19
[22] 1 Corinthians 2:14
[23] Mosiah 3:19 – "the natural man is an enemy to God…unless he yields to the enticings of the Holy Spirit, and putteth off the natural man and becometh a saint through the atonement of Christ"
[24] Moroni 7:45

carnal mind; it negates the natural man by living the word of the Lord Jesus, which says *"It is more blessed to give than to receive."*[25] The center of selflessness is an overriding desire that gives praise rather than seeks it, that foregoes power, pleasure, and substance in order to give strength and satisfaction to others.

The pure love of Christ not only places the lusts of the flesh on the altar of sacrifice, it places the whole soul. Yet, how does one make an offering of their entire soul? Those 'offering their whole soul as an offering unto God'[26] must be willing to give up the bad as well as the good. This means a disciple may have to willingly sacrifice dreams, aspirations, friendships or even family in order to 'submit to all things which the Lord seeth fit.'[27]

Mankind's uniqueness is found in the ability to interrupt closed chains of cause and effect. Being endowed with the gift of agency, man is able to create new causes with overriding effects – effects that can supersede circumstance, setting, genes and experiential instruction. Our individuality most clearly manifests itself through the heavenly gift of agency. Agency is a precious and good gift, but it is also one that we must be capable of placing on the altar. The law of sacrifice may demand offerings of the sacred and the profane, the flesh and the blood, the body and the spirit. It may demand our entire soul for *"whoso is not willing to lay down his life for my sake is not my disciple."*[28]

Christ taught, *"He that findeth his life shall lose it: and he that loseth his life for my sake shall find it."*[29] However, life not death is the divine endowment. The most pressing implication of Christ's instruction to 'lose our life for His sake' is that we must lose our selfishness. Our true, immortal self is buried beneath the egotistical instincts of the natural man; your divine nature is hidden by the indulgent life he desires.

Only by denying and discarding our carnal nature can we uncover our true self. This is man's great objective! We must work to eliminate the natural man's control over our choices. We must reverse the carnal reflexes presently restraining our spirit and the Spirit of God which dwells in us.

To accomplish this, we must emulate our Lord Jesus who *"made*

---

[25] Acts 20:35
[26] Omni 1:26 – "I would that ye should come unto Christ, who is the Holy One of Israel…Yea, come unto him, and offer your whole souls as an offering unto him"
[27] Mosiah 3:19 – "and becometh as a child, submissive meek, humble, patient, full of love, willing to submit to all things which the Lord seeth fit to inflict upon him even as a child doth submit to his father."
[28] D&C 103:28
[29] Matthew 10:38,39

himself of no reputation."[30] The words "*no reputation*" are a translation of the Greek word *kenoo*[31] which means *to abase, neutralize or be made nothing. Kenoo* comes from the word *kenos*,[32] meaning *empty, either literally or figuratively.* Many different translations of this verse exist, but a particularly intriguing one is an alternative version that states, Christ 'emptied Himself.'

In what is called the "*condescension of God,*"[33] Jesus made Himself as nothing. In love and service Christ completely 'emptied Himself' until He, The Son of Man "*descended below all things.*"[34] Though a God, worthy of the highest prestige Jesus made himself of "*no reputation.*" The condescension of God is not only a description of Jesus's mortal birth, it portrays His complete life of servitude, for He "*made himself of no reputation, and **took upon him the form of a servant**, and was made in the likeness of men.*"[35]

In a world where "*all seek their own* [and] *not the things which are Jesus Christ's,*"[36] will you resist the ease of your brute instincts? Will you indulge or deny the self-centered cries of the natural man? No feast can fill the famished feelings of the flesh. It thirsts and never finds relief. This uncontrollable, lawless lust makes the emotions of the flesh radioactively destructive. His heart is a restless river. Finding no joy in what is there; he stirs in agitation for not having more. The flesh's frantic hunger is not something to be treated lightly, for as *"the eyes of a man are never satisfied"* so too "*Hell and destruction are never full.*"[37] A selfish man, by means of his insuppressible hunger, "*enlargeth his desire as hell, and is as death and cannot be satisfied.*"[38] Simply stated, selfishness is death. It is the portal to hell and the most pervasive source of human suffering.

Our divine nature and the power of God are impeded by egocentric pride. Since selfishness subdues the godliness in our spirits, mortal lusts must be subjugated in order to surface our godly desires. Our view of virtue is veiled by our vanity. Carnality corrupts our cognition, and the ever-asserting ego contaminates our sight. Pride, repugnant and putrid pride, represses man's potential. Only by emptying ourselves of selfishness can we lift the fogging film that frustrates the correct view of God, our

---

[30] Philippians 2:7
[31] Greek Strong's Dictionary #2758 –(Ken-o-o)
[32] Greek Strong's Dictionary # 2756 –(Ken-os')
[33] 1 Nephi 11:16
[34] D&C 88:6 – "He that ascended up on high, as also he descended below all things, in that he comprehended all things, that he might be in all and through all things, the light of truth."
[35] Philippians 2:7 – Emphasis added
[36] Philippians 2:21 – Brackets added
[37] Proverbs 27:20 – "Hell and destruction are never full: so the eyes of man are never satisfied."
[38] Habakkuk 2:4

Father.

One will never grasp Eternal truth so long as they desperately clutch to their current self. For *"verily I say unto you that it is your privilege, and a promise I give unto you ... that inasmuch as you strip yourselves from jealousies and fears, and humble yourselves before me, for ye are not sufficiently humble, the veil shall be rent and* **you shall see me and know that I am** *– not with the carnal neither natural mind, but with the spiritual."*[39] This greatest of all revelations is reserved for those who relinquish themselves of all selfish desires and embrace the sainthood of servitude. If we desire to fulfill this destiny, we must have *"no other object in view ... but to glorify God;"* we *"must not be influenced by any other motive than that of building his kingdom."*[40] If we cannot do this, these things will remain hidden forever.

In life there are gods and men and they can be distinguished one from the other – the children of men will be seen serving themselves; but it is the *"offspring of God"* [41] who will be found serving others. How much time do you spend carving a graven image of a worldly identity? The form of the flesh must be forfeited in order to take on the image of God. The natural man is not the self. You are not your flesh! Chemical lusts must be distinguished from your divine nature. Your identity is so much deeper than the shallow skin and brittle bones which house your immortal spirit. You are a child of God, not some clump of carnal clay or heaps of hormones. Again, the flesh is not the self! It is a force and an influence, but it is not you. It is a shell, not your soul. By suppressing the flesh's arrogant ego, your confidence will not be destroyed. Rather, a confidence in Christ will bloom. Do not settle for seeing yourself in the form of a man, for you were created in the image of God.

Jesus, who *"put all things in subjection under his feet,"* [42] subjected himself to the sacrifice of an everlasting suffering. Jesus 'did spend and was spent for us' and because of His abundant charity He sought not His own saying, *"Father ... not my will, but thine, be done."*[43] Herein Christ had His will *"swallowed up in the will of the Father."*[44] Herein is sacrifice. Herein is selflessness. Herein is love. *"If any man have ears to hear, let him hear,"*[45] let

---

[39] D&C 67:10 – Emphasis added
[40] See JSH 1:46
[41] Acts 17:29
[42] Hebrew 2:8 – "Thou hast put all things in subjection under his feet. For in that he put all in subjection under him, he left nothing that is not put under him"
[43] Luke 22:42
[44] Mosiah 15:7 – "Yea, even so he shall be led, crucified, and slain, the flesh becoming subject even unto death, the will of the Son being swallowed up in the will of the Father."
[45] Mark 7:16

them see and comprehend this – the mystery of godliness. Jesus who "*hath poured out his soul unto death,*"[46] emptied Himself of every carnal persuasion and "*took upon him the form of a servant, and was made in the likeness of men: And being found in fashion as a man, he humbled himself, and became obedient unto death, even the death of the cross.*"[47] Through a sacrifice of selflessness the "*Son of Man hath descended below them all. Art thou greater than he?*"[48]

"*Behold, are ye stripped of pride ... Behold, I say, is there one among you who is not stripped of envy?*"[49] To this I would add: have you stripped yourselves of vanity, lust, sloth and anger. Empty yourself of all the ungodliness contained in the natural man. Free yourself from the selfish lusts of the flesh which now confine you. After the manner of the Holy Messiah, empty every selfish desire from your heart and God will most assuredly fill your whole soul with light; "*Which light proceedeth forth from the presence of God to fill the immensity of space.*"[50] Remember the promise of God which says, "*if your eye be single to my glory, your whole bodies shall be filled with light, and there shall be no darkness in you; and that body which is filled with light comprehendeth all things. Therefore, sanctify yourselves that your minds become single to God, and the days will come that you shall see him; for* **he will unveil his face unto you***,*"[51] for once the image of man has been emptied – only the image of God remains. "*And this word, Yet once more, signifieth the removing of those things that are shaken, as of things that are made, that those things which cannot be shaken may remain.*"[52]

---

[46] Isaiah 53:12
[47] Philippians 2:7,8
[48] See D&C 88:6 – "He hath ascended up on high, as also he descended below all things"
[49] Alma 5:28,29
[50] D&C 88:12
[51] D&C 88:67,68 – Emphasis added
[52] Hebrews 12:27

Humility

    Every attribute of the divine nature is honed by humility. Humility engenders a softer side of godliness. Though Heavenly Father is omnipotent, because of His humility, He is still mild. Though God is omniscient, because He is perfectly meek, He does not parade His powers. Because God is meek, He delights in inconspicuous service. He requires no credit for the gifts He gives; neither does He wait around for an applause after every miracle He performs. Being stabilized by meekness, God is neither manipulative nor cocky. God is not consumed by His greatness, rather because He is Humble. He expends His greatness in service.

    Though we can use the words meekness and humility interchangeably, the word meekness highlights a special aspect of humility. In the scriptures meekness denotes mildness or gentleness. God's meekness can be perceived in the tranquility of his presence. It can be heard in the tenderness of His tone. With a *"still voice of perfect mildness,"*[1] the Father subdues anxious souls with a soothing whisper.

    The shaping of our world has been sustained by soft submissiveness more than sharp assertiveness. The cultures of the world have had a long history of favoring rugged strength, aggressive power and dominating talent over the unassuming manifestations of godliness. Nevertheless, considering that the Savior said of His own personality, *"I am meek and lowly in heart,"*[2] we cannot overlook the immense importance that the mild qualities of meekness have in the heavenly hierarchy of virtues.

    What causes the meek to behave mildly? The foundation of humility's meekness is a firm feeling of nonmaleficence. Nonmaleficence is the desire to not cause harm, hurt or damage to another. To use the words of the scriptures, nonmaleficence is to *"not have a mind to injure one another, but*

---

[1] Helaman 5:30
[2] Matthew 11:29

to live peaceably."³ The lowly and humble in heart bear a special caution of conscience, one that deters them from bringing harm to others in any way. This penetrating attitude of meekness tempers the actions and temperament of the humble.

Those who are meek avoid every form of abuse. They resist gossip, violence, name-calling, yelling and profanity. They refrain from bullying, manipulations, insults and passive aggressive tactics. Inspired by love and consideration the meek avoid causing pain, injury and inconvenience to others. Such is why the meek step carefully. They compute the consequences of their choices, and take the time to consider how their actions affect those around them.

Being watchful of their words, the meek are careful to *"talk no more so exceeding proudly"* and to *'let no arrogancy come out of their mouth.'*⁴ For *"most men will proclaim everyone his own goodness: but a faithful man who can find?"*⁵ Oh how loud the haughty blast the trumpets of triumph, while the meek are given to gain without all the noise. Just because humility is not overtly assertive or pokingly pretentious, we should not assume that it is always passive. The meek prefer passivity; however, meekness is more than capable of planting itself firmly in principle. Meekness does not imply cowardice. It is not sheepish submission. It is a conscious yielding motivated by love.

Smuggish pride persuades gullible legions into being inconsiderate and slanderous; however, having humility does not suggest that one will always sponge accusatory attacks. The humble will stand silent as Christ did before the contemptible priests, yet they will also stand with the tenacious confidence Christ exhibited when He rebuked the wicked from the temple. Similarly, Moses who *"was very meek, above all the men who were upon the face of the earth,"*⁶ exhibited the indomitable poise of meekness when facing the bitterness of hell. Without forsaking meekness, Moses commanded the devil, *"Depart from me, Satan, for this one God only will I worship, which is the God of glory."*⁷

In like manner the Prophet Joseph upheld humility as he stood wrapped in chains before the unscrupulous barking of degenerate guards declaring, "SILENCE, ye fiends of the infernal pit! In the name of Jesus

---

[3] Mosiah 4:13
[4] See Samuel 2:3 – "Talk no more so exceeding proudly; let not arrogancy come out of your mouth:"
[5] Proverbs 20:6
[6] Numbers 12:3
[7] Moses 1:18

Christ I rebuke you, and command you to be still."[8] The ever yielding nature of humility is not submissive to circumstance. The center of its submission is to the Father's will – whether it be unto brashness or bashfulness.

Another side to meekness is described by Jacob, who praised the *"chaste and delicate before God"* saying such are *"pleasing unto God."*[9] This delicate nature often noticed among women and children, describes a love that is open to vulnerability. Godly delicateness empathetically endures whereas the proud, like porcelain, swiftly shatter into self-pity. In like manner, the arrogant are fragile in faith; their shallow roots[10] being seeded in selfishness are not grounded deeply in discipleship.

Pertaining to 'shallow roots,' a saint's devotion can be dug up by fame as well as by affliction. Faith can just as easily be fractured by fortune as from failure. Prosperity and praise have proven sometimes to be a great adversary to discipleship. The day may come when we must face the oft fatal tests of popularity, status or acclaim. We are advised, *"Let another man praise thee, and not thine own mouth; a stranger, and not thine own lips."*[11] When all eyes are upon you, will you also start staring at yourself? At such a time will we remember that the command to be a light to the world, is not a call to obsess over social spotlights.

Those demanding roles on the center stage are like those whom Isaiah spoke, who *"kindle a fire"* and *"compass* [themselves] *about with sparks."*[12] Lacking the full illumination of the light of Christ, these are left to *"walk in the light of* [their] *fire, and in the sparks that* [they] *have kindled."* Being guided by the brightness of their own sparks instead of the 'Light of the World,' these souls are susceptible to being blinded by the *"mists of darkness."*[13]

Nevertheless, humility is not ignorance. It is not living in a stupor so as to avoid coming to terms with your talents and achievements. We should be aware of our accomplishments and gifts. As long as we are humble, we can be conscious of an accomplishment without obsessing over it. We can be familiar with our faculties without fixating on them.

---

[8] Haight, David. Joseph Smith, the Prophet. *Ensign*, Dec 2001,
[9] Jacob 2:7
[10] See Matthew 13:21 – "Yet hath he not root in himself, but dureth for a while: for when tribulation or persecution ariseth because of the word, by and by he is offended."
[11] Proverbs 27:2
[12] Isaiah 50:11
[13] 1 Nephi 12:17 – "And the mists of darkness are the temptations of the devil, which blindeth the eyes, and hardeneth the hearts of the children of men, and leadeth them away in to broad roads, that they perish and are lost."

We should embrace our talents and gifts, for it is written, *"Behold he rejoices not in that which is given to him, neither rejoices in him who is the giver of the gift."*[14] Since the humble are not engrossed by success, they perceive praise proportionally, remembering always their Eternal Provider. Amidst praise, honor and power, we must tame carnal aspirations with the wisdom of the humble King who taught *"I, whom ye call your king, am no better than ye yourselves are."*[15]

Meekness must not be limited to a monthly meditation or an item on a daily to do list. Humility should meticulously be incorporated into all of our perceptions, emotions, and social manners. Because humility is a quality of softness it manifests in very subtle ways. The disciple's task is to develop what the Greek's named *tapeinophrosune*;[16] a word meaning *lowliness or humbleness of mind*. These 'small and simple acts of humility will bring many great things to pass.'[17] Qualities resulting from a 'lowliness of mind' include: gratefulness, redirecting praise, obedience, being easy to be entreated, and being prayerful. Through these meek mannerisms we " [Cast] *down imaginations, and every high thing that exalteth itself against the knowledge of God, and* [bring] *every thought to the obedience of Christ"* [18] – such is the delicate art of humility.

"Blessed are the poor in spirit … Blessed are they that mourn … Blessed are the meek."[19] Suffering has the ability to mold meekness into our minds. Yet suffering itself does not make one more sensitive to spiritual things. Only when affliction makes us humble do we become receptive to spiritual truth. As the mortal body is able to sense its surroundings, your spirit has a sense for celestial things. The soul feels experiences in ways that escape the chemistry of your nervous system. Our spirits are particularly receptive to suffering. In the profound depths of pain, we feel a lingering stir which arouses our spirits. Suffering surfaces an awareness that we exist in a way that transcends our mortal figure. Like the proverbial pinch that assures us we are not dreaming, suffering pinches our spirit reminding us that that we are natives to Heaven and only tourists of this world.

Along with a heightened awareness of our spiritual existence, pain can improve our ability to detect the invisible ambience of the Holy Spirit.

---

[14] D&C 88:33
[15] Mosiah 2:26
[16] Greek Strong's Dictionary #5012 –(tap-i-nof-ros-oo'-nay)
[17] See Alma 37:6 – "behold I say unto you, that by small and simple things are great things brought to pass; and small means in many instances doth confound the wise."
[18] 2 Corinthians 10:5 – Brackets added: original – Casting
[19] Matthew 5:3-5

When suffering shakes our souls, we become attentive to previously indiscernible impressions of the Spirit. It requires humility to sense the whisperings of the Spirit. If we remain humble, spiritual promptings will grow till they overpower the reasoning and feeling of our natural man. Therefore, do not fight against the function that suffering serves, for suffering thins the veil and unravels the secret glories of the Celestial world.

Having a superb sense of selflessness, it is the humble who are keen to the command, *"whatsoever ye would that men should do to you, do ye even so to them."*[20] Being more aware of the feelings, thoughts and views of others, the humble are quick to develop a love for others for the good that is in them. Those who are *"sufficiently meek"* no longer 'seek to excel'[21] above their brethren; they measure other people's perspectives with the same weight they measure their own. Thus, it is the humble who tolerate contrary viewpoints without violence, and therewith transform opposition into peace.

Meekness prevents competition from consuming compassion. It opens the door to empathy and sympathy. Since the humble are not 'puffed up' with pomp or pride, they resist the temptation to see themselves as better than another. Unsurprisingly, the larger we make ourselves to be in our own eyes, the smaller other people appear. Instead of looking down on others from a high throne of lofty position, the humble meet the eyes of others on an equal plane.

Here we see a significant contributor to the humble perspective. The humble believe and live the words of the ancient King who said to his people, *"I am like as yourselves, subject to all manner of infirmities in body and mind."*[22] Such a sense of meekness aligns our experiences with one another. It creates a tempered togetherness; one that sees others as brothers and sisters instead of as rivals. Oh what an unparalleled revolution it would be, if men would remember that others exist in the same way that they themselves exist!

Obedience can be a common form of humility. Nevertheless, obedience is a principle that especially should never be considered outside of the parent virtue of love. Describing the relationship between love and obedience the scriptures say, *"If a man love me, he will keep my words,"*[23] for *"this is the love of God, that we keep his commandments: and his commandments are not*

---

[20] Matthew 7:12
[21] D&C 58:41 – "And also he hath need to repent, for I, the Lord am not well pleased with him for he seeketh to excel, and he is not sufficiently meek before me."
[22] Mosiah 2:7
[23] John 14:23

grievous."[24]

God's desire has never been to develop mindless, militaristic, obligatory conformity. God has no glory in senseless sacrifices. *"To what purpose is the multitude of your sacrifices unto me? saith the LORD: I am full of the burnt offerings of rams ... Bring no more vain oblations."*[25] Grimacing service, or duty performed out of ignorant habit is not God's plan. Obedience is best appreciated as an ancillary characteristic of humility, for within a humble spirit all the positive traits of obedience are embodied. When we obey, we are expressing humility, and when humility is the provoking source of our submissiveness, obedience is done for the right reasons. Humility is not an act of fearful submission to a suppressive power; it is grateful obedience. Being ever aware of their debt, when the meek provide voluntary service, they do so willing, appreciatively and affectionately.

The process of developing faith may require obedience to stand alone; however, this obedience only holds the place for higher principles. Adam demonstrated this function of obedience when he kept the commandment to offer the firstling of his flock unto the Lord. When asked why he was offering these sacrifices he stated, *"I know not, save the Lord commanded me."*[26] Such humility is honorable; but blind obedience is scaffolding for informed obedience. Even so, both eventually give way to the virtue of willing obedience, for *"the Lord requireth the heart and a willing mind."*[27] Though blind obedience does serve a role, it is worth noting that God hardly leads us blindly. Most of life's difficult "why questions" are directly answered in the scriptures. As God's word teams together with the invaluable, individual impressions of the Spirit, we have more than enough insight to navigate through the difficult whys of life.

Love, selflessness and humility are woven tightly together. Without love, humility turns into treacherous timidity – a silent conceit, soft sneers coupled with quiet scorn. Like the contemptuous kiss of Judas, some store secret malice in hushed hearts. For some their silence is strategically nefarious, concealing animosity beneath a mask of modesty. Thus, not all gentleness is meekness. One can be calm and yet cruel. Though one tempers the volume of their tone, they may fail to mute mockery, gossip or insult. There are those who are soft, but selfish. When lacking strong roots, gentleness is disfigured into a flimsy, fragile figure that is frustrated

---

[24] 1 John 5:3
[25] Isaiah 1:11,13
[26] Moses 5:6
[27] See D&C 64:34 – "and the willing and obedient shall eat the good of the land of Zion in these last days."

and offended easily. These types may not display their offense with outright combativeness, heated tongues, or fiery tempers. Instead, theirs is that unacceptable, vengeful selfishness of silence. No matter how extensive the deceptive display of cordial manners may be, contrived conduct can never stretch wide enough to cover one's secret sins from God's *"all searching eye."*[28]

Gratitude and humility have a significant reciprocating relationship. Gratitude engenders humility by accenting an awareness of the debt we owe God. Contemplating God's majesty, compassion, and mercy has a way of inspiring those same feelings within our self. On the other hand, the humble are more grateful. Humility drives feelings of gratitude deep into the soul, kindling the question, *"What shall I render unto the LORD for all his benefits toward me?"*[29] When we are humble, gratitude does not cease after a single, appreciative supplication. Instead, our thankfulness supercharges a desire for service. This does not suppose that the humble omit *"the sacrifice of praise to God continually, that is, the fruit of our lips giving thanks to his name."*[30] Rather, this highlights an acuity of gratitude known only to the truly humble.

In *"nothing doth man offed God, or against none is his wrath kindled, save those who confess not his hand in all things, and obey not his commandments."*[31] How silly it is to see ungrateful persons strut their independence like a cavalier, naïve teenager who glories in his magnificent triumphs while forgetting to pay tribute to the supplier of his food, home, clothes and other daily amenities. We would do well to remember the wisdom of John the Baptist who said, *"A man can receive nothing, except it be given him from heaven."*[32] Entitlements are devastating distortions that steal the grace of God that is supplied in every second, sense and breath. Each moment of life is an unearned heavenly treasure, therefore whatsoever you receive, *"account it of God; and … rejoice that* [you are] *accounted of God worthy to receive."*[33]

The humble are haunted by their indebtedness to God. It troubles them so profoundly that merely professing appreciation hardly seems sufficient. Thus, the humble practice pragmatic forms of praise. Because a humble heart ever searches for ways to 'render thanks to the Lord for all

---

[28] Mosiah 27:31 – "then shall they confess that he is God…and they shall quake, and tremble, and shrink beneath the glance of his all-searching eye."
[29] Psalms 116:12
[30] Hebrews 13:15 – Emphasis added
[31] D&C 59:21
[32] John 3:27
[33] D&C 50:34 – originally: "let him account it of God; and let him rejoice that he is accounted of God worthy to receive."

His benefits,' they regularly offer sincere *"sacrifices of thanksgiving."*[34] Not being content to simply discuss their gratitude, the humble convert thanks into works and turn their gratitude into actions and covenants. We observe this behavior in the record of Jesus healing the ten lepers. We read, *"And one of them, when he saw that he was healed, turned back, and with a loud voice glorified God, And fell down on his face at his feet, giving him thanks ... And Jesus answering said, Were there not ten cleansed? But where are the nine? There are not found **that returned to give glory to God**, save this stranger."*[35]

It is nearly inconceivable to imagine a realistic scenario where all ten of these people, who had been chronically afflicted with such a devastating disease, do not instantly fall to the earth shouting halleluiahs for the wondrous miracle that just occurred. It is beyond reason to think that anyone could have their life so immediately and conspicuously changed without paying an equally immediate and conspicuous tribute.

However, it is both plausible and common to see, as the story records, only one of the ten 'turning back' to 'return' to the giver of the gift. Perhaps what distinguished this single beneficiary from the nine was that this man gave his gratitude a second thought. Humility makes thanks more than a couple choral halleluiahs. The meek linger on gifts of grace in a way that transforms their admiration into discipleship. This is the proper way *"to thank your heavenly King!"*[36]

Service is the tongue of gratitude. Through service the meek communicate their concern; it is their primary means of voicing their devotion; it is a language of their love. Emphasizing the virtue of service Christ taught, *"whosoever will be chief among you, let him be your servant."*[37] Service is instinctual for the meek; it is a reflex of their love, not some clever way of paradoxically exalting one's self into position and status. It does not require external prompting or persuasion to motivate the meek to service or sacrifice. No, the meek are ever *"anxiously engaged in a good cause, and do many things of their own free will, and bring to pass much righteousness."*[38]

However, there are less obvious forms of service that are not as detectable as giving time, talents or work. The Prophet Benjamin, himself an epitome of humility exemplified this special form of service by laboring diligently *"that thereby, he might not become burdensome to his people."*[39] By

---

[34] Psalms 107:22
[35] Luke 17:15-18 – Emphasis added
[36] Mosiah 2:19 – "O how you ought to thank your heavenly King!"
[37] Matthew 20:27
[38] D&C 58:27
[39] Mosiah 6:7

monitoring the movements of the meek, we see somewhat of a subconscious desire to avoid adding to the burdens of others. Often, not adding weight to one's yoke is equally serviceable as decreasing the load of another's burden. Similarly, limiting self-indulgence can be a special type of service – sometimes taking less is as great a blessing as giving more.

In order for men to repress the swollen swagger of pride, they must learn that they are not the sole architect of their autonomy. The humble understand God's intervening role behind man's supposed independence. To *"say in thine heart, My power and the might of mine hand hath gotten me this wealth,"*[40] is not simply unappreciative; it is dreadfully appalling. *"Can ye say aught of yourselves?"*[41] Our respective movements are as independent as those of our planet. Both planets and people are propelled in their orbits by a greater force. It is the meek who comprehend that every decision and action requires God's mutual involvement.

Though our autonomy causes us to bear the accountability of our choices, we desperately depend on God for the remaining ingredients of action. Were it not for God's contributions of life, law, truth and morality, our agency would be nullified. We intensely depend on God for the structure and conditions of our current station. As Jesus humbly stated, *"I can of mine own self do nothing,"*[42] so too we must acknowledge God's influence in all we do. *"Surely your turning of things upside down shall be esteemed as the potter's clay: for shall the work say of him that made it, He made me not? Or shall the thing framed say of him that framed it, He had no understanding?"*[43] *"For if a man think himself to be something, when he is nothing, he deceiveth himself."*[44]

Because the humble understand their reliance upon God, their humility engenders tolerance for others. Heavenly Father is *"peaceable, gentle, and easy to be entreated, full of mercy and good fruits, without partiality, and without hypocrisy."*[45] Consider the following questions – how approachable are you? Do people have to reroute to avoid running into your rough personality traits, or do you have a charisma that welcomes company, conversation and inquiry? How well do you stomach criticism? Can you handle instruction and reproof? The scriptures advise, *"now, I would that ye should be humble, and*

---

[40] Deuteronomy 8:17
[41] Mosiah 2:25 – (Aught: meaning anything, just as the negative form – naught means nothing.)
[42] John 5:30
[43] Isaiah 29:16
[44] Galatians 6:3
[45] See James 3:17 – "But the wisdom that is from above is first pure, then peaceable, gentle, and easy to be entreated, full of mercy and good fruits, without partiality, and without hypocrisy."

be submissive and gentle; easy to be entreated."[46]

Being 'easy to be entreated' is another branch of humility. The meek do not grumble when service is needed, rather they are ready and responsive to requests. Meekness makes us more accessible. It makes us swift to serve and happy to help. When we are humble, new ideas are not seen as attacks, nor are inquiries viewed as assaults. Debate, even heated debate, does not qualify as an excuse to become offended or angry. Such is not the way of the humble, for they have the self-restraint that allows others to see things differently.

The gentle hand of humility receives inquiry, information, and even correction with tenderness and tolerance. Perhaps humility's most practically relevant reaction is its response to reproof. Of all life's situations, none tries our humility as acutely as reprimand, evaluation, and critique. On these occasions, will you remain 'easy to be entreated' or will you crumble at correction?

We cannot be easy to be entreated if we are easy to be offended. We cannot be meek if we *"will not bear chastisement."*[47] How are you supposed to approach people who are disgruntled over differences of opinion? Somehow even harmless informing interactions have a way of provoking these prickly people. Trying to approach those who are easy to be offended can require absurd levels of caution. Thankfully, such character traits have no place in God's divine nature.

True offense is uncommon, whereas making others offenders for benign mistakes or careless commentary is more mainstream. Too many people react like those described by Isaiah and *"make a man an offender for a word."*[48] It is almost as if these individuals want to be offended; they *"watch for iniquity,"*[49] patiently waiting like paparazzi to turn pebbles of opinion into rocks of offense.

Whether correction is given lovingly or bitterly, if we are easy to be entreated it is all received the same. By seeing past poorly chosen words or jagged manners, the humble are not offended by harsh counsel or even misguided condemnation. With meekness they accept the love and good will behind the gesture. They receive any and all instruction as an opportunity to re-evaluate their decisions and improve their self. It is

---

[46] Alma 7:23
[47] D&C 136:31 – "My people must be tried in all things, that they may be prepared to receive the glory that I have for them, even the glory of Zion; and he that will not bear chastisement is not worthy of my kingdom."
[48] Isaiah 29:21
[49] Isaiah 29:20

extremely difficult to be offended while being empathetic. Such is why they who are easy to be entreated are also fast to forgive.

There is another side of being easy to be entreated – the truly humble know how to ask for help, as well as offer it. It is important for us to know our limitations and humbly recognize as Moses did, "*I am not able to bear all this people alone, because it is too heavy for me.*"[50]

It is ironic to consider how much time we spend on our knees imploring God for help, while ignoring the predictable promptings to ask those around us for help. As we look for answers and blessings from God, do not be shy to search for them among the immense masses of willing disciples, disciples who have taken "*upon them the name of Christ, having a determination to serve him to the end.*"[51]

Sometimes our pride would wait for the veil to rupture, and an army of angels to aid us before imploring a mortal ministering angel who lives across the street. It can be extremely difficult to humble ourselves to ask another person for help, but the meek are not ashamed of their mortal limitations. They 'glory in their infirmities that the power of Christ may rest upon them.'[52]

Just as the humble are easy to be entreated, they are also easy to be educated. Teachability is a notable trait of the humble. The door to every godly attribute swings on the hinges of humility. Just as pride detonates all the deadly sins, humility initiates the development of all the godly attributes. The prophet Moroni observed how humility triggers the traits of faith and hope saying, "*behold I say unto you that he cannot have faith and hope, save he shall be meek, and lowly of heart.*" Without humility men do not feel the need to further furnish their faith; without humility men cease their study of godliness and stop improving.

The premise of pressing forward on the straight and narrow path, presupposes that one hasn't yet reached the precipice they were pressing towards. It is the meek who retain the inner responsibility for building the Kingdom of God, remembering that pressing forward implies that this journey will not be an effortless ride on an escalator.

Before one is teachable, there must be sufficient space to accommodate new teachings. Humility helps us empty our selfishness. It excavates the pride which prevents us from receiving instruction. By

---

[50] Numbers 11:14
[51] Moroni 6:3
[52] See 2 Corinthians 12:9 – "My grace is sufficient for thee: for my strength is made perfect in weakness. Most gladly therefore will I rather glory in my infirmities, that the power of Christ may rest upon me."

'humbling ourselves and acknowledging to God the things which we have done which are wrong,'[53] we increase our awareness of our weaknesses. It is humility that opposes the damning arrogance which says, *"I am rich, and increased with goods, and have need of nothing."*[54] A person who feels that he has 'need of nothing,' like a full vessel cannot receive additional substance. Only those with open hands are able to receive *"all that* [the] *Father hath."*[55]

Honestly and humbly appraising our standing and progress, prepares our character to be shaped by the Spirit. Confession carves the space in our soul that can subsequently be filled with learning and revelation. Therefore, the humble not only ask *"… Lord, is it I"*[56] and *"what lack I yet,"*[57] they also have every intention of filling the 'spots in their feasts of charity.'[58] Admitting our own faults and weaknesses is never easy because confession uncovers our vulnerabilities. Vulnerability is a key aspect to confession as well as a pivotal part of all education. In order to advance socially, intellectually or spiritually we must open ourselves to our vulnerabilities. We must come to terms with our imperfections and errors.

Remember that repentance will not be wrought without facing stubborn resistance from the natural man. Satan has at his disposal an array of tools to turn us away from making spiritual modifications. Having the immature mentality of a child, the natural man repels change. He is obstinate and prepared to throw a tantrum if we try to put an end to his habits. One common approach he wryly whispers in our ears is to get us to note the faults and inadequacies of a messenger. Sadly, in this regard Satan has no need to recruit the help of his devilish minions. Not while men are lining up past the doors to have their turn at tearing down others. Satan emphasizes every blemish, including strange gestures, monotonous inflections and even points out the physical imperfections of a teacher.

Satan does this because he knows that if he can effectively distract our focus toward the person giving the message, he may prevent us from evaluating the message itself. If Satan can successfully do this, he destroys any chance we have at change. Just as the young may resist the wisdom of an elder, the old may pay no heed to the perspectives of some youths. The

---

[53] D&C 5:28 – "And now, except he humble himself and acknowledge unto me the things that he has done which are wrong … I will grant unto him no views of the things of which I have spoken."
[54] Revelation 3:17
[55] D&C 84:38 – "And he that receiveth my Father receiveth my Father's kingdom; therefore all that my Father hath shall be given unto him."
[56] Matthew 26:22
[57] Matthew 19:20
[58] Jude 1:12 – "These are spots in your feasts of charity…clouds they are without water, carried about of winds; trees whose fruit withereth, without fruit …"

prejudice of the natural man is ageless. Just as the young may dismiss the old for being out of touch, the old may dismiss a youth thinking that an inexperienced child could offer him no further wisdom.

Yet is a messenger really so relevant to the message? Do we cast aside a message if the speaker does not fit our every expectation? Do you require a voice of thunder in order to be receptive? Do you require articulations spoken with crystalline perfection, or spectacular sermons designed to dazzle and entertain your mind? Those who think they can justifiably disconnect under the rationale that, 'I have heard this lesson before,' would place God at the level of a court jester, whose sole duty is to entertain and thrill his audience.

Of all the applications of humility there is one particular setting where disciples must master a meek attitude – prayer. Prayer is an outward manifestation of humility; however, we also become more humble as we *"worship and bow down and kneel before the LORD our maker."*[59] Therefore prayers need to be more than a morning mantra. Instead prayer should be a daily method of offering praise and sacrifice. Prayer is not meant to be a pulpit for voicing and appeasing our appetites. Though petition has its place in prayer, a prayer should not be completely composed of pleading. Similarly, there is more to prayer than weeping. Because prayer is the most basic of Christian rituals, it is helpful to consider prayer in the context of worship.[60]

How do we incorporate praise and worship into prayer? For the most part disciples are well trained in the tradition of giving gratitude as a respectful prologue to their petitions. However, many disciples are far less experienced in the art of praise. Gratitude primes one's soul to be more receptive to the Spirit; yet praise is another instrument that can be played as prelude for our prayers.

Praise speaks with a subtly different sound than gratitude, which acknowledges items, blessings and gifts. Illustrating the tone of praise Jacob exclaims, *"O the wisdom of God, his mercy and grace!"*[61] Praise looks past the blessing itself to extol the One responsible for our blessings. With a unique intensity, praise does more than admit the hand of God, it adores God himself. In praise we do not only notice our gifts, we exalt the Giver. With praise we do more than count our blessings; we acclaim our courteous

---

[59] See Psalms 95:6 – "O come, let us worship and bow down: Let us kneel before the LORD our maker."
[60] See Alma 33:3 – "Do ye remember to have read what Zenos…has said concerning prayer or worship?"
[61] 2 Nephi 9:10

benefactor.

Sometimes I wonder if we go about prayers in the wrong way. Joseph Smith stated, "Having a knowledge of God, **we begin to know how to approach Him**, and how to ask so as to receive an answer."[62] What do we need to do 'to ask so as to receive an answer?' How are we supposed to approach this 'being we have got to worship?' Do we approach Him as a friend, a Father or a God? Yes, the Eternal Father functions in each of these roles, but what is the correct way to balance them? Truly, in prayer we need to be as open and comfortable with God as we are with close friends. However, this principle does not imply invocations should digress into chummy chit-chat. We must remember that though God is our friend, He is also our God.

Imagine approaching that heavenly throne spangled with gems and gold. As you proceed down the decorated courts, a flurry of lights and glories tease your every sense. This dazzling dance of colors captivates you, sending your spirit into a state of childlike enchantment. But even this terrific, calligraphic mixture of marvels is curtailed by the beaming countenance of God. Have you ever taken a moment to consider this type of setting in your prayers? Have you ever considered the recipient of your prayers and the absolute respect, awe and adoration He deserves?

When you kneel, do you realize whom you bow to? The universe rests gently in the palm of His mighty hand. It is nothing but an instrument of His delight. Would you, a pathetic particle dare superciliously strut toward this throne with cocksure swagger and cavalier confidence? When you stand in this sacred setting, it will not require persuasion to force your knees to the floor. Hoping to blend in with the dirt, you will exclaim, "*now, for this cause I know that man is nothing, which thing I never had supposed.*"[63] Such a sublime scenario has a way of making humility rapidly reflexive.

When you pray, your immediate setting may not seem so lofty, but prayer transforms a crowded closet into a majestic extension of the cosmic courts of the Celestial Kingdom. Thus, the physical choreography we select for our prayers should reflect the utmost reverence that naturally attends the place and person we are approaching. Due to the prideful posture and casual carriage selected by some, they hardly make it past Heaven's outer walls.

But why worry so much about posture. You may be thinking God is omniscient and thus will be in attendance regardless of my actions. Yet,

---

[62] Joseph Smith. The King Follett Sermon. Published Ensign April 1971 – Emphasis added
[63] Moses 1:10

this is not the issue at hand. Though God is present regardless of our stance, we need to have the courtesy to show up to our own prayers as well.

Haste will quickly dishonor our homage. In contrast, the humble are reverent and do not hurry their worship. Some pray as if they were leaving a message on an answering machine. In these cases, no indication is given in language, tone or feeling that the person is presently communicating with a REAL entity.

To avoid this pitfall, take a moment before you speak, pause to remember the Being to whom you are talking. Bring His majesty and Spirit into your consciousness. Reverence is key to revelation. Speak to God as if He were really before you, then to your surprise you may realize – 'His eyes are upon you. He is in your midst though ye cannot see Him.'[64]

Humility makes our prayers penitent! We are admonished, "*exercise your faith unto repentance*;"[65] but faith unto repentance is most frequently attained by praying unto repentance. So long as we are self-absorbed in our prayers, it will not be possible to hear the Spirit's soft whispers over the sounds of our own prerogatives. George Bernard Shaw commented on such prayers saying, "*Most people do not pray; they only beg.*"[66] Some people don't even beg, they just whine. Prayer should not be emphasized as a microphone for carnal complaints. Instead prayer should be seen as wrestling mat – one where pride is pinned into submission.

Effective prayer requires effort. There is sure to be some struggle as we grapple against our egos. God is aware that inside of us is a constant conflict between the flesh and the Spirit. It is not helpful to ignore this conflict. Rather we should wrestle to resolve these conflicts through prayer. Penitent prayers are a 'wrestle before God,' with the intent to 'receive a remission of our sins.'[67] Because prayer is part of the process of repentance, we must anticipate that pain will accompany a productive prayer.

An unresolved a prayer is a "*double minded*"[68] prayer; one dissociatively split between definitive decisions. However, indecision is not the only form of double mindedness. The hidden deception of hypocrisy not only divides our prayers, it desecrates them. With pretend

---

[64] D&C 38:7 – "mine eyes are upon you. I am in your midst and ye cannot see me"
[65] Alma 34:17 – "exercise your faith unto repentance, that ye begin to call upon his holy name"
[66] Quote attributed to George Bernard Shaw
[67] See Enos 1:2 – "And I will tell you of the wrestle which I had before God, before I received a remission of my sins"
[68] James 1:8 – "A double minded man is unstable in all his ways."

righteousness, hypocrites subtract sincerity by 'multiplying many words.'[69] Vain invocations can be dramatic as well as dull. We see this in those who pray with an attitude of teenage martyrdom expecting miraculous compensation for their sacrificial sobs. Nevertheless, humility counteracts hypocrisy by sharpening our sincerity and honesty. Such is why humility produces repentance, for a humble prayer by definition is honest. Sincere supplications have a special way of becoming submissive.

The storybook character Huck Finn is a great example of how humble sincerity influences prayer. Describing Huck's attempt to pray, Twain wrote, "I about made up my mind to pray, and see if I couldn't try to quit being the kind of a boy I was and be better. So I kneeled down. But the words wouldn't come. Why wouldn't they? It warn't no use to try and hide it from Him. Nor from ME, neither. I knowed very well why they wouldn't come. It was because my heart warn't right; it was because I warn't square; it was because I was playing double. I was letting ON to give up sin, but away inside of me I was holding on to the biggest one of all. I was trying to make my mouth SAY I would do the right thing ... but deep down in me I knowed it was a lie, and He knowed it. You can't pray a lie – I found that out."[70] God is not a fool. He can discern the difference between a 'yes man' prayer and a *"thy will be done"* prayer.

A prayer does not always refer to those expressions contained within a single session. Multiple prayers offered over a period of time can connect together to compile an entire prayer. With persistent appeals to God over days and weeks, we progressively peel back layer after layer of our pride. As it is with any hard-fought wrestling match, the struggle for submissiveness may require multiple rounds before the champion is crowned. It is only after our desires have fused with the Father's will that a prayer is truly complete. Perhaps then, many of our prayers remain unanswered simply because they are not yet finished; they are ineffectual only because they are incomplete.

Since the conclusion of a prayer falls on yielding to the Fathers will, the focus of our prayers needs to shift from our self to the Savior. If this is not accomplished, how can we in good conscience add the closing clause, "in the name of Jesus Christ?" The Bible Dictionary explains the significance of this finishing phrase saying, "Christians are taught to pray in

---

[69] 3 Nephi 19:24 – Brackets added – "and they did not multiply many words" See also Matt 6:7 – "But when ye pray, use not vain repetitions, as the heathen do: for they think that they shall be heard for their much speaking."

[70] Mark Twain. The Adventures of Huckleberry Finn (Tom Sawyer's Comrade). Harper and Brothers Publishers. New York and London 1912. Chapter 31 p.295

Christ's name. We pray in Christ's name when our mind is the mind of Christ, and our wishes the wishes of Christ … Many prayers remain unanswered because they are not in Christ's name at all; they in no way represent His mind but spring out of the selfishness of man's heart."[71]

Prayers need to be a consecration not a confrontation. As we conclude our prayers, we should ponder – in what way have I submitted myself to God? Prayer is not meant to be a means of celestial shopping. Prayer is an altar of sacrifice where we lay our sins for the slaughter. Where have the pledges gone in prayer? Where have the vows and covenants gone? Swear not by the heaven or the earth which is God's footstool, but do not hesitate to commit yourself in prayer.

Right now there are changes that need to be made in each of our lives. The changes required by Christianity are much more than a makeover; they are a complete reconstruction. At this moment each of us are aware of some of the changes we need to make, while there are others yet to be revealed to us. Concerning those changes which currently camp at the fore of your consciousness, it is appropriate to ask – What are you waiting for? It is time to change the attitude of our prayers. It is time to conclude our prayers not with sloth or sleep, but with service and sacrifice.

It is within your power to be humble. Whether or not you are meek is completely dependent upon your desires. By mixing the gifts of agency and time, you can choose to be humble as did the Lord, Jesus. The choice is yours. You can humble yourself because life 'compels you to be humble,'[72] or you can proactively humble yourself *"because of the word."*[73] By exercising faith in God's teachings we can become humble, *"without being compelled to be humble"* by external forces.[74] Regardless of the stimulating source or situation; all cases testify that humility results from potentiating our internal autonomy.

In the end, your humility must be deeper than desperation. One of life's most difficult tests is to be humble when life is calm and pleasant. What a shame that during life's summer seasons, our dependence on God gets drained by the unremitting warmth of favorable conditions. Since our potential to be humble does not disappear on good days, what is the secret

---

[71] Bible Dictionary – Prayer
[72] Alma 32:13 – "And now, because ye are compelled to be humble blessed are ye; for a man sometimes, if he is compelled to be humble, seeketh repentance."
[73] Alma 32:14 – "And now, as I said unto you, that because ye were compelled to be humble ye were blessed, do ye not suppose that they are more blessed who truly humble themselves because of the word?"
[74] Alma 32:16 – "Therefore, blessed are they who humble themselves without being compelled to be humble"

to sustaining meekness through periods of success? Can we learn which principles are responsible for motivating those, *"who would humble themselves, let them be in whatsoever circumstances they might?"*[75]

Submissiveness need not be a respecter of circumstance. Thus, we wonder what "word," when planted in our hearts, brings humble behaviors in every conceivable circumstance? Is there some idea or doctrine that this trait can be attributed to? In response to this question, recall Christ's great Sermon on the Mount. Here Jesus revealed 'interrelated and progressive precept that flow together to form the refined and spiritual character.'[76] Therefore take note that this progressive spiritual process starts by being *"poor in spirit."*[77] If improving our spiritual character is conditional on us being poor in spirit, we wonder what the phrase *"poor in spirit"* means?

In this verse the Greek the word for poor is *ptochos*,[78] a word meaning *a beggar, vagrant or mendicant*. When used as an adjective the word means *to crouch* giving us a powerful image of a crouching, desperate, and withered beggar. This image is neither mistake nor coincidence. The illustration of a beggar is as intentional as it is instructive. There is no doubt that being poor in spirit, or a beggar in spirit recognizes that 'we are all beggars,' and *"depend upon the same Being, even God, for all the substance which we have."*[79] Consider what profound effects this single doctrine could have, were it 'written in your heart.'[80]

When one is poor in spirit, they are stirred by the sense that *"ye are eternally indebted to our heavenly Father, to render to him all that you have and are."*[81] As Christ observed, *"to whom little is forgiven, the same loveth little."*[82] The feeling of our infinite debt to God inspires an equally infinite source of gratitude and love. Similarly, being aware of the *"God, who has created you, on whom you are dependent for you lives and for all that ye have and are,"*[83] makes one more apt to *"always retain in remembrance, the greatness of God, and your own nothingness, and his goodness and longsuffering towards you, unworthy creatures, and humble yourselves even in the depths of humility, calling on the name of the Lord daily."*[84]

---

[75] Alma 32:25
[76] See Bible Dictionary – Beatitudes
[77] Matthew 5:3 – "Blessed are the poor in spirit: for theirs is the kingdom of heaven."
[78] Greek Strong's Dictionary #4434 – (pto – khos')
[79] Mosiah 4:19 – "For behold, are we not all beggars? Do we not all depend upon the same Being, even God"
[80] See Jeremiah 31:33 – "I will put my law in their inward parts, and write it in their hearts"
[81] Mosiah 2:34 – "Ye are eternally indebted unto your heavenly Father, to render to him all that you have and are"
[82] Luke 7:47
[83] Mosiah 2:21
[84] Mosiah 4:11

By discerning their tremendous debt owed to God, the humble do not see themselves as the sole owners of their agency. It is the humble who believe the word, "*Ye are not your own? For ye are bought with a price.*" Thus, the meek feel inclined to 'glorify God in their body, and in their spirit,' "*which are God's.*"[85] Here is the key to keeping meekness. Here is the doctrine that produces the unconditional, resilient humility we seek. 'Hath God not made thee, and established thee?' "*Is not he thy father that hath bought thee?*"[86] God has claim on you, for He has "*created you from the beginning, and is preserving you from day to day, by lending you breath, that ye may live and move and do according to your own will, and even supporting you from one moment to another.*"[87] But this is not all. Christ the Savior spent His soul in serving the sentence of our sins, and therewith 'purchased' us "*with His own blood.*"[88]

Jesus endured mutilating torture of mind, spirit, and body – an agony which ruptured the vessels in every one of His pores. Therefore, we should never debate the totality of the debt we owe God. Our debt spilled more than a few drops of blood; it cost a life of perfection. Therefore as the Prophet Peter taught, it is a 'damnable heresy to deny the Lord that bought you, which denial will bring upon you a swift destruction.'[89] Feelings of humility may be fostered in different ways, but no other method presses upon one's thoughts, behaviors and devotion to the extent that this truth does. "*O then, how ye ought to impart of the substance that ye have one to another,*"[90] which includes all the substance of your soul and self, for all these things do "*not belong to you but to God, to whom also your life belongeth.*"[91]

Consider God the Almighty, "*the God of our Lord Jesus Christ, the Father of glory ... Far above all principality, and power, and might and dominion, and every name that is named, not only in this world, but also in that which is to come.*"[92] Consider how God, who has all power, governs galaxies with a gentle hand. He is not absorbed by His omnipotence; instead He prefers to use His power to empower others. Father does not command control of all His creations, He manages the universe with meekness. Does not the silent

---

[85] 1 Corinthians 6:19,20 – "ye are not your own? For ye are bought with a price: therefore glorify God in your body, and in your spirit, which are God's"
[86] See Deuteronomy 32:6 – "Is not he thy father that hath bought thee? hath he not made thee, and established thee?"
[87] Mosiah 2:21
[88] Acts 20:28 – "to feed the church of God, which he hath purchased with His own blood."
[89] 2 Peter 2:1 – "But there were false prophets also among the people...who privily shall bring in damnable heresies, even denying the Lord that bought them, and bring upon themselves swift destruction."
[90] Mosiah 2:21
[91] Mosiah 4:22
[92] Ephesians 1:21

spin of planets and stars speak of the Father's sweet humility?

"For thus saith the high and lofty One that inhabiteth eternity, whose name is Holy; I dwell in the high and holy place, with him also that is of a contrite and humble spirit, to revive the spirit of the humble, and to revive the heart of the contrite ones."[93] Take note of the word 'also' in the verse above. The message states that God dwells with those who are **also** of a contrite and humble spirit – implying that God himself is humble.

God is not some hard-hearted dictator whose delight is in hoarding massive amounts of enslaved souls. Though Heavenly Father is Supreme, He whispers with the softness of *"a still small voice."*[94] The gentle nature of God invites rather than demands. He counsels instead of controls. He comforts instead of intimidates. Can you sense the gentle charm of His warming welcome inviting you with peace and serenity? Have you felt the sweet caress of His meekness tenderly still your boisterous soul? Therefore let the world praise the gentleness of God, for our Father truly is mild. He is meek. He is Humble.

---

[93] Isaiah 57:15
[94] 1 Kings 19:12

Faith

The veil is a taunting sheet coating our consciousness. With absolute disregard it apprehends our memories and sends our senses into obscurity. This unsympathetic sentinel guards God's intergalactic glow of glory – a glory which governs and gives light[1] to all things. Yet perhaps the veil is not solely sent for provocation, but to protect us from the brightness of perfection; a brightness that could 'cause the very elements to melt with fervent heat.'[2] Despite this bullying barrier, the spirit of man shares an indivisible bond with God. For *"The Spirit itself beareth witness with our spirit, that we are the children of God."*[3]

Mark how Paul uses the word *"with"* in the verse above. The Holy Spirit bears witness not only <u>to</u> our spirit, but <u>with</u> our spirit. This implies that your spirit also takes part in testifying that you are child of God. Your spirit has a witness, one buried beneath the veil. By the touch of the Holy Ghost this forgotten consciousness awakens and then if only for a moment we clearly behold our eternal identity and heritage.

Underneath our veiled memories is a remarkable revelation of the Father's existence and character. This echoing declaration can be recaptured when eternal truths are spoken. When the Spirit witnesses of the content in a truth, it concurrently evokes that deep yearning within us to be near Father once more. This is the witness of our spirit. Our spirits have ever been captivated by God's majesty and drawn into it. Your *"soul [longs] to be there."*[4]

Can we comprehend such doctrines contained in our own spirits? Can we uncover our own forgotten testimony of the living God? Every word from God, every revelation from the Holy Ghost, is accompanied with a witness that we are not strangers to spirituality. Godliness and nobility are not foreign principles. Virtue carries a feeling of familiarity, a nostalgic warmth like the hearth of a home.

The witness within our spirit is the very sense of recollection that accompanies the touch of the Holy Ghost. Within His whispers we feel the

---

[1] See Facsimile No. 2 Explanation Paragraph 5: to borrow its light … receiving light
[2] See 3 Nephi 26:3 – "even until the elements should melt with fervent heat, and the earth should be wrapt together as scroll, and the heavens and the earth should pass away"
[3] Romans 8:16 see also vs17 – "And if children, then heirs; heirs of God, and joint heirs with Christ"
[4] Alma 36:22 – "Yea, methought I saw…God sitting upon his throne…and my soul did long to be there."

testimony that God is our home, and divinity our original estate. We feel an internal record that God is not some obscure former acquaintance, but that we knew Him being once encircled about *"in the arms of His love."*[5] You knew the Eternal Father, being one who once existed with Him in an eternity of marvels and wonders.

Underlying every miraculous manifestation from the Spirit is a gentle undertone that there is still much more to be had. The Spirit is a restrained power, and while it resides within us we may recognize that its strength is subdued; for as we feel its influence, we sense a force that could completely consume us if it were fully released. This power was noticed and described by Nephi who said, *"He hath filled me with his love even unto the consuming of my flesh."*[6] The fullness of the Father presses firmly against the veil. By faith we push against the veil and feel the pressure of immortality and infinity pushing back at us from the other side. Such overwhelming power leads us to exclaim, *"for this cause I know that man is nothing, which thing I never had supposed."*[7]

By faith men pierce the veil. But how do we define faith? Faith is a multi-faceted process built by many individual, but interconnecting pieces. Consequently, we can't pin faith down to one definition without omitting some steps in the whole process. Some say faith is a belief, while others describe it as a hope. Faith has been associated with knowledge, action and power. Faith is said to be a gift, a feeling, an idea and even a personality. Aspects of faith feed into patience, courage, happiness and integrity.

Faith is not a singular event; instead it is a flowing process wherewith we plant ideas in our soul.[8] Faith emerges from meekness, the open mind and heart. Ideas seeded in the soil of curiosity, inquiry and exploration are allowed to grow. If nourished, the process of faith progresses from the inception of an idea to contemplation. After contemplation, faith moves onward to an experimentation. By faith ideas continue to be nurtured past the threshold of thought to action. Overtime actions progress into habits and continue onward till the original idea fuses with our personality and merges with our soul.[9] Faith is inner conviction that progresses us through this process.

Faith is a principle of action; it is a principle of change. Whenever

---

[5] 2 Nephi 1:15
[6] 2 Nephi 4:21
[7] Moses 1:10
[8] See Alma 32:28 – "if ye give place, that a seed may be planted in your heart"
[9] See Alma 32:42 – "And because of your diligence and your faith and your patience with the word in nourishing it, that it may take root in you, behold, by and by ye shall pluck the fruit thereof, which is most precious"

a doctrine or principle is taught, what is most important is how the idea will change us. Thus, we need to consider how an idea evolves from the seed of a single thought into a fruit bearing branch capable of altering perceptions, reactions, emotions, behaviors and ultimately one's being?

Our study begins by examining some of the ideas anciently associated with faith. In the Old Testament, two words are primarily used to portray faith: *aman*[10] and *emuwnah*.[11] *Aman* is predominately translated as *believe* and is responsible for about half of the appearances of the word *faith*. *Aman*, like our word *amen* means *to be firm, true, enduring, faithful, believing and permanent*. Additionally, the consistency connoted in *aman* was intended to evoke the image of a caring parent or nurturing nurse.[12] Whether nurse or parent, we can better understand faith by recalling scenes of those whose care is constant; those whose love is enduring and presence permanent in our time of need.

The other word translated as faith is *emuwnah*. *Emuwnah* with its related term *emuwn*,[13] denotes similar ideas of firmness, being faithful, trustworthy, established and steady. In Greek, the word almost exclusively used for faith is *pistis*.[14] *Pistis* comes from a word *peitho*[15] which means *to persuade, convince, pacify, conciliate or win over*. Like the other words we've considered thus far, *pistis* means faith and belief; however it also connotes conviction. Those with faith or conviction are those who are truly convinced of a concept or idea. Conviction comes as ideas are carried from the mind to the heart, and it is by faith that ideas are engrafted into our character.

Faith is proportional to the degree to which the idea persuades us. It is possible for ideas to be indifferent. An idea can be solely academic without being convincing. Such is why persuasion is an important component of faith. The very instant that we become persuaded by an idea, our thoughts, feelings and behaviors change. When we are convinced of a doctrine or principle, the concept consequently becomes a part of us. They then inevitably leak into our actions, thoughts, perceptions and personality.

---

[10] Hebrew Strong's Dictionary #539 –(Aw-man)– "a primitive root: properly, to build up or support, to foster as a parent or nurse, figuratively to render or be firm or faithful, to trust or believe, to be permanent or quiet; morally to be true or certain."

[11] Hebrew Strong's Dictionary #530 –(emuwnah (em – oo – naw')

[12] See 1 Thessalonians 2:9 – "But we were gentle among you, even as a nurse cherisheth her children"

[13] Hebrew Strong's Dictionary #529 –(emuwn – aymoon')

[14] Greek Strong's Dictionary #4102 –(pis'-tis)

[15] Greek Strong's Dictionary #3982 –(pi'-tho)

So we contemplate the following questions: Do the principles of the gospel persuade you to piety, or are you unconvinced of the validity of the doctrines? *"Do you exercise faith in the redemption of him who created you?"*[16] How firm is your faith? Are you as constant as a parent or as trustworthy as a teen? Are you dependable, established, steady and permanent in the things you profess, or are you the sort that exhibits fair-weather faith? Are you casual or constant in your convictions? Are you truly persuaded? Do you really believe?

Mortality is a stranger to certainty. *"For now we see through a glass, darkly; but then face to face: now I know in part; but then shall I know even as also I am known."*[17] The world in which we live is a darkened stage of unpredictability. Amidst the shade and shadow of uncertainty, life forces us to place our trust in the unseen. Inextinguishable remnants of doubt glaze over our telestial understanding, and these residual elements of unsurety will forever remain with us so long as we are mortal. *"Wherefore, no man can behold all my works, except he behold all my glory; and no man can behold all my glory, and afterwards remain in the flesh on the earth."*[18]

Since certainty escapes us, faith does not necessarily destroy doubts, rather it defies them. The subtle difference in the wording implies that doubt will still exist. Faith is not a *"perfect knowledge of things,"* but rather a *"hope for things which are not seen, which are true."*[19] Faith is not action motivated from knowledge and surety; instead faith is action against uncertainty. This is why we cannot expect the critical conclusions about God and His kingdom to come to us without taking any chances. Though God will give us sufficient persuasion through the power of the Holy Spirit, this does not suggest that He will immediately eradicate all of our reservations.

Though faith accepts ideas amidst lingering elements of unsurety, as long as there is faith there is never any ambivalence in behavior. When there is faith, our decisions are detectable and our opinions are observable. Faith is the moment where an idea is taken to create causality. The spirit of faith is a spirit of adventure, an energy of exploration that answers the clarion call to leave rationalization at home and take the ballistic plunge into the unknown.

What is so marvelous about faith is that it allows us to act without

---

[16] Alma 5:15
[17] 1 Corinthians 13:12
[18] Moses 1:5
[19] Alma 32:21 – "And now as I said concerning faith – Faith is not to have a perfect knowledge of things"

having all the facts. At a most critical point, faith is an experiment. *"But behold ... awake and **arouse your faculties, even to an experiment upon my words**, and exercise a particle of faith."*[20] Experimentation always exists at the great juncture between belief and action. Faith is that component which enables us to proceed along uncertain paths. However, know that this experiment cannot be safely carried out in a calm and controlled laboratory. No, the experiment of faith requires risk.

"But without faith it is impossible to please him: for he that cometh to God must believe that he is, and that he is a rewarder of them that diligently seek him."[21] The test of faith will assess whether you are willing to jump into jeopardy, *"not knowing beforehand the things which* [you] *should do."*[22] Will you gamble godliness against the glory of the world even when the stakes are high? You will face periods where God will challenge you to step outside traditional rationale and reason.

Experiences where we must defy conventional logic are important and inescapable parts of God's program. The framework of all man's intellect originates from a trust in unseen principles. There are those who place their trust supremely in their own self and understanding; while others trust in a supreme being whose, *"thoughts are not your thoughts"* and whose *'ways are not their own ways.'*[23] *"... thine heart is lifted up, and thou hast said, I am a God, I sit in the seat of God, in the midst of the seas; yet thou art a man, and not God, though thou set thine heart as the heart of God:"*[24] This is the great divide between faith and atheism. This is the basic critical trust of Christianity. We must believe that *"as the heavens are higher than the earth, so are my ways higher than your ways, and my thoughts than your thoughts."*[25] If we are equipped with a belief in a higher order that supersedes mankind's best comprehensions, we will no longer *"dispute not because* [we] *see not,"*[26] but will *"look forward with an eye of faith."*[27]

We cannot anticipate all the outcomes of our decisions. God has intentionally designed life to have uncertainty, for the scriptures attest that

---

[20] Alma 32:27 – Emphasis added
[21] Hebrews 11:6
[22] 1 Nephi 4:6 – Brackets added
[23] See Isaiah 55:8 – "For my thoughts are not your thoughts, neither are your ways my ways, saith the LORD."
See also vs. 9
[24] Ezekiel 28:2
[25] Isaiah 55:9
[26] Ether 12:6
[27] Alma 32:40 – "And thus, if ye will not nourish the word, looking forward with an eye of faith to the fruit thereof, ye can never pluck to fruit of the tree of life."

it is *"by faith ye stand."*[28] We will not be able to destroy every drop of doubt floating in our minds, but because of faith we can still produce actions against uncertainty and shadow. Can you take that step into the dark? Can you press forward *"not knowing beforehand the thing which"*[29] you should do? Faith is decisive amidst doubts. Doubt disables decisions. When doubt is given pre-eminence, it blocks behaviors and prevents virtues from coming into existence. That we might know our self and our enemy, the study of faith must include an analysis of its antithesis – doubt.

Upon seeing the Savior standing above an unstable sea as if it were land, Peter boldly leaped off a ship to meet him. Instead of splashing into the waters, Peter's feet landed atop the waters without sinking. With his steps somehow being miraculously supported, Peter started walking on the water toward the Savior. Then being startled by a boisterous wind Peter began to sink. Seeing the struggle of His friend and student, Jesus stretched out His hand to catch Peter. After securing Peter, Jesus counseled him saying, *"O thou of little faith, wherefore didst thou doubt?"* [30]

There are only four instances in the scriptures where Jesus uses the word *doubt*. This verse in particular is the only case where the Greek word *distazo*[31] is used to signify doubt. *Distazo* means to be caught in between two things. It essentially represents the message Elijah spoke to the children of Israel, *"How long halt ye between two opinions."*[32] Being unable to make a decision, those who doubt, waver *"like a wave of the sea driven with the wind and tossed."*[33] This pause, this halting hesitancy is fatal for faith, for the *"double minded man is unstable in all his ways."*[34]

How long do you stall before you choose to follow Gods commands? Do you falter when asked to trust Heavenly Father? The faithful "[stagger] *not at the promise of God through unbelief.*"[35] They are not only decisive, but there is hardly a shred of reluctance in their actions. The faithful do not pause to brood over the promptings of the Spirit; instead they run in response to spiritual impressions.[36] The faithful do not need to second guess or double check, neither do they feel a need to 'look back.'[37]

---

[28] 2 Corinthians 1:24
[29] 1 Nephi 4:6 – I was led by the Spirit, not knowing beforehand the things which I should do.
[30] Matthew 14:31
[31] Greek Strong's Dictionary #1365 –(dis-tad'-zo)
[32] 1 Kings 18:21
[33] James 1:6
[34] James 1:8
[35] Romans 4:20 – Staggered – Greek Strong's Dictionary #1252 – diakrino – To waver
[36] Acts 8:30 – "And Philip ran thither to him, and heard him read the prophet Esaias"
[37] See Genesis 19:26 – "But his wife looked back … and she became a pillar of salt."

Though the faithful do not fully know the course they embark upon, their actions are decisive – a display of definitive confidence.

Self-doubt is the most pervasive and powerful paralytic to a person's progress. Every act of faith an individual makes must be cleared by their self-confidence. Faith in God, regardless of its measure is negated when there is no faith in our own abilities. It is easy to exclaim, "*I know, O Lord, that thou hast all power, and can do whatsoever thou wilt for the benefit of man.*"[38] But what is God's **specific will** as opposed to His general will? What does God want you to do at this moment in time? What can God do through you here, now and today? These are the difficult questions of faith. Anyone can believe in God's omnipotence, but the true test of faith is to believe that God's omnipotence can impose on your particular set of circumstances.

Laman and Lemuel are the traditional cautionary examples of how belief and even knowledge can be undone if we lack faith in our own capacities. Notice where Laman and Lemuel place themselves in the following statements: "*And they said unto me: We have not; for the Lord maketh no such thing known unto* **us**,"[39] and "*How is it possible that the Lord will deliver Laban into* **our** *hands*."[40] Even after seeing an angel of heaven, the faith of Laman and Lemuel could not fathom how God's influence would function for them. Amidst undeniable revelations, incredible visions, and miraculous events, their tragic impediment may have been an inability to believe that God would, or could cause these same miracles for them.

Failures of faith are not always the result of a disbelief in God. Instead, they are frequently a result of disbelieving that God intends to accomplish something **through us**. In order for our faith in God to be efficacious, it needs to be accompanied by a faith in our self and situation. You must believe that God will answer *your* prayers. You must believe that God will give *you* strength; that He will lead you and reveal His wonders to *you* specifically. God's power will remain mostly inert until we learn express faith in gospel principles in a personal way.

Remember that the veil does exist; and because the veil exists, we will not have a perfect knowledge of all things in mortality. Not only are the odds against you, the program itself is against you. A major purpose of mortal life is to test our faith, for the scriptures say "*The just shall live by faith.*"[41] The frequency which God tests faith is a testament to its

---

[38] Ether 3:4
[39] 1 Nephi 15:9 – Emphasis added
[40] 1 Nephi 3:31 – Emphasis added
[41] Romans 1:17

significance! Life is designed to test our faith. All of the uncertainty inherent in mortality helps accomplish this purpose. God intentionally places us in situations where we will have to exercise faith against doubt. We are trapped in a state where we must "*walk by faith, not by sight.*"[42]

Faith is not the stuff of fantasy. Faith is the fuel for action. Wishful words are no substitute for the substance of service. Though faith is not action itself, faith is the agent largely responsible for producing action. If beliefs fail to convert into action, there is no faith, as the scriptures say, "*For as the body without the spirit is dead, so faith without works is dead also.*"[43] Doubt deadens beliefs, whereas ideas are animated by the force of faith. By faith we take inanimate, invisible, and intangible thoughts and make them real. Though thoughts do not exist in the physical world themselves, the process of faith takes immaterial ideas and gives them a physical creation.

This precept was penned by the Apostle James: "*But be ye doers of the word, and not hearers only, deceiving your own selves.*"[44] The Greek word translated as "*doers*" is *poietes*.[45] *Poietes* means *to make, do or perform*. *Poietes* is a doer; in special instances *poietes* is rendered as the word *poet*. In fact, the origin of our word poet is found in this Greek word. Though James may not have intended the following subtleties, the principles demonstrated in the word play are still true.

The image of a poet contained in the word *doer* illustrates how faith works. In an artistic sense, the goal of a poet is to express transcendental thoughts – ideas that are so powerful, so immense that they cannot be bottled up in common communication. Through clever devises, a poet shapes superior and sublime concepts using mortal materials. Similarly the work of faith is *poietes*. Faith is that which converts ineffable ideas into action. Faith is a creation, a process that gives ethereal concepts life in the physical realm. Faith is the "**substance** *of things hoped for.*"[46] As the substance in our hope, it is faith that gives shape to heavenly thoughts, doctrines and desires.

There is a statement that "faith and doubt cannot exist in the same mind at the same time, for one will dispel the other."[47] This is true in the phenomenal or physical realm. Just as the pop culture wisdom of Yoda observed, "do or do not – there is no try." Pertaining to tangible, earthly

---

[42] See 2 Corinthians 5:7 – "(For we walk by faith, not by sight:)
[43] James 2:26
[44] James 1:22
[45] Greek Strong's Dictionary #4163 –(poy-ay-tace') "from poieo to make or do, a performer. Specially, a poet – doer"
[46] Hebrews 11:1 – Emphasis added
[47] Thomas S. Monson. "Come unto Him in Prayer and Faith." *Ensign*, March 2009

existence there is either faith or doubt. You either do or you doubt because they cannot materially co-exist. However, in the nominal or mental realm there is a ferocious battle between faith and doubt as they vie for physical expression. If one has no doubts, then there would be no faith, for these would be replaced by knowledge and surety. *"Now, as I said concerning faith – that it was not a perfect knowledge – even so it is with my words. Ye cannot know of their surety, unto perfection, any more than faith is a perfect knowledge."*[48]

Though knowledge sounds lofty, a perfect knowledge does not ensure perfect practice. Knowledge is not the climax of faith. Knowledge alone does not consistently and accurately predict conduct. Luke records, *"And devils also came out of many, crying out, and saying, Thou art Christ the Son of God, And he rebuking them suffered them not to speak: for they knew that he was Christ."*[49] If a devil's knowledge is greater than our own, why is it that the knowledge of God and Christ fails to redeem the damned legions of hell?

One may know of a surety that God exists, yet this knowledge[50] does not automatically cause a complete knowledge of all things, nor does it excuse the necessity of faith. Laman and Lemuel had a knowledge of God's existence perfected with the visitation on an angel, yet they still murmured *"because they knew not the dealings of that God who had created them."*[51] They knew that God was there, but they did not know His nature. They had no doubt that God was real, but they still misunderstood His plan and doctrines.

Trust is a potentiation of faith. *"What confidence is this wherein thou trustest?"*[52] How does your trust in God manifest? Of all matters pertaining to trust, the most pressing for the saints of *"the household of God"*[53] is to trust in Christ's atonement and redemption. Sins have a way of sticking to our self-image, and Satan is more than happy to see us perpetuate corrupt pictures of our identity. Satan persistently points out our past. He exhausts his efforts reminding us about who we once were. In contrast, God continually reminds us who we can be and points us toward the future. God inspires us with our divine potential, whereas Satan discourages us with our problematic moral failings.

Can the vile really become virtuous? Can the perverse really be

---

[48] Alma 32:26
[49] Luke 4:41
[50] See Alma 32:32 – "And now, behold, is your knowledge perfect? Yea, your knowledge is perfect in that thin, and your faith is dormant; and this because you know, for ye know that the word hath swelled your souls"
[51] 1 Nephi 2:12
[52] Isaiah 36:4
[53] Ephesians 2:19 – "ye are no more strangers and foreigners, but fellowcitizens with the saints, and of the household of God."

made pure or the shameful be made respectable? Can you see past the scarified wounds which once spotted your soul to see the light of divinity within yourself? So many good souls struggle to fully accept all the implications of God's grace. And we are not talking about imperfections, short-comings or mistakes. No, we are speaking of aggressive recalcitrance, gross ungodliness and seditious lust. God's *"grace is sufficient!"*[54] The effigy of a most reprobate, hideous human being can have the *"image of God"* restored to them; but first they must trust in grace. They must trust in God.

"We believe that the first principles and ordinances of the Gospel are: first, Faith in the Lord Jesus Christ ... ."[55] We all *"rely upon the merits of Jesus Christ;"*[56] therefore we must trust that forgiveness and sanctification are real and available to us as well as others. Receiving a revelation of a renewed self rarely comes easily. Transformation is a challenging task. It takes a tremendous amount of time and effort to combat deeply ingrained mentalities and manners. Un-doing habits can take more than a day, week or month. Though we may feel wrenched mentally, emotionally and spiritually, with faith in Christ's redemption we can trust that *"if our heart condemns us, God is greater than our heart, and knoweth all things."*[57] As the sun rises and falls, cycling from darkness to light, death to regeneration, we too can be reborn each day. We can awaken *"out of a deep sleep"* and "[awake] *unto God "*[58] as 'a new creation'[59] – a creation illuminated by the light of the risen Son. *"It is of the LORD'S mercies that we are not consumed, because his compassions fail not. They are new every morning: great is thy faithfulness."*[60]

Christ has said, *"blessed are they that have not seen, and yet have believed."*[61] Regardless of the degree of doubt that exists within a person, the only thing that matters is whether or not faith coverts concepts into action. Action is the true measure of faith, *"But wilt thou know, O vain man, that faith without works is dead!"*[62] In essence, when there is faith there is action. When there is doubt people pause, hesitate and stand still. If faith does not manifest in an extrinsic form, whatever amount of faith one professes is

---

[54] 2 Corinthians 12:9
[55] Articles of Faith 1:4
[56] D&C 3:20
[57] 1 John 3:20 – See 1 John 3:20
[58] Alma 5:7 – "Behold, he changed their hearts; yea, he awakened them out of a deep sleep, and they awoke unto God."
[59] See 2 Corinthians 5:17 – "Therefore if any man be in Christ, he is a new creature: old things are passed away; behold, all things are become new."– Greek word for Creature is ktisis: which is the act of creating, can also be rendered as creation.
[60] Lamentations 3:22,23
[61] John 20:29
[62] James 2:20

futile. Because faith's entire purpose is to produce action; action is the most important aspect of faith. All other measurements do not matter. Let your actions speak your convictions, for action is the conclusion of faith.

Though actions are the conclusion of faith, love is the beginning of faith. Love is the foundation of faith. Beliefs without love become begrudging and dissonant. Without love we stammer and stutter to trust. Without love one never reaches that totality of conviction which defiantly tosses aside respite, leaps into the dark mystery and fully 'commends itself unto God.'[63]

Concerning the interplay between love and faith Paul writes, "*faith worketh by love.*"[64] But how does faith work by love? The Greek word for *worketh* is *energeo*;[65] which means to work by, operate by, activate, energize, or make efficacious. Love is that initial "*desire to believe,*" that 'works in us, to prepare a place for a portion of God's words.'[66] Not only does love plant the seed of faith, love gives life to our faith. Love's activating energy nourishes faith so that it may "*get root, that it may grow up, and bring forth fruit.*"[67] The love of God is the persuasion. Love is what convinces us to believe. The Spirit of God brings to our remembrance the Holy Father's perfect love. Conviction does not come from a cognitive recollection of fantastic facts; rather faith is born from the spiritual nostalgia remaining from God's embrace.

Therefore, "*Believe in God; believe that he is, and that he created all things, both in heaven and in earth; believe that he has all wisdom, and all power, both in heaven and in earth; believe that man doth not comprehend all the things which the Lord can comprehend.*"[68] Have faith in God, your Eternal Father and His son Jesus Christ, "*whom having not seen, ye love; in whom, though now ye see him not, yet believing, ye rejoice with joy unspeakable and full of glory: Receiving the end of your faith, even the salvation of your souls.*"[69]

---

[63] Ether 6:4 – "and it came to pass that when they had done all these things they got aboard their vessels or barges, and set forth into the sea, commending themselves unto the Lord their God."
[64] Galatians: 5:6 – Built from the Greek words – Pistis (faith) energeo (worketh) and agape (love). Pistis – As mentioned earlier is a firm faith; it is conviction. Agape – Can be translated as charity and love and represents the highest form of love or Godly love.
[65] Greek Strong's Dictionary #1754 –(en-erg-eh'-o)– To be active, do or be effectual, fervent, mighty, work)
[66] Alma 32:27 – Brackets added – "…if ye can no more than desire to believe, let this desire work in you, even until ye believe in a manner that ye can give place for a portion of my words."
[67] Alma 32:37
[68] Mosiah 4:9
[69] 1 Peter 1:8,9

Courage

We have entered into an examination that is both specific and real. Concerning the reality and scope of this test, God has said, "*I will prove you in all things, whether you will abide in my covenant, even unto death, that you may be found worthy.*"[1] Life is a test – what a profound, yet terrifying truth. It is essential to settle our perspective that settings, circumstances, coincidence, and irony are all part of God's curriculum for soul shaping.

Life's various tones and atmospheres each have their purposeful place in your telestial tutelage. Whether life is monotonous or spectacular, up-tempo or dragging, painful or happy; everything you experience in life funnels through this precept. Understanding that life is a test is a teaching that imposes itself on every second of life. Have we taken the time to consider this curriculum that comprises our lives?

God has created a world that is not indifferent, therefore we are not able to truly be indifferent – though some may try. Mortal life is not a prolonged layover en route to Heaven. Agency is a brutal battlefield fought in the trenches of time. Within this warfare emotions, experiences, principles, theories and concepts explosively collide. In the "*wrestle ... against principalities, against powers, against, the rulers of the darkness of this world, against spiritual wickedness in high places,*"[2] one cannot hide underneath neutrality. It is impossible for man to live his life without forming an allegiance to one side or another. As beings endowed with a gift to 'to act and not merely be acted upon,'[3] we are forced to respond to our situations. We are constrained to make choices and generate responses. It is here in the arena of agency that the virtue of courage emerges.

God is intent on challenging every holy virtue to its threshold. Thus, every godly principle must meet and eventually triumph over adverse conditions. Resistance, both constant and terrible will be positioned against

---

[1] D&C 98:14
[2] Ephesians 6:12
[3] See 2 Nephi 2:26 – "… they have become free forever, knowing good from evil; to act for themselves and not be acted upon…"

our determination to do what is right. Life pits good against evil, and there is no protective cover beneath complacency; for apathy, pause, and indecision are inevitably decisions. Ideas swirl about us; they brush up against our consciousness and provoke reactions which surface moral agency. Because we exist in time, time demands us to choose a course. Therefore, ready yourself, for courage will be required on that day when Christ will call, *"Who is on the LORD's side? Let him come unto me!"*[4]

In the scriptures, the call to faith is often actually a call to courage. Courage is a companion to faith. Like faith, courage carries a connotation of decisiveness and action. Yet, for the sake of distinction, we may say that faith is decision against doubt, whereas courage is action against opposition, fear and dread. Laman and Lemuel had a knowledge beyond faith; yet they lacked the courage to 'carry the cross of Christ.'[5] It is possible for one to have a great understanding of truth, or even a burning belief in virtue, yet still fail to act because they fear the consequences of their conviction.

Courage is the inward causal force which conquers dread and anxiety. It is the moment of action. Courage is the power in faith that pushes against fears, pressures and risks. Because courage requires conflict, courage carries us into a territory of inconvenient Christianity. Sainthood isn't fashioned on pristine Celestial stages; it is sculpted on the frontlines of the telestial battlefield.

Boldness is not automatically bravery. Sometimes ignoring caution can be cowardly. Courage gives us decisiveness, surety, persistence, and unflinching faith. However, the way courage manifests is often counter intuitive. For example, history has proven chastity to be a greater challenge and of more merit than many military conquests, for *"He that is slow to anger is better than the mighty; and he that ruleth his spirit than he that taketh a city."*[6] Men wear weakness when they attempt to control and rule over others, *"but he that is greatest among you shall be your servant."*[7] Faithfulness is a more ferocious fight than football, service will strain us more severely than athletics, and there are times when kindness can be as risky as combat. Likewise, meekness requires more muscle than domineering and real heroism is often had in humility –true valor is in virtue.

Because courage can be used to accomplish good and evil, love needs to be at the core of our courage. The Apostle John has provided us

---

[4] Exodus 32:26
[5] See Matthew 10:38 – And he that taketh not his cross, and followeth after me, is not worthy of me."
[6] Proverbs 16:32
[7] Matthew 23:11

insight on the association between love and courage saying, *"there is no fear in love; but perfect love casteth out fear: because fear hath torment.*[8] *He that feareth is not made perfect in love."*[9] But why is there no fear in love? Will a person be immune to the feelings of fear because of love? Or is the lesson that love courageously counteracts the consequences of fear? If the latter is true, what are fear's detrimental consequences?

The Greek word for fear in the verse above is *phobos*,[10] a word that first meant *flight* but was later given to mean *the source which underlies flight and terror*. Retreat is the destructive result of fear. Fear is any idea, doubt, or resistance that makes one flee from faith. If the fatal effects of fear are unopposed by courage, fear can coerce us to leave virtue, avoid covenants and withdraw from discipleship.

But *"God hath not given us the spirit of fear; but of power, and of love, and of a sound mind."*[11] Love evokes a spirit of adventure in our souls and emboldens us in an epic way. No power on earth or heaven can overcome the courage created by compassion, charity and love. The courage in love is the required catalyst for transforming our character. Without this power no man would have the tenacity to change or the audacity to sacrifice. Courage is the backbone of our beliefs. It is only because of courage that men dare to take on the difficult duties of discipleship. Because of the courage in love, disciples of Christ *"Fear not to do good;"*[12] they accept the cost of their covenants and pay the price of their principles.

Our world continues to accept crude customs that are contrary to God's commandments. The tides of culture constrain us to shrink from or cast aside our covenants. But those who exercise the gallantry of godliness *"do good continually;"*[13] they *"suffer* [Christ's] *cross and bear the shame of the world."*[14] Valor for virtue has the nerve to *"deny* [itself] *of all ungodliness,"*[15] such is the heroics of heaven.

The courageous resist the societal pressures to renounce righteousness. They deny the crookedness of nations and confront the corruption in cultures. True, latter-day saints must be able to believe in the

---

[8] Greek Strong's Dictionary #2851: kolasis –(kol'-as-is)– kolasis means punishment.
[9] 1 John 4:18 – "There is no fear in love; but perfect love casteth out fear: because fear hath torment. He that feareth is not made perfect in love."
[10] Greek Strong's Dictionary #5401 – "phobos first had the meaning of flight, that which is caused by being scared; the, that which may cause flight, fear dread terror."
[11] 2 Timothy 1:7
[12] D&C 6:33 – "Fear not to do good, my sons, for whatsoever ye sow, that shall ye also reap; therefore, if ye sow good ye shall also reap good for your reward."
[13] Mosiah 5:2
[14] Jacob 1:8 – Brackets added – Originally: his
[15] Moroni 10:32 – Brackets added – Originally: yourselves

dark; yet there are also times when we must be able to believe against the clan. Choosing discipleship despite cultural pressures is not unique to our generation. In the days of Christ there were many "*among the chief rulers*" who "*believed on him; but because of the Pharisees they did not confess him, lest they should be put out of the synagogue: For they loved the praise of men more than the praise of God.*"[16] Followers of Christ must develop a courageous conviction that is willing to "[hazard their] *lives for the name of our Lord Jesus Christ.*"[17] This precept can apply to our physical wellbeing as well as the social seat in our comparative synagogues.

Are you capable of endangering your reputation for the sake of righteousness? Would you jeopardize power, prestige, or position to keep the principles of discipleship? Do your covenants take precedence over your standing and esteem with men? Know also that the tests of life do not always manifest as minorities holding their ground against immoral majorities. When God corrected the Prophet Joseph saying, "*you should not have feared man more than God,*"[18] He spoke in regards to an exchange only involving him and a friend, a friend who was even of the same faith. Not only should we fear God more than the expectations of our civilization, but our reverence toward God should exceed friends and friendships when necessary.

We who "*shine as lights in the world*"[19] will have to learn the craft of courageous conversation. As it pertains to sharing the gospel, people would gasp at the thought of de-emphasizing the role of being an example. Hiding a candle under a bushel is a serious crime in Zion; however, it has become completely acceptable to shove that same bushel in your mouth. 'Letting your light so shine before men'[20] has come to mean let your light so silently shine. So many members of Christ's ministry are content to be missionary mimes. They are a mute museum quietly containing the marvelous mysteries of Heaven. Yet, this tendency for doctrinal timidity is counted as an acceptable victory to the devil who despises the sound of voices speaking virtue.

In order to match the furious noises of wickedness blasting the earth, saints must acquire skills that surpass their current state of evangelical glowing. We must learn some of the offensive maneuvers of missionary

---

[16] John 12:42,43
[17] Acts 15:26 – "Men that have hazarded their lives for the name of our Lord Jesus Christ."
[18] D&C 3:7
[19] Philippians 2:15
[20] Matthew 5:16 – "Let your light so shine before men, that they may see your good works, and glorify your Father which is in heaven."

work. In contrast to the cultural cliché, as it pertains to missionary work, a thousand pictures cannot compare with the worth of our words. The current game of gospel charades is oft a weak display of courage and an embarrassment to our baptismal covenant to *"stand as* [a witness] *of God at all times and in all things, and in all places that ye may be in."*[21] There is a reason the word *"loud"* is used over and over again when God speaks of sharing the gospel. Our covenants contain a promise to be more than streetlight saints shedding occasional flashes of faith to a darkened world. God desires megaphones as much as he desires light bulbs. Being an example is an important part to missionary work, but that severely limits the amount of routes we can run if that is only play in our playbook.

God has issued the call, *"Who will rise up for me against the evildoers? Or who will stand up for me against the workers of iniquity?"*[22] How could we be content to merely sit in the stands and watch as 'the servants of the Lord labor with all diligence, even until the bad is cast away out of the Lord's vineyard.'[23] *"Therefore ... we should waste and wear out our lives in bringing to light all the hidden things of darkness, wherein we know them; and they are truly manifest from heaven – These should then be attended to with great earnestness."*[24] Disciples of Jesus Christ are not the idle audience of celestial events. They are the initiators, the activators; even the builders of the kingdom of God.

Traveling the higher road requires more than a casual commitment. In contrast, the ways of the natural man often requires minimal effort. He is slowly sinking down entropy's lazy slope. *"Woe unto them that are at ease in Zion."*[25] Too many travelers on the straight and narrow road are growing *"weary in well doing."*[26] They drift from the disciple's path seeking to cozy up in the camps of mediocrity. Followers of Christ's shouldn't settle for some perceived climax of spirituality. For when one thinks they have reached their personal summit, they all too often stop *"striving against sin."*[27]

Courage is oft a casualty to ease and complacency. It is a fickle, informal faith that expects to coast through Christian discipleship without getting any cuts or bruises. *"Lukewarm"*[28] members are bystanders not

---

[21] Mosiah 18:8 – Brackets added
[22] Psalms 96:16
[23] See Jacob 5:74 – "And thus they labored, with all diligence ... even until the bad had been cast away out of the vineyard."
[24] D&C 123:13,14
[25] Amos 6:1
[26] Galatians 6:9 – "And let us not be weary in well doing, for in due season we shall reap, if we faint not."
[27] See Hebrews 12:4 – "Ye have not yet resisted unto blood, striving against sin."
[28] Revelation 3:16 – "So then because thou art lukewarm, and neither cold not hot, I will spue thee out of my mouth."

servants; their synthetic show of discipleship is nothing more than an automated reaction. This sort of lukewarm, relaxed love results in commitments of convenience not consecration.

Courage is the attribute that fights against the entropic forces of the flesh. To truly be alive is to fight against these inherent impulses for idleness. An obscure translation in the book of Joshua poetically illustrates this principle. The verse states, *"And as soon as we heard these things, our hearts did melt, neither did there remain any more courage in any man."*[29] Here the Hebrew word used for courage is *ruwach*.[30] *Ruwach* means *spirit, wind* or *breath*. It is the symbolic representation of life as seen in the following verse from Genesis: *"And behold I even I do bring a flood of waters upon the earth, to destroy all flesh, in which is the* **breath of life** *from under heaven."*[31] Even though these scriptures indirectly connect the concepts of life and courage, there is great power and truth in the idea.

To have courage is to be alive. Comatose cowards who attempt to discard their power of autonomy are hardly better than decomposing carcasses. The daily fight of faith is the soul's breath of fresh air. It is a reminder that we are truly alive and possess free will. By activating your faith, you will see how your spirit, which directs your actions, originates from a grander world and a higher order. Therefore, it is imperative that we perform conscious actions every day; for these acts are the evidence of the existence of our individuality and soul.

Courage is more than a concept. As our understanding moves beyond academics, we discover the actual phenomenon of courage. Courage is a rousing elevation of affect. It is a flaring fortitude, a blaze of bold bravado. Courage is that burning in our hearts which incinerates apprehensions. It is the virtue that counters and conquers fear.

The word courage is only used once in the New Testament. The Greek word for courage is *tharsos*,[32] which is associated with the group of words *tharseo*[33] and *tharrheo*.[34] *Tharseo* means *confidence and courage*. It is the phrase *"good cheer"* spoken by Jesus when He said, *"In the world ye shall have tribulation: but be of* **good cheer***, I have overcome the world."*[35] *Tharrheo* gives us a

---

[29] Joshua 2:11
[30] Hebrew Strong's Dictionary # 7307 – "from 7306 wind, by resemblance breath…figuratively, life"
[31] Genesis 6:17 – Emphasis added
[32] Greek Strong's Dictionary #2294 –(Thar'-sos) akin (by transposition) to thrasos daring; boldness (subjectively): – courage.
[33] Greek Strong's Dictionary#2293 –(Thar-she'-o) to have courage: – be of good cheer.
[34] Greek Strong's Dictionary #2292 –(Thar-hreh'-0)
[35] See John 16:33

broader understanding of boldness, confidence and courage, as the root word of *tharrheo* means to be warm. Courage is the warmth of living. It is the heat of our spirits. With this virtue man sears the freedom freezing forces of apathy, entropy, and passivity; particularly the inactivity that arises from terror.

Life's intensity frequently fluctuates. Some days trickle down like autumn leaves, while other periods move so slow that time seems stuck. On these occasions it may feel as though the cogs of time are rusted over, and each individual tick of the clock is a tortuous battle. What do we make of these undulations in life? Is there reason for life's spontaneous shifts of momentum? Is there purpose in time's dramatic pauses?

When these uninvited changes in tempo slow life to a stop, we are compelled to ponder the purpose behind the pause. Settings themselves may be malignant or benign, therefore the situation alone cannot completely account for our spirit's swells of awareness. During periods of pause we sense some strange, ominous feeling; one that opens our soul to the hidden enormity of eternity.

God arranges our circumstances to form peaks – pivotal moments where everything in life converges on a single decision. This moment of decision is the moment of courage. It is a time where the flow of one's life will turn on a hinge. In the moment of courage all previous pledges you've made mean nothing. In fact, everything you have professed in the past will hang in the balance. The tremendous pressure produced by such heavy circumstances squeezes out our true character. Then, for better or worse our responses will dramatically determine the future course of our lives.

While we are caught between the conflicting pulls of contrasting ideals, we have the opportunity to become better acquainted with the light of Christ. In the moment of decision, standard logical thinking generally persuades us to retreat from righteousness simply on the premise that virtue is more difficult. Next the world and its extravagant culture chimes in only to add another voice against godliness. But something inside of us resists these pressures. If nothing were there, man would simply succumb. But before we would surrender to these vulgar gospels, another voice intervenes. What is this voice that speaks in these final seconds? And why … why must it make its presence known at the most inopportune moment? Not only this, it comes with no fanfare, no lavish logic, or statistical persuasiveness. Despite being the softest of whispers, it has the audacity to toss every instinctual craving to the wind?

How is it that so much weight is woven into a whisper? Though its sound is almost imperceptively soft, it speaks with a peculiar authority, one with a faint yet familiar undertone. Daring to oppose natural logic, this whispering conscience heralds a truth which eludes the wisdom of the world. All it takes is one moment, one flicker of light to turn our every natural impulse on its head. Baser reactions yield to the radiance of our divine nature. No justification can win an appeal against this subtle light. In this moment we can no longer play the fool, for our senses are illuminated to comprehend the right from the wrong. Against the backdrop of this "*light of Christ,*"[36] the rationales of the natural man are exposed as sycophantic deceptions. When these moments awaken our spirit, we must answer the call to courage and brave virtue against the conflicting tugs of convenience and culture.

Actions alone do not define courage. Instead the context in which actions are made largely determines whether or not they are truly courageous. The setting is as important as the act. Constructing the appropriate stage for courage has ever been the poet's art. Their stories carve courage from opposition. The hero's story tells of defiant bravery against impossible odds. We measure the hero's courage by the magnitude of counterforce set to impede his will. The hero must battle fierce winds working to blow him off course. When he looks to the skies to sustain him, the lights are clouded by fog and storm. As the hero nears the summit, he is deserted by all external supports. Then in the silence of his thoughts that abysmal Cerberus is summoned – doubt, regret and loneliness. The path stretches onward. Every step tempts him to turn back, to forsake his quest. Every painstaking breath begs him to abandon his mission.

Whatever fire once burned within the hero is squelched by the heinous darkness which swallows the horizon. His quest was pure; his calling divine. So how could he now be left weary, alone and at the brink of failure? Beneath a mask of stoicism, his heart has shattered and weeps within him saying, "*When I looked for good, then evil came unto me: and when I waited for light, there came darkness.*"[37]

The rational mind can no longer clasp naivety. Logic lets loose and fiendishly advertises the odds of success against the remaining flickers of faith. The terror of his situation entices him to retreat. It is here as he begins to fear that he sees and experiences the 'bitterness of hell.'[38] Such anguish is far too great for any words to convey. Stories never succeed to tell the tortures of time. Sentences are read in seconds; but pain, affliction,

---

[36] See Moroni 7:19 – "Wherefore, I beseech of you brethren, that ye should search diligently in the light of Christ that ye may know good from evil"
[37] Job 30:26
[38] See Moses 1:20 – "and as he began to fear, he saw the bitterness of hell."

horror and grief are not so fleeting. Hours, days, months, years – these are the most tormenting tools that will test the courage of our love.

Serious discipleship is demanding. Its dues were described by Jesus, *"And whoso is not willing to lay down his life for my sake is not my disciple."*[39] So long as God's 'work and glory is bringing to pass the immortality and eternal life of man,' our lives will not be bereft of drama. The sharpness of affliction's edge has a way of surfacing our spiritual senses. Suffering is not strictly a training program for divine attributes. In seasons of suffering there is no question as to whether or not life's test is real. Suffering lifts the veil. We touch the reality of the test, and by so doing, we sense the reality of our Tester.

The test of life is real. This is not an exam that we can breeze by with some last-minute cramming. It is not a one and done test, you will have to retain the lessons long after the final exams are finished. Your life is a test. Every second of every minute is under the radar. This is a far more serious issue than being included on Santa's naughty or nice list. Each mortal climax we encounter is weighing whether we have the courage to sacrifice. No one is exempt from the stretching that accompanies life's test. *"The Son of Man hath descended below them all. Art thou greater than he?"*[40]

The holiness of the Messiah did not shield Him from suffering. His purity compounded, not protected Him from pain and His innocence only made His agony more irkingly ironic. *"And lo, [He suffered] temptations, and pain of body, hunger, thirst, and fatigue, even more than man can suffer, except it be unto death; for behold, blood cometh from every pore, so great shall be his anguish for the wickedness and the abominations of his people."*[41] And *"they scourge him, and he suffereth it; and they smite him, and he suffereth it. Yea, they spit upon him, and he suffereth it."*[42] *"Which suffering caused [Christ], even God, the greatest of all, to tremble because of pain, and to bleed at every pore, and to suffer both body and spirit."*[43]

This was the Christ, the Savior of all mankind. Yet He *"was [polluted]*[44] *for our transgressions"* and *"was [crushed]*[45] *for our iniquities."*[46]

---

[39] D&C 103:28
[40] D&C 122:8
[41] Mosiah 3:7 – Brackets added originally: he shall suffer
[42] 1 Nephi 19:9
[43] D&C 19:18 – Brackets added originally: myself
[44] See Hebrew Strong's Dictionary # 2490 – Chalal –(khaw-lal'): most frequently this word means to pollute or defile. Chalal also means to profane and can be translated as dissolve, wound. The word may be have reference to a ritual of defilement, such as when one anciently would come into contact with a dead body.
[45] See Hebrew Strong's Dictionary # 1792 – Daka –(daw-kaw'): means to crumble, bruise literally or figuratively, daka means to break in to pieces. It is related to the word dakka #1793 which means to dash in into pieces or crush into powder.

During this inexplicable, soul scalding torture, what thoughts and feelings could possibly have run through Jesus's mind and heart? Reflecting on this most violently poignant period in all eternity, Christ said, *"and I would that I might not drink of the bitter cup, and shrink."*[47]

The fear of the bitter cup's fullness left Christ *"sore amazed,"*[48] and He *"began to be sorrowful and very heavy."*[49] In this revelation, Jesus divulges the concern of shrinking from the size of His mission. 'Encompassed'[50] by the pressure of billions and billions of souls depending on His sacrifice, we see a menacing fear arise to challenge Christ's capability to fulfill the full task He was sent to accomplish. No man can conceive the hostile terrors that tempted Jesus in those final hours leading to Gethsemane and Calvary. Some of this emotional turmoil is disclosed in Christ's statement, *"Now is my soul troubled; and what shall I say? Father, save me from this hour; but for this cause came I unto this hour."* [51] And when the time was finally come He *"being in an agony ... prayed more earnestly: and his sweat was as it were great drops of blood falling to the ground."*[52] Here Luke uses an unusual phrase. Instead of saying "He being in agony," the scripture says, "He being in **an** agony." Why the peculiar placement of the word *"an"*?

The Greek rendering of the word *agony* is *agonia*.[53] This word was a substitute for the Greek word *agon*, which had reference to a place of gathering or assembly. *Agon* alludes to the sporting competitions which occurred at these gathering places. *Agon* intentionally brings to one's mind the ancient Olympic and Pythian tournaments. During these contests men were stretched to their physical and physiological limits; their mental and emotional capabilities were pushed to the maximum.

Today we still relate to the intense sentiments of the Olympic Games. As it was in olden times, our current Olympics represent an exploration of human achievement. It is a spectacle where sport toys with the boundaries of human potential. This is *agonia*– the agony of extreme emotional and physical strain. It is the arena where a man's full potential is challenged. It is the stadium where men must face the peak of their

---

[46] Isaiah 53:5
[47] D&C 19:18
[48] Mark 14:33 – "And he taketh with him Peter and James and John, and began to be sore amazed, and to be very heavy"
[49] Matthew 26:27 – "And he took with him Peter ad the two sons of Zebedee, and began to be sorrowful and very heavy."
[50] See Psalms 118:11,12 – "The compassed me about; yea they compassed me about..."
[51] John 12:27 – "Now is my soul troubled; and what shall I say? Father, save me from this hour; but for this cause came I unto this hour."
[52] Luke 22:44
[53] Greek Strong's Dictionary # 74 –(ag-o-nee'-ah) #73 (ag-one')

capabilities. So when we read that Jesus was in *"an agony,"* we contemplate the cruel colosseum which Christ was placed in. Jesus was in *"an agony."* Before the assembly of eternity, Christ was strained to the threshold of His potential – *"how sore you know not, how exquisite you know not, yea, how hard to bear you know not."*[54]

Jesus was stressed to the emotional, physical, mental, and spiritual limits, *"which suffering caused myself, even God, the greatest of all, to tremble because of pain and to bleed at every pore, and to suffer both body and spirit."*[55] Nevertheless, despite the intimidating distress and anxiety accompanying this moment where infinity turned on a hinge, Christ faced the challenge and conquered it with courage. He didn't retreat! Though His soul was troubled, Jesus did not shrink! In the most pivotal point in all eternity He heroically stated, *"Father, if thou be willing, remove this cup from me: nevertheless not my will, but thine, be done."*[56] Jesus did not flee from His promise to redeem mankind, He did not retreat from His calling. He did not cower from keeping His covenants.

Though the awful dread of Hell *"encompassed [Him] about,"*[57] Het met it and courageously defeated it. Because Jesus was perfect in love, He did not fear or flee from the prospect of pain and failure. Our Lord Jesus felt the complete sharpness of the test of life and triumphed.

"Now thanks be unto God, which always causeth us to triumph in Christ, and maketh manifest the savour of his knowledge by us in every place."[58] And though, *"We are troubled on every side,"* we are not distressed; *"we are perplexed, but not in despair; Persecuted, but not forsaken; cast down, but not destroyed."*[59] Therefore, *"shall we not go on in so great a cause? Go forward and not backward. Courage, brethren; and on, onto the victory!"*[60]

Heavenly Father is a God of courage. We know this because His Holy Spirit has ever been the source of courage in our lives. His Spirit resonates an inspiration within each of us. His power has emboldened families, communities and nations. By this Spirit we are bolstered up to meet the daunting demands of discipleship. We know that God is courageous, for when we are near Him we feel brave.

---

[54] D&C 19:15
[55] D&C 19:18
[56] Luke 22:42
[57] See Psalms 118:10,11 – "All nations compassed me about…They compassed me about; yea they compassed me about: but in the name of the Lord I will destroy them."
[58] 2 Corinthians 2:14
[59] 2 Corinthians 4:8,9 – "We are troubled on ever side, yet not distressed; we are perplexed, but not in despair…"
[60] See D&C 128:22

Hope

What moves the man mauled by misery and loneliness? What unseen strength upholds his heavy heart and loaded legs? When sadness strikes the soul with unsympathetic resolve, how does the shattered man press onward? His mind dissociated, blasted beyond vaporous breath. Within his countenance is a concealed grimace and a silent groan. Behind his eyes is a despondent stare – a glazed gaze sunken by some invisible burden. Yet, the mangled man moves forward, taking one shuffled step after another. What convert conviction continues to carry this ruined traveler? Reason may have departed long ago, but not hope for it is far more resilient. And though unaware, the inanimate wayfarer walks toward an unknown world of wonder.

Hope is an essential part of your identity. Hope is an evidence that heaven has not wholly withdrawn itself from your spirit's memory. Your former life and *"the glory which you had with* [God] *before the world was"*[1] is irremovably implanted in your soul. It is from here hope resonates. When darkened by distresses or downtrodden with feelings of depression, we may quietly utter, 'I will not make mention of God, nor speak any more in God's name.' But hope has a ghastly resilience and haunts our hearts 'as a burning fire shut up in our bones.' At the peak of desperation, hope propels the stunned and exhausted soul.

Hope is not an accessory. It is part of your divine nature. Like your soul, hope is immortal for both have emerged from the Eternal. Such is why those who resist the pull of hope eventually confess as Jeremiah did, *"I was weary with forbearing, and I could not stay."*[2] Since hope is seeded in our divine disposition, it does not depart gently. Only a merciless ripping of repetitive recalcitrance can remove hope from the heart. These continual mutinies tortuously tear away hope from a spirit. At the end of this process

---

[1] John 17:5 – "O Father, glorify thou me with thine own self with the glory which I had with thee before the world was."
[2] Jeremiah 20:9 – "Then I said, I will not make mention of him, nor speak any more in his name. But his word was in mine heart as a burning fire shut up in my bones, and I was weary with forbearing, and I could not stay."

what is left is a disheveled corpse, something hardly recognizable as human; for it is only the devils who have fully forfeited hope. These wretched demons are not the image of a flaring hellish fury, which *"didst weaken the nations."*[3] Rather, these despicable, pathetic worms depict decrepitly cold, listless carcasses cast out from *"the heights of the clouds."*[4]

The devils, bereft of the gift of hope, have a deep void carved into their being. Inside this hole we discover the dark emptiness described in scriptures as *"the bitterness of hell."*[5] Hell is the opposite of hope. As a state of mind, hope is the conceptual antithesis to the state of mind we call hell. For in hell all dreams disappear, visions vanish and miracles are lost. In hell, the reality individuals chose not believe in becomes forever lost to them, and the reality they created through their choices becomes their everlasting habitation. Life perpetually presents a constant battle between hope and hell, and we will feel them frequently and ferociously tug on our thoughts and feelings. However, as long as we still draw breath, hope will not ever be wholly expelled, even if it only remains in particles.

Of all worldly sights, none awakens hope so significantly as children. Children are a nostalgic glance of the celestial realm. Their undefiled, radiant spirits have a way of transferring magical remembrances of Heaven. Being in their presence rouses slumbering sparkles of hope. In that instant our dreams are changed into something more, something so great we can hardly comprehend it. *"For since the beginning of the world men have not heard, nor perceived by the ear, neither hath the eye seen…what* [God] *prepared for him that waiteth for him."*[6] When caught in these moments, the potential 'prepared for them that wait upon the Lord' transforms fantasy into something tangible.

Hope shares a symbiotic interaction with all the godly principles. Hope's multiple meanings are due to a widespread intermingling with other virtues – which in turn dilutes its definition. For example, hope is used to express desire and therefore blends with the principle of love. Many hopes project desires into an unseen, uncertain, future scenario which inter-mixes hope with faith. An optimistic outlook is associated with hope connecting hope to happiness. The Hebrews understood how hope is largely

---

[3] Isaiah 14:12 – "How art thou fallen from heaven, O Lucifer, son of the morning! How art thou cut down to the ground, which didst weaken the nations!"
[4] Isaiah 14:14 -13) For thou (Lucifer) hast said in thine heart, I will ascend into heaven, I will exalt my throne above the starts…14) I will ascend above the heights of the clouds: I will be like the most High."
[5] Moses 1:20 – "Moses began to fear exceedingly; and **as he began to fear, he saw the bitterness of hell.**" (Emphasis added)
[6] See Isaiah 64:4 – Brackets added

responsible for patience, as exemplified in their word *yachal;* [7] a word meaning *waiting, patience and hope*. But hope does not only empower patience. Hope has a definite presence in all courage, love, justice and all other virtues.

Ironically contemporary connotations put a pessimistic spin on hope, denigrating it to display doubtful dreams and whimsical wishes. But hope is not purely imagination. Neither is it uncertainty. Hope should not be confused with guesswork or gullibility. Hope is both observable and substantive, for it is the force of our faith and a provoking drive behind all virtues. Still, critics will continue to be absolutely puzzled by people with genuine hope. They have no way of explaining hope, so they contrive a label and call the hopeful naïve. It was a terrible day when optimists became heretics and idealists were considered neurotic.[8] But without dreams or visions, existence is not just trite – it is utterly empty.

We may experience failure after failure after failure; but as long as we retain hope, we will never forfeit our path. Nor do we surrender enthusiasm. When hope is present, mistakes will not smother our excitement, nor will disappointments stay our productivity. Such is why we rightfully associate hope with an optimistic attitude. However, the hopeful would more appropriately be labeled realists, since none are as centered in reality as the hopeful. Someday the righteous of the world may rescue the term 'realist' from the cynics, for the day shall come when those who have mocked Christ will confess the reality of Christian hope.

The *"hope of the gospel"*[9] is as real as it gets; because it is a perspective established by *"things as they are, and as they were, and as they are to come."*[10] Even so, we should not confuse this realism with the common use of the term realism, a term which has become salted with pessimism. Hope stands opposite to the ideals, motivations and actions of the pessimist. Not only do pessimists fixate on the negative, it is as if they want things to be as bad as they think they are. In some cases, pessimism is used as a planned approach to justify bad behaviors. Their cunning plot imagines that if life is as bad as they think it is, their poor choices are excused.

Just as hope carries multiple semantics in the English language, hope has had a broad variety of meanings in the past. In the scriptures over

---

[7] Hebrew Strong's Dictionary #3176 –(yaw-chal')
[8] Sigmund Freud. *The future of an illusion*. New York: W.W. Norton and Company. 1961 "Religion would thus be the universal obsessional neurosis of humanity"
[9] Colossians 1:23 – "If ye continue in the faith grounded and settled, and be not moved away from the hope of the gospel."
[10] D&C 93:24

ten different words are translated as hope. Standing out from those various definitions is the Greek word *elpis*,[11] a word meaning *confident anticipation or expectation*. *Elpis* is to look forward with certainty. To use the words of Paul the Apostle, hope or *elpis* is *"earnest expectation … my hope, that in nothing I shall be ashamed, but that with all boldness."*[12] If hope is an excited anticipation, what exactly are we expecting? What is in hope that causes people to look forward with unashamed, bold confidence?

Perhaps the best way to cognitively grip the concept of hope is to assign it the meaning of motivation. Seeing hope as a motivation helps us see how it correlates with faith, desire and love. Love is the purpose, but hope is its spirit. Faith is the belief, but hope is the pep. Desire is the emotion, whereas hope is the energy. Here the old adage – "a picture is worth a thousand words" is especially pertinent. The visual symbols associated with hope are worth as much as any articulate description we can concoct. Attaching our understanding of hope to images of light, fire, flame and sparks is useful. Doing so allows us to sufficiently visualize hope as the burning motivation that emits energy and life into our ethics. Keeping this picture in mind, we can picture those 'people which sit in darkness' finding the great light of hope. We see hope cause 'those in the shadow of death,' to have 'light to spring up.'[13]

Hope does not only reside at the heart of Christian virtues; it is the heart of Christian virtues. Hope is the flame of faith and the light of love. Hope kindles courage and sparks our spirits to service. By hope we ignite humility and keep our convictions constant. Hope is the very vigor of virtue. It is responsible for the burning of belief and the stamina of patience. Just as electricity gives power to a light bulb, hope charges our charity. It has been said that *"faith without works is dead,"*[14] but faith without hope is empty; righteous fervor becomes vacant.

Without hope love is limp and lifeless. If hope fades, sympathy and compassion become stale. Can courage be sustainable without hope? Can one maintain zest or zeal if hope perishes? When hope fails all the other virtues become vacant. As it is written, *"Where there is no vision, the people perish."*[15] Yet, similarly when there is no hope, civilizations stagnate and all progression pauses. Thus we see that hope is the great bridge

---

[11] Greek Strong's Dictionary #1680 – (el-pece')
[12] Philippians 1:20
[13] See Matthew 4:6 – "The people which sat in darkness saw great light; and to them which sat in the…shadow of death light is sprung up."
[14] James 2:20
[15] Proverbs 29:18

between the present and the future. If we demolish this bridge, we lose that essential connection we must maintain with the future.

Without hope a person is dead while they are yet alive. As the proverb says, *"A merry heart doeth good like a medicine: but a broken spirit drieth the bones."*[16] Hope pumps life giving blood of love into every attribute; making hope the pulse of piety. God is the source of hope. Spiritual invigoration comes to man through the medium of the Holy Spirit. It is written, *"Now the God of hope fill you with all joy and peace in believing, that ye abound in hope, through the power of the Holy Ghost."*[17] Truly, we abound in hope through the Holy Ghost, *"the record of heaven; the Comforter"* that which **"*maketh alive all things.*"**[18]

Therefore, watch the frequency wherewith God magnifies your motivation and stimulates your desires. By doing so you will greater realize the extent Heavenly Father participates in your life. Available amongst God's magnificent spiritual gifts, He may bless us with the gift of hope; a gift which enlivens action and arouses righteousness. Within the power of this gift, even beaten, battered and broken spirits can be 'made alive' again.

But what is the substance of our hope? What does the hope in Christ entail? The Prophet Mormon responds, *"And what is it that ye shall hope for? Behold I say unto you that ye shall have hope through the atonement of Christ and the power of his resurrection, to be raised unto life eternal, and this because of your faith in him according to the promise."*[19] First and foremost we have hope in Christ and the power of His resurrection.

Without the resurrection, life is merely a prolonged embalming and our planet a tomb. It is not possible to appreciate how essential and effectual this hope is until one has experienced the loss of a loved one. When long-time friends and family pass, it does not simply sting; it crushes. It sucks the spirit dry and surfaces that hideous hopelessness of hell. Yet, death need not drown hope. Instead, these periods should make us ponder; for God will use suffering to cause remembrances of eternity to emerge. Amidst solitude's silence, the Spirit will stand near to us with whispers of loving consolation. Then by the power of the Holy Ghost, the Eternal Father will come to you speaking His *"pleasing word ... yea, the word which healeth the wounded soul."*[20]

---

[16] Proverbs 17:22
[17] Romans 15:13
[18] Moses 6:61 – Emphasis added
[19] Moroni 7:41
[20] Jacob 2:8 – see Jacob 3:2 – "O all ye that are pure in heart, lift up your heads an receive the pleasing word of God, and feast upon his love; for ye may, if your minds are firm, forever."

Know that the healing therapy of God's word can be administered in ways other than thoughts. The Spirit submerges souls in soft serenity; it circulates inside us as a soothing ointment. Father's sacred words are given to us not solely by sight or cerebral understanding, they are given through your soul's special facility to sense the sublime. The transcendent power of the Holy Spirit penetrates the despairs of hell and plant these words in our heart – "[Christ] *breaketh the bands of death, that the grave shall have no victory, and that the sting of death should be swallowed up in the* **hopes of glory**."[21]

When discussing hope, we must avoid the pitfall of projecting hope solely in unreachable futures so that it becomes the stuff of fantasy. Some unwittingly banish hope's relevance to a vague whimsical paradise prepared only for celestial populations. For example: we hope to return to the presence of God, we hope to overcome our sins, we hope to see the faces of loved ones who have departed this life. We hope for the day when joy will not be fleeting; that day when all sorrows will end, we hope for the day when 'swords will be beaten into plowshares and spears into pruning hooks;'[22] the time when war will be no more. As we reach the conclusion of this list, we are left to confront the question of – when? When will 'the year of the redeemed come?'[23] When will these things be possible?

Please understand that hope is not death. It is not a gift from the grave. It is disturbing to see people direct all their hopes to that undefinable date of their demise. Hope is not only to be enjoyed as a distant guiding star; it is also an adjoining fiery flame. When hope is pushed too far into foreign futures one cannot enjoy the heat emanating from hope's immediate presence. Resigning hope to dreams of untouchable destinies, ones only obtainable in death is as nourishing as an incandescent light. If we do this we may partake of the brightness of hope, but not its warmth. Therefore, it is crucial for us to find uses for hope that are valid and applicable in our present circumstances.

A particularly pertinent part of the "*hope of glory*"[24] is "*the glory of Zion*;"[25] a grandeur which can be gained despite the weaknesses of the flesh.

---

[21] Alma 22:14 – Brackets and emphasis added
[22] Isaiah 2:4 – "they shall beat their swords into plowshares, and their spears into pruning hooks: nation shall not lift up sword against nation, neither shall they learn war anymore."
[23] See Isaiah 63:4
[24] Colossians 1:27 – "To whom God would make known what is the riches of the glory of this mystery among the Gentiles which is Christ in you, the hope of glory:"
[25] D&C 136:31 – My people must be tried in all things, that they may be prepared to receive the glory that I have for them, even the glory of Zion; and he that will not bear chastisement is not worthy of my kingdom."

Not only do we have hope for *"a better world,"* [26] we can have hope in a better tomorrow and a better today. Hope is relevant in the now! With the power of hope, we can discover and create innovative ways to improve and beautify our world, our self and our conditions.

With Zion in our sights, we become *"sure and steadfast, always abounding in good works, being led to glorify God."*[27] Enjoyments and noteworthy accomplishments are available to us every day. When we understand the reality and pertinence of daily hope, we will see how hope truly is the *"anchor of the soul."*[28] Hope is applicable in every situation and struggle. It is by hope that we are kept *"grounded and settled"*[29] so that no form of tribulation will remove us from our righteous aspirations.

How does hope specifically accomplish the role of securing our convictions? Illustrating how hope is capable of fastening our faith, we read of a people who **"never did look upon death with any degree of terror**, *for their hope and views of Christ and the resurrection; therefore, death was swallowed up to them by the victory of Christ over it."*[30] At its peak, hope sweeps away both the pain and fear of death. However, hope is not limited to taking away the terror of the tomb. It soothes the suffering of seeing loved ones pass on. It is capable of soaking up distress and every shade of sadness.

Hope can be derived from our motivations. Our motivations are the outward manifestation of an inward hope. This being true, we see what prompted Paul's statement, *"be ready always to give an answer to every man that asketh you a reason of the hope that is in you."*[31] What is the reason behind your hopes? Why do you have hope and where did it come from? What is the underlying cause responsible for your motivation? Can you explain the ideas and feelings which propel you along the path of life? Do you know why you get up in the mornings or do your daily work. Is there an internal reason you act out the choice to continue to fight for survival, justice or life itself?

Hope is born as the soul resurfaces remembrances of familiar feelings we had of living in God's presence. Just as our mortal memories

---

[26] Ether 12:4 – "Wherefore, whoso believeth in God might with surety hope for a better world, yea, even a place at the right hand of God"
[27] Ether 12:4 – "which hope cometh of faith, maketh an anchor to the souls of men, which would make them sure and steadfast, always abounding in good works, being led to glorify God."
[28] Hebrews 6:19 – "Which hope we have as an anchor to the soul, both sure and stedfast"
[29] See Colossians: 1:23 – "If ye continue in the faith grounded and settled, and be not moved away from the hope of the gospel.
[30] Alma 27:28 – Emphasis added
[31] 1 Peter 3:5

are a part of us, this spiritual sub-consciousness cannot be separated from us. With whispering brushes of influence, the Comforter which *"shall ... bring all things to your remembrance,"*[32] works tirelessly on our souls to uncover those memories of a former affection we felt from and towards the Father.

The dimmed memory of our former feelings toward the Father are not the primarily factor for the 'hope that is in us.' Hope emerges from resurging remembrance of God's love for us. Hope is that first faint, but refreshing recollection of the Father's love for your soul. It is this love which ignites the fire of hope in our hearts. The love of the Holy Father awakens the sleeping wish of our soul to be wrapped once more *"in the arms of* [His] *love."*[33] As love is the central source of hope, we must strive to *"come to* [this] *knowledge of the glory of God,"* and strive until we have *"known of his goodness and tasted of his love."*[34]

Truly, hope is born of love. We hope to remember Father again. We hope to recall the features of His face. We hope to feel the power and warmth of His hands once more. Yet, these faded photographs, blurred by the veil are only a prelude to the *"perfect brightness of hope."*[35] Even the slightest taste of God's love ignites a burning flame that fights to regain the fullness of the Father's affections. When the seed of hope is sewn it is permanently planted in our spirits. Even so, these stirrings are only a sample of sublime love.

Just as forgiveness acts as the arm of mercy, prayers are the hands of hope. Each plea that leaves our lips is an emblem of our hope. No other practice or rite reveals one's hopes so purely as prayer. Hope spills out of each petition as we 'pour out our soul to God.'[36] Hope's relationship to prayer manifests in an important way through the companion concepts of motivation and expectation. When we pray, we should routinely consider what we are specifically anticipating from a prayer. Once your 'amen' has been said, you get off the floor, open your eyes and ... now what? What are you hoping to happen? What do you expect for a prayer, specifically and in general? When you are down on your knees, what are

---

[32] John 14:26 – "But the Comforter ... he shall teach you all things, and bring all things to your remembrance"
[33] D&C 6:20 – "Be faithful ... in keeping the commandments of God, and I will encircle thee in the arms of my love."
[34] Mosiah 4:11 – "as ye have come to the knowledge of the glory of God, or if ye have known of his goodness and have tasted of his love...even so I would that ye should...always retain in remembrance, the greatness of God."
[35] 2 Nephi 31:20 – "ye must press forward with a steadfastness in Christ, having a perfect brightness of hope"
[36] Alma 58:10 – "Therefore we did pour out our souls in prayer to God, that he would strengthen us and deliver us"

you trying to accomplish? Similarly, we wonder – what it is we anticipate God that is going to accomplish from our prayers? If all that you expect is that you can finally put your head down and sleep, there may be significant improvements left to be made. Do the words 'amen' complete a prayer or are additional step left undone?

Too often prayers are offered with the same far-flung outlook of burying a time capsule. Some plant their petitions deep in the earth with a haphazard hope of God ever discovering them or responding to them. It isn't until our prayers cease to be drifting messages in a bottle, bobbling about in backwater whims, that will we be able to awaken God's wonders.

When was the last time you entered a prayer with "*full confidence in obtaining a divine manifestation?*"[37] "*If any of you lack wisdom, let him ask of God … But let him ask in faith, nothing wavering. For he that wavereth is like a wave of the sea driven with the wind and tossed.*"[38] Never waver in faith or diligence, for Heavenly Father who 'upbraideth not' rewards the resilient! Know that it is most often our own doubts which sets limit on the Lord. We are oft like them of old who "*… turned back and tempted God, and limited the Holy One of Israel.*"[39] Ultimately, we are the ones primarily responsible for apprehending our possibilities. It is our doubt that diminishes God's omnipotent power. The Father does not withhold His hands to bless; rather, we are the ones holding back His hands by our lack of trust, hope, confidence and courage.

Though all of this may seem boorishly basic. It is astounding to see how frequent the fundamental aspects of prayer are forgotten. Sadly, intent is among the commonly omitted components of prayer. In prayer, you need to always speak to God as if He were really before you! Mindless monologues and hustled, chattered chants do us little good.

Remember that 'God's eyes are upon **you**. He is in **your** midst though ye cannot see Him.'[40] Never rush a personal prayer! Do not allow your words to speak faster than your feelings. So often people sprint through prayers; but speedy prayers tend to be spoken without plan or purpose. Before entering the heavenly realm to entreat God, consider the reason you are approaching Him. Recall the word which says, "*When ye come to appear before me, who hath required this at your hand, to tread my courts?*"[41] As this verse suggests, make and take the time to consider what brought you to

---

[37] Joseph Smith History 1:29
[38] James 1:5,6
[39] Psalms 78:41
[40] See D&C 38:7 – "I say unto you that mine eyes are upon you. I am in your midst and ye cannot see me;"
[41] Isaiah 1:18

pray to God in the first place. Center yourself in your intention. Ask yourself, 'why am I praying and what is my purpose?'

Is there a reason you have come before the Lord, or have you arrived at the heavenly halls by shear happenstance? Sometimes we enter our prayers with as much regard of an idling loaf, we mindlessly dawdle our way to the throne of God, having no design or intent. The scriptures record such a prayer made by Oliver Cowdery. However, Oliver was neither the first or last person to offer an aimless prayer. The chiding remarks given to him continue to serve as rebuke to countless others who lazily implore the Lord. And God said, *"Behold, you have not understood; you have supposed that I would give it unto you, when you took no thought save it was to ask me. But, behold, I say unto you, that you must study it out in your mind; then you must ask me."*[42]

Before one embarks on a journey, they first need a plan and an objective to direct their actions. Our individual journeys require a guiding reason, lest we encounter the wonderland dilemma of trying to decide which road to take without having a destination in mind. Before we even open our mouth to address our Father in Heaven, it would be best to have premeditated about "which way [we] ought to go from here."[43] The moment we are unable to adequately respond to the question – 'why am I praying,' the prayer we are offering becomes vain.

Jesus warned, *"But when ye pray, use not vain repetitions, as the heathen do; for they think that they shall be heard for their much speaking."*[44] For some reason most people get hung up over the word repetition in this admonition. They would grab their pitchforks and run repetitions straight out of their prayers. But are the repetitions the particular problem we are being warned about? The truth is, repetition should not disturb us as much as vanity.

It is vanity which regularly corrupts our prayers. Yet this vanity speaks not only to the self-aggrandizing shows of spirituality or facades of faith. Facades of faith have many other faces. The real core of vanity is emptiness.[45] The emptiness of vanity is shown in hollow oaths, shallow statements and meaningless multiplying of words. Empty devotion occurs when there is disconnect and dissonance from our purpose and our

---

[42] D&C 9:7,8

[43] See Lewis Caroll. Alice's Adventures in Wonderland. "Would you tell me, please, which way I ought to go from here? That depends a good deal on where you want to get to, said the Cat, I don't much care where – Said Alice. Then it doesn't matter which way you go, said the Cat. – so long as I get SOMEWHERE, Alice added as an explanation. Oh, you're sure to do that, said the Cat, if you only walk long enough."

[44] Matthew 6:7

[45] The word 'vain' used in the phrase 'vain repetitions' is Kenos. See Greek Strong's Dictionary #2756 – Kenos: means empty, either literally or figuratively.

presentation. Vanity is a deception; it is a synthetic show of saintliness. Vanity is demonstrated in pageantry patience, exhibition humility, policed piety and table mannered meekness. Vanity makes mercy subterfuge, courage counterfeit, and faith fraud. Vanity is at its essence the progenitor of inauthenticity. Vanity produces pulseless prayers. Why do some coat their prayers with fake or fancy phrases? God does not need our supplications to be coated with fancy sayings in order to swallow the whole truth. Ironically, these occasions commonly reflect an inward desire to sweeten our shame so that it can be swallowed easier.

Jesus' rebuke was not targeting repetition so much as it was villainizing insincerity. It is entirely possible for a person to recite the same words over and over again without compromising their intent. Doubt should not be denoted from repetition, since repetition may just as easily an represent a real resilience and determination. Such was the case in the parable of the unjust judge. Here even a crooked arbiter rewards a widow's persistence saying, *"Thou I fear not God, nor regard man; Yet because this widow troubleth me, I will avenge her, lest by her continual coming she weary me."*[46] Shall not God then *"avenge his own elect, which cry day and night unto him, though he bear long with them?"*[47]

Prefacing the story of the widow and the unjust judge are the words, *"And* [Jesus] *spake a parable unto them to this end, that men ought always to pray, and not to faint."*[48] As it pertains to fainting, the warning is not directed against episodes of syncope causing one to fall unconscious to the floor. (Though sadly, this could describe some our attitudes toward worship.) In this verse the Greek word for faint is *ekkakeo*,[49] which means *to lose courage or fail in heart*. With this in mind, can you hear the Savior's encouraging call to pray always and don't lose heart? *"And let us not be not weary in well doing: for in due season we shall reap, if we faint not."*[50] Never lose your hope, never stop praying for that which is right – take strength in the call of the Holy Spirit that urges you to never give up!

Strive to allow hope to change your prayers. Before appealing to God, ponder the purpose of your prayer. Be decisive about what you want to accomplish and do not wander or drift into empty petitions. When it is difficult or painful to hold on to hope, and you are tempted to let go, hold

---

[46] Luke 18:4,5
[47] Luke 18:7 – "And shall not God avenge his own elect, which cry day and night unto him"
[48] Luke 18:1
[49] Greek Strong's Dictionary #1573 –(ek-kak-eh'-o)– "to be weak, by implication to fail in heart, faint or be weary."
[50] Galatians 6:9 (The Greek word translated as faint in this verse is also ekkakeo)

fast to your convictions, hold fast to the hope that is in you. Refuse to bury your dreams and temper your ambitions. When you must *"against hope* [believe] *in hope,"* [51] recall the qualities of the Being you are worshiping and entreating. Remember that God's nature and love is the very source of your hope. When you bow to God, you do not worship a being that looks at you as a puppet or a pet. He sees you as a person. He looks upon you as His precious child.

What do you anticipate when you pray? *"If any of you lack wisdom, let him ask of God, that giveth to all men liberally, and upbraideth not; and it shall be given him."*[52] When James penned these words, his intention was not to inform us about a celestial liquidation of wisdom. Instead, James is trying to teach us about lack and God's liberality. Could we not also say, if any of you lack courage, let him ask of God? If any of you lack patience, let him ask of God. If any of you lack hope, charity, strength or anything virtuous – let him ask of God! Whatever the lack may be, the advice is the same – ask God. God truly gives liberally! He wants to bless you, He *"delight*[s] *to bless with the greatest of all blessings."*[53]

Heavenly Father has so many incredible gifts awaiting us, but they are "conditional on our asking for them"[54] – So ask! *"Why art thou cast down, O my soul? and why art thou disquieted in me? hope thou in God."*[55] For God *"spared not his own Son, but delivered him up for us all,* **how shall he not with him also freely give us all things?** *"*[56] The Father offered up His only begotten Son as an Eternal emblem of His love and liberality. Oh then, He who spared not His own Son shall truly give you all things freely. Therefore, *"gird up the loins of your mind, be sober, and* **hope to the end** *for the grace that is to be brought unto you at the revelation of Jesus Christ."*[57]

---

[51] Romans 4:18 – Brackets added
[52] James 1:5
[53] D&C 41:1 – Emphasis and brackets added
[54] Bible Dictionary 'Prayer'
[55] Psalms 42:5
[56] Romans 8:32
[57] 1 Peter 1: 13 – Emphasis added

Joy

All the wandering hordes of humanity seem connected by a shared quest. This universal motivation has no respect to age, culture, gender or personality. From the moment moral consciousness awakens, so too does that everlasting pursuit for a sustainable, satiating source of joy. This piercing longing to obtain lasting happiness significantly shapes all human behaviors.

Happiness has ever acted as a ridiculing carrot, hung at the end of a long stick taunting man's fantasy. Secretly stored in the soul's inmost core is a coercing craving to return to the supernal bliss we once shared with God. Thus, it is more than the idea of *"a state of never-ending happiness,"*[1] that compels us. It is the remembrance of the former exultation we knew with Heavenly Father which urges us forward on *"the way of holiness."*[2]

Fleeting joy is spiritually insufficient. True happiness is not some short acting, evaporating chemical. Nor is it some hormonal induced euphoria. The immortal soul seeks for a joy that is greater than brief elations of pleasure. Sustainable satisfaction for the soul will not come from any earthly treasure; only the *"treasures in heaven"* [3] have the longevity to create complete contentment. Ultimately, love is the treasure of heaven that stills the starving spirit. Love is both the key and conclusion to God's *"great plan of happiness."*[4] Love is not transient. Neither is love enduring; it is eternal. When love is in full bloom it produces fruit which is 'most sweet, above all that has ever been tasted before.'[5] Joy is the taste of the fruit of love, and since joy stems from the *"love of God, which sheddeth itself abroad in the hearts of the children of men … it is the most desirable above all things."*[6]

Who on earth holds the mysteries of heaven? Do you search for them in widely appraised psychologists? Are they the secrets know to powerful politicians or accomplished athletes? Is it possible they could be

---

[1] Alma 28:12
[2] Isaiah 35:8
[3] See Matt 6:20 – "But lay up for yourselves treasures in heaven, where neither moth nor rust doth corrupt, and where thieves do not break through nor steal:"
[4] Alma 42:8
[5] 1 Nephi 8:11
[6] 1 Nephi 11:22

found from men lacking prestigious accolades? Maybe the riddle can be solved by the academically decorated surgeon. Or perhaps some special wisdom can be learned from the simpletons who live what some would call uneventful lives, yet do so with a smile and with the praise and adoration of their family. Where is wisdom? Where is Heaven? Where is joy?

Have you been looking for happiness in a mystical, magical idea? Do you suppose that the mighty change of change of heart comes from the charm of an enchanting teaching? Are Heaven's mysteries contained in metaphysics and deep doctrines? Were you able to recreate the origins of the universe – including the formation of galaxies, planets and people; would you have any advantage in re-creating your conduct? Can stockpiles of facts improve your character or give you the greater love which leads to greater happiness?

Love is the mystery of heaven. This revelation comes not in words, but in selflessness and service. The revelation of love arises from the bonds we make in human relationships. With love we unveil Eternity's most sacred secrets; not of the mind or heart, but of the spirit. The revelation of love is not desirable because it uncovers new knowledge, rather because it results in a newness of one's nature.

Happiness isn't simply something we search for; it is something we create. *"All the days of the afflicted are evil: but he that is of a merry heart hath a continual feast."*[7] Joy and Heaven are better understood as a personality than as a possession or place. Happiness is not a foreign, far away possession that heckles us with its absence. True happiness is an inward ability, and a necessary part of our divine nature. The components for generating joy are already part of you; they are there now, waiting to be accessed. An ability to be happy is a gift from God. It is something that is sculpted into our immortal constitutions. Since happiness is a part of your soul, *"then may God grant unto you that your burdens may be light, through the joy of his Son. And even* **all this can ye do if ye will**.*"*[8]

Creating happiness is not a unique topic. There are countless recipes from prominent people claiming some mastery of this process. We are surrounded by seas of philosophical, self-help hypotheses. Maybe somewhere in these vast pools of principles is a fully perfected blueprint mapping the necessary steps to produce happiness; if so, I would be as eager to get ahold of these instructions as anyone else. I openly confess that there are gaps in my own understanding of how to maximize our joy in

---

[7] Proverbs 15:15
[8] Alma 33:23 – Emphasis added

this fallen world. My soul has not yet reached the celestial shores where I can endlessly splurge on succulent, savory smoothies. With the rest of you I am working on solving this puzzle hoping that someday the wise of the world will unravel this enigma. Nonetheless, whatever small portion which I have discovered I will share. If anything, so that we can compare notes.

A most vital truth tied to our measure of happiness is summed up in the scriptural statement, *"ye are in the hands of God."*[9] Prophets, preachers and speakers of all varieties have dabbled with this idea, but only when we embrace the full implication of this truth can we grasp happiness with a firm grip.

When I was a child there was a memorable analogy that illustrated what it means to be 'in the hands of God.' The lesson began with a mysterious bag sitting on a table in the front of the classroom. The teacher says she has a test for us as she carefully pulls a water bottle and a clear cup out of the bag. She fills the cup with water up to a line drawn about midway on the cup. Once the water reaches the mid line the teacher stops pouring and displays the final product for everyone in the class to see. With curious eyes watching her, she asks her students, "How full is the cup?"

One by one, the teacher asks the students to state how much is in the cup. Some newcomers to the lesson fell prey to the trap and responded, "It's about half empty." Then there were those who had this lesson in the past, who either quickly stated that it was half full, or decided to raise a sarcastic voice and join the half-emptiers. At the conclusion of this lesson, we are taught the following moral – the cup and its contents can be described in two ways: we can say that it is half empty or half full.

If we focus on what we don't have or what we are missing, we see life like a cup that appears half empty. However, if we pay attention to what we do have, and acknowledge what has been given to us, life and the cup are seen as half full. It is the same cup, sow how you describe the experience is ultimately your choice.

Being older and much more sarcastically clever, I have decided to tweak this object lesson to make an additional point. Among the principles taught in Chemistry is the composition of non-living materials – such as water and air. In Chemistry we learn about atoms, elements and molecules which are some of the tiniest, most basic forms of matter. Even the air we breathe, though imperceptible is composed of matter – we are ever immersed in an invisible ocean of Oxygen, Hydrogen, Nitrogen and Carbon

---

[9] Mormon 5:23

atoms and molecules. Thus, the scientist looks at the glass and says it is not half empty or half full, it is completely full. It is half full of water and half full of air.

Here is true optimism – the cup that is your life is not half empty, neither is it half full. Your life is always completely full! Life is full of significant experiences, every moment of it. Your life is filled with constant meaning. Because your entire life is in 'God's hands,' then it is as the scriptures say, "***in everything ye are enriched by him***."[10] Every experience in life has a potential to enrich us. God and His works manifest even in life's smallest particles. So whether 'the Lord gives or takes away' we can declare "*blessed be the name of the LORD.*"[11]

Now some periods of life will be richer, just as the water is denser than the air. When you are metaphorically immersed in water you feel every moment massaging your senses. During these times, truth, love and happiness are easily recognizable. For this reason, our discussion won't be focused on how to find happiness when the sun is out. The higher goal will be to learn how to access joy on rainy days.

We will encounter times where life feels like air. On these days it may take a forced effort to realize that there is something around us. Though it is difficult to perceive, we are still surrounded by matter during these phases. Even then, spiritual substance is all around us capable of bringing us joy. Because life has periods of humdrum, boredom and monotony, finding substance in periods of what appears as seemingly nothingness is an unavoidable part to being joyful.

Continuing with the chemistry object lesson, when we look closer at the composition of both water and air, it is remarkable how much empty space exists between individual particles. For all the tangible reality we visibly perceive, there is an enormous amount of empty space in between the actual material substance. Likewise, there are proverbial particles of matter in every period of life. This substance is what gives meaning to each moment. Everything that seems like empty space is still part of the structure of your life's purpose. When our perceptions are properly oriented by God's plan the matter or things that matter is ever before us. Seeing the substance behind our circumstances allows us to respond to situations with freedom, optimism, hope and joy.

The book of Genesis contains a scriptural parallel to this point. Summarizing the difficult events in his life, Joseph, son of Israel says, "*But

---

[10] 1 Corinthians 1:5 – Emphasis added
[11] Job 1:21 – "Naked came I out of my mother's womb, and naked shall I return thither: the LORD gave, and the LORD hath taken away; blessed be the name of the LORD."

as for you, ye though evil against me; but God meant it unto good."[12] Joseph was cast into a pit, sold into slavery and separated from the people he loved, and not just for days but for years and years.

Joseph's entire world was destroyed multiple times. He was surrounded with uncertainty, sadness, and loneliness. There was great evil wrought upon Joseph. And maybe the whole time Joseph wasn't out playing hopscotch, doing summer saults and sipping lemonade. He may have shed a tear or two. But, amidst all his suffering, Joseph retained a meaningful measure of joy because he understood there was purpose in his pain. Because Joseph believed that there was a plan behind his particular experiences, he moved forward with hope and happiness.

"What? shall we receive good at the hand of God, and shall we not receive evil?"[13] We will all assuredly experience tribulation, heartbreak and tragedy; but all things are for our sakes and God has designed *"that all things work together for good to them that love God."*[14] It is necessary for us to *"taste the bitter, that [we] may know to prize the good."*[15] *"Men are, that they might joy,"*[16] and "the cavity which suffering carves into our souls will one day also be the receptacle of joy."[17] When we interpret life's events in the context that 'we are in the hands of God,' all our experiences and circumstance are fixed and oriented in truth. For the hands that hold your fate are the same hands which were placed on your head to bless you. They are the hands that *"bear you"* and will be the same hands that *"carry you"* through difficulties.[18] This hope gives us happiness. It magnifies our ability to create joyful and happy experiences. Such makes us suppose that happiness may be more of a skill than a state.

Because God tailors the tests of life to fit our measurements, it is not possible to outline the purpose behind every specific situation. Those revelations are expressly reserved for the individual in their particular circumstances. However, most experiences generally facilitate the same outcome. The scriptures illustrate this principle, in a story about a drifting, wayward ship. We read: *"And it came to pass that the Lord God caused that there should be a furious wind blow upon the face of the waters, towards the promised land;*

---

[12] Genesis 50:20
[13] Job 2:10
[14] Romans 8:28
[15] Moses 6:55 – Brackets added – Originally: "and they taste the bitter, that they may know to prize the good."
[16] 2 Nephi 2:25
[17] Neal A. Maxwell. But For a Small Moment. From a speech given September 1, 1974
[18] See Isaiah 46:4 – "And even to your old age I am he; and even to hoar hairs will I carry you: I have made, and will bear; even I will carry, and will deliver you."

and thus they were tossed upon the waves of the sea before the wind. And ... they were many times buried in the depths of the sea, because of the mountain waves which broke upon them, and also the great and terrible tempests which were caused by the fierceness of the wind. And ... **the wind did never cease to blow towards the promised land.**"[19]

All the traumatic tossing produced by the storms and waves was a device intended to propel these sailors toward 'the promised land.' Every type of boisterous wind, all tumult and turmoil is the thrust pushing us toward heavenly lands. Though times will certainly come where you feel as though a 'mountain wave' has fallen upon you, though waters bury you deeply and crash down over your entire vessel; despite all of this, everything and every experience directs you to the promised land. "*If thou art accused with all manner of false accusations; if thine enemies fall upon thee; if they tear thee from the society of thy father and mother and brethren and sisters ... if thou shouldst be cast into the pit, or into the hands of murderers, and the sentence of death passed upon thee ... if the heavens gather blackness, and all the elements combine to hedge up the way; and above all, if the very jaws of hell shall gape open the mouth wide after thee, know thou, my son, that all these things shall give thee experience, and shall be for thy good.*"[20] When you accept this, joy will always remain near you.

In contrast, too many people pathologically worry over things that are out of their control. It is crucial to distinguish what is within our control and what is not. Disciples of Christ ever struggle to balance how to "*cheerfully do all things that lie in our power,*" and then 'stand still and wait for God's arm to be revealed.'[21] If either of these principles is askew, we open ourselves up to misery.

Those trying to carry things outside their control set themselves up for failure and frustration. Why would one fight against 'the law which moves the times and the seasons?'[22] Though these "*courses are fixed, even the courses of the heavens and the earth,*"[23] some individuals strain to control these kingdoms. Similarly, there are they which stress over time's currents and resist the courses of the seasons, which includes the course of free will. When problems lie outside the power of these people, instead of standing still with a posture of peace, their restless soul anxiously paces over their

---

[19] Ether 6: 5,6,8 – Emphasis added
[20] D&C 122:6,7
[21] D&C 123:17 – "Therefore, dearly beloved brethren, let us cheerfully do all things that lie in our power; and then may we stand still, with the utmost assurance, to see the salvation of God, and for his arm to be revealed."
[22] See D&C 88:42 – "And again, verily I say unto you, he hath given a law unto all things, by which they move in their times and their seasons;"
[23] D&C 88:43

non-manipulable predicaments.

In order to have joy, we must trust God. We must trust His strategic timing, His planned scenarios and His purposeful placements. We must trust that 'we are in God's hands!' By *"commending* [ourselves] *unto the Lord* [our] *God,"*[24] we find the stillness, peace and happiness that comes from staying connected to Eternity. If we desire enduring joy, we must have faith in the word which says, *"A man's heart deviseth his way: but the LORD directeth his steps."*[25] Heavenly Father surely, with nearly indiscernible tenderness directs the destiny of each individual, just as He does the *"destinies of all the armies of the nations of the earth."*[26]

God, our Father is not sluggishly glued to His throne content to live out His omnipotence in idle observation. His all searching eye does not search the span of the universe for the sake of His eternal entertainment. When this blinding veil is removed from our eyes and we review our lives without mortal restraints, nothing will impress us more than the constant, immeasurable extent of God's imposing influence. You will be amazed at His omniscient orchestration of events. You will reverence His subtle, yet intervening presence which softly straightened your paths and gently guided the course of your life. Instead of haphazard happenings and chaotic coincidence, you will see a marvelous genius strategically intersecting our situations. We will observe Father's omniscience weaving circumstances into a masterful tapestry of interconnecting causes and effects.

So let go! Let go of the urge to control all of your surroundings. Yours is not to bear the burden of Atlas. Do your best to utilize the talents which God has given to you, *"magnify the calling whereunto* [God has] *called you, and the mission with which* [God has] *commissioned you."*[27] When you feel that things are out of control; trust that God is in control. Trust that your steps are being directed down a path God has prepared for you. *Man's goings are of the* LORD; *how can a man then understand his own way?"* [28]

God directs us, but we still have to pick up our legs and walk. Unhappiness follows imbalances on either side of this principle. When misguided mercy corrupts a person's ability to act, they erroneously eliminate the very experiences intended to bring them joy. By failing 'to do all that is in our power' or by serving with blunted enthusiasm, we will

---

[24] Ether 6:4 – "they got aboard of their vessels … and set forth into the sea, commending themselves unto the Lord their God."
[25] Proverbs 16:9
[26] D&C 117:6
[27] D&C 88:80 – "… magnify the calling whereunto I have called you, and the mission with which I have commissioned you."
[28] Proverbs 20:24

inevitably reap a life haunted by regrets. There is no joy in giving half-hearted effort, only remorse. So if you are living lukewarmly, the degree of joy you will have at your disposable will be severely limited.

In contrast, every man should learn to *"enjoy the good of all his labour, it is the gift of God."*[29] Few things compare to the satisfaction that comes from honest work. Just as the heavens rejoice over the penitent sinner, we should learn to rejoice with heaven over our accomplishments. Work is the medium for men to create – either in his surroundings or within himself. As stewards of the earth, ours is the duty and opportunity to improve and beautify the world around us. *"Wherefore I perceive that there is nothing better, than that a man should rejoice in his own works."*[30] Man cannot have joy without work.

Always do your best. For all God requires is that, *"every man shall give as he is able, according to the blessing of the LORD thy God which he hath given thee."*[31] After you have done *"all* [you] *can do,"*[32] the gift of God, even the Holy Spirit, will speak these jubilant words to your soul – *"I will accept you, saith the Lord God."*[33] This highly individual revelation is available to you! By faith you can have the same testimony given to the Prophet Enoch, *"for before his translation he had this testimony, that he pleased God."*[34] According to the liberality of the Lord which he has toward His children, you can know your standing before him. As it is the gift of God to have joy in your labor, this gift can grant us the knowledge that our efforts are acceptable to God. This brilliantly burning rapture of knowing that you and your life please the Eternal Father is the sustaining *"joy of the saints."*[35]

True happiness does not need to gorge on games in order to experience joy. Surrounding yourself with every manner of entertainment and comfort will not make you happy. We cannot play our way into happiness. Glutting one's self with games cannot compensate for the joys of service. Nor can it replace the innate joy of hard-fought accomplishment. The devils have joy in chaos, adolescents take joy in pleasures, men will find joy in work, but it is the gods who have joy in service.

---

[29] Ecclesiastes 3:13
[30] Ecclesiastes 3:22
[31] Deuteronomy 16:17
[32] See 2 Nephi 25:23 – "For we labor diligently to write to persuade our children, and also our brethren, to believe in Christ, and to be reconciled to God, for we know that it is by grace that we are saved, after all we can do."
[33] Ezekiel 43:27
[34] Hebrews 11:5
[35] See Enos 1:3 – "I had often heard my father speak concerning eternal life, and the joy of the saints"

Joy is not made from musing. Happiness is induced by righteous activity. The pattern for managing spiritual health is similar to the care of our physical bodies. As it is with physical health, prohibitions are only part of the picture. People cannot be physically well by only abstaining from harmful or unhealthy things. What we do with and take into our bodies is just as important as what we refuse.

The pattern for both physical and spiritual health is centered on activity. In both cases, what we do is as important as what we avoid. Therefore, we should feed the famished spirit with love. We should nourish our souls and others with charity, compassion, kindness, and service. In these we practice a pattern of cultivating ecstasy that can be everlasting. *"For bodily exercise profiteth little: but godliness is profitable unto all things."*[36]

Neal A. Maxwell similarly observed, "Once we are settled in terms of the direction of our discipleship and the gross sins are left firmly behind –'misery prevention' it might be called–then the major focus falls upon the 'thou shalt' commandments. **It is the keeping of the 'thou shalt' commandments which brings even greater happiness.**"[37]

Joy is had in righteousness living. If we are 'living contrary to the nature of God, we will be without God in the world and therefore are in a state contrary to the nature of happiness.'[38] *"Behold thus saith the Lord unto my people – you have many things to do and to repent of; for behold …* **your hearts are not satisfied***. And ye obey not the truth, but have pleasure in unrighteousness."*[39] The stimuli created by wickedness are merely decoys. Such fleeting elations do not have the capacity to satiate your immortal spirit. Such is why the pleasure produced in *"wickedness never was happiness."*[40] For *"the wicked are like the troubled sea, when it cannot rest, whose waters cast up mire and dirt. There is no peace, saith my God to the wicked."*[41]

Selfishness is not happiness. Happiness is not had in hoarding massive amounts of substance for one's self. No! it is had in distributing the substance of your self in service. The scriptures say, *"she that liveth in pleasure is dead while she liveth."*[42] Hell has an unsustainable appetite. The

---

[36] 1 Timothy 4:8
[37] Neal Maxwell. The Pathway of Discipleship. *Ensign* Sept.1998. From a talk given at BYU on January 4, 1998 – Emphasis added
[38] See Alma 41:11 – "…they are without God in the world, and they have gone contrary to the nature of God; therefore, they are in a state contrary to the nature of happiness."
[39] D&C 56:14,15 – Emphasis added
[40] Alma 41:10
[41] Isaiah 57:20,21
[42] 1 Timothy 5:6

selfish feast but are never full. This overwhelming appetite is not only an impediment to happiness. It is the source of so much suffering. Only selflessness and service can counteract the hunger pains produced by pride. As the Messiah taught, *"If I then, your Lord and Master, have washed your feet; ye also ought to wash one another's feet ... If ye know these things,* **happy are ye if do them**.*"*[43] Therefore, give yourself in the service of others, for service is the soul's sweetest source of satisfaction.

Another important trait of the joyful is that they are less demanding. Happiness slips away as preferences turn into expectations and expectations to entitlements. Stable happiness finds pleasure in the simple things of life. By training our spirit to feast on simplicity we are able to become *"content with the things which the Lord hath allotted unto* [us]."[44] Happiness is furnished by taming our desires instead of fighting to feed the frequent demands of the flesh. *"The full soul loatheth an honeycomb; but to the hungry soul every bitter thing is sweet."*[45] The happy are less disappointed because they have fewer entitlements. They are less worried about what they deserve and are more occupied with whom they can serve.

For some, the speed of their displeasure and discontentment is damning. Not only are their attitudes swayed by showers and storms, but for them the sun may be too bright or the breeze too cool or too windy. Maybe if life were a perfectly orchestrated flow of ideal events, scenarios and people this sort could behave saintly. But even in heaven, it will not take long for the habitually discontent to be bothered by the bright lights or get bored with the background music. A narrow and rigid reception of enjoyments is antithetical to the treasures of heaven. God's gifts are diverse. By broadening our field of appreciation to reach the vast varieties which virtue and beauty manifests, we improve our ability to create and cultivate joy.

Heaven itself will never meet some people's expectations. In the world to come, chronic complainers will quickly become concerned with the shape of their crown, the color of their robes or the size of their mansion. Heaven is not so much about moving into a celestial climate, but changing ourselves into celestial beings. Those who are godly, are able to construct a heaven from a wide variety of settings; whereas pessimists, murmurers and the overly controlling quickly make a hell out of heaven.

Beware not to fall victim to that devastating type of death, the kind

---

[43] John 13:14,17 – Emphasis added
[44] Alma 29:3 – "for I ought to be content with the things which the Lord hath allotted unto me."
[45] Proverbs 27:7

that comes when life ceases to captivate us. Sadly, something in man's brute nature dislikes repetition, as if hearing or doing something multiple times diminishes its significance. If this poor habit goes unchecked, it will prevent us from attaining many important truths. We must be aware of this human tendency to devalue things that are repeated, lest this spoil our ability to taste and savor spiritual things.

Monotony must not ruin one's ability to relish. This is especially true in matters of worship. Do we spiritually savor our Sunday services, or do your Sabbath feasts resemble mindless movie theatre munching? Feasting on the word of God is an invitation to treasure every flavor of faith, not obliviously absorb precious principles as one does a bag of popcorn. It is the discontent carnal nature that demands extra spices to be sprinkled on top of every lesson to satisfy its tastes. In contrast, the content don't require every gathering to be a gourmet meal, nor do they need to tantalize their testimony with constant fantastic thrills in order to be appreciative and happy.

Contentment does not only apply to material comforts; it is also relevant in matters of spirituality. Nonetheless, when we speak of being spiritually content, it must be clear that this does not suggest that one should only *"desire to know the truth in part, but not all."*[46] Being spiritually content does not imply that we should stop searching for God, nor does it imply that we should stop trying to improve our standing before God. At all costs, we must avoid the *"carnal security"* that tantalizes with the voice, *"All is well in Zion, yea, Zion prospereth, all is well."*[47] Disciples must not become pacified by the damning contentment that says, *"I am rich, and increased with goods, and* **have need of nothing***."*[48]

Contentment does not negate the need for work, nor does it demand that we drop every ambition. Instead, as we 'learn to be content in whatsoever state we are in,'[49] we will learn to have peace in the pace that God has set for our progress. In effect, when one is spiritually content, they will *"murmur not because of the things which thou hast not seen, for they are withheld from thee and from the world, which is wisdom in me in a time to come."*[50] Since gratitude is a companion to happiness, murmuring is directly opposed

---

[46] D&C 49:2
[47] See 2 Nephi 28:21 – "And others will he pacify, and lull them away into carnal security, that they will say, All is well in Zion; yea, Zion prospereth, all is well – And thus the devil cheateth their souls, and leadeth them away carefully down to hell."
[48] Revelation 3:17 – Emphasis added
[49] See Philippians 4:11 – "Not that I speak in respect of want; for I have learned, in whatsoever state I am, therewith to be content."
[50] D&C 25:4

to joy. Do you count your complaints or numbering your blessings? *"And when the people complained, it displeased the* LORD*."*[51]

"Every man that striveth for the mastery is temperate in all things."[52] Mastering contentment requires some restraint on ambition. Our drive, even for godliness can mutate into the dangerous territory of covetousness or envy. Both envy and jealousy steal one's ability to have happiness. Jealousy creates a fidgeting anxiety in the soul, the covetous are ever restless and envy is always uneasy.

We learn an important truth about happiness by observing how envy, jealously, lust and covetousness operate. In order for these vices to function, a social setting is required. Envy, jealousy, and lust do not exist in solitude. Rather these are relationships gone awry. Instead of magnifying our joy with brotherhood, love and unity, some allow happiness to become warped by selfishness and ire. In order to access the 'exceeding joy' known only to the *"truly penitent and humble seeker of happiness,"*[53] we must learn how to share joy with others.

Are you capable of taking joy in other people's accomplishments, or is your happiness contingent on how full your trophy case is? Do you measure happiness by the number of medals you've won? Maybe you measure it by friends, money or diplomas? The great key to increasing our happiness is being able to have happiness with others. The Prophet Alma taught this principle saying, *"I do not joy in my own success alone, but* **my joy is more full because of the success of my brethren***."*[54] When happiness is resigned to moments of personal gratification our supply will be scarce. But when we discover how to take joy in other people's accomplishments, there is no limit to the joy we can experience in life.

Laughter is a perfect illustration of how sociality and relationships enlarge our joy. When a person is alone their laughter is somewhat hindered. Its sound is submerged and shallow. But when the same stimulus occurs in the presence of others, especially friends, people burst out in shouts and snorts; they release uncontainable cackles and caws. Just as laughter is amplified when it is shared with others, so too is joy. However, as long as we are strangers with one another, we will not be able access to this secret. Therefore, do not settle for only having acquaintances for relationships. Give yourself to others and connect with them. By creating more and tighter bonds with the people around you, by deepening

---

[51] Numbers 11:1
[52] 1 Corinthians 9:24
[53] Alma 27:18
[54] Alma 29:14 – Emphasis added

your relationships through love and service, you will improve your ability to feel joy in the success of others.

The family is the fundamental laboratory where we learn and practice how to have joy with others. Parents and grand-parents gradually master this technique as their enjoyment over their children and grandchildren's work is as great as if they did the task themselves. Brothers and sisters are not excluded from this group. From their example we see similar empathetic links. Because of the love developed between family members, one cannot help but weep for joy in seeing each other smile, succeed and rejoice. Nevertheless, the day will come when our love for all men in this world will be as binding as blood, for they are our brethren in Christ. Likewise, we await that time when a shared sense of sisterhood will seal strangers together. On this day the family of God, finally united in love, will fulfill the words, when *"one member be honoured, all the members rejoice with it."*[55]

For this reason, we know that Father in Heaven has a fullness of joy. As God's love is limitless, so also is His joy without end. Our Father is a God of happiness. Oh to know once more *"the ways of life,"* to have 'God make us full of joy with His countenance.'[56] Like the overzealous parent on the sidelines, God excitedly cheers us on through life. Hiding somewhere in the background of chortling companies and groups gathered together in gladness is a sense that our rapture is shared. When we feel true joy, the Holy Spirit awakens us to a resounding remembrance of our festive Father and the aura of merriment that surrounded His courts. Father's sweet sentiments spread mirth across the universe and His jovial smile turns the stars to shame. It is God's bright temperament that illuminates *"the path of life: for in* [His] *presence is fullness of joy;"* and *"at* [His] *right hand there are pleasures for evermore."*[57]

---

[55] 1 Corinthians 12:26
[56] Acts 2:28 - "Thou hast made known to me the ways of life; thou shalt make me full of joy with thy countenance."
[57] Psalms 16:11 – "Thou wilt shew me the path of life: in thy presence is fullness of joy; at thy right hand there are pleasures for evermore."

Longsuffering

"*For since the beginning of the world men have not heard, nor perceived by the ear, neither hath the eye seen, O God, beside thee, what he hath prepared for him that waiteth for him.*"[1] "*But they that wait upon the* LORD *shall renew their strength; they shall mount up with wings as eagles; they shall run, and not be weary; and they shall walk, and not faint.*"[2] "*And it shall be said in that day Lo, this is our God; we have waited for him, and he will save us: this is the* LORD; *we have waited for him, we will be glad and rejoice in his salvation.*"[3] Therefore, "*May Christ lift thee up, and may his sufferings and death, and the showing his body unto our fathers, and his mercy and long suffering, and the hope of his glory and of eternal life, rest in your mind forever.*"[4]

Divine love "*suffereth long.*"[5] Longsuffering is the longevity of love. It lengthens love's reach from mortality to eternity. Father, who is perfect in love, is "*merciful and gracious, longsuffering and abundant in goodness and truth.*"[6] "*O how marvelous are the works of the Lord, and how long doth he suffer with his people.*"[7] Just as obedience is secondary to humility, longsuffering is an appendage to larger principles. Longsuffering is born of love. It is empowered by hope. It is activated with faith and executed with compassion.

Most commonly we speak of longsuffering in terms of patience. Either word will suffice for both describe the same flavor of virtue. Yet, there are other attributes associated with longsuffering and patience that should not be forgotten, namely peacemaking and perseverance.

Longsuffering through time is patience, whereas longsuffering through trials or challenges is perseverance. In either case, peace is the product of patience and perseverance; it is the conclusion of longsuffering. "*Mark the perfect man, and behold the upright: for the end of that man is peace.*"[8]

---

[1] Isaiah 64:4
[2] Isaiah 40:31
[3] Isaiah 25:9
[4] Moroni 9:25
[5] Moroni 7:45
[6] Exodus 34:6
[7] Mosiah 8:20
[8] Psalms 37:37

When we learn to be patient with the Lord we are at peace, for God will *"keep him in perfect peace, whose mind is stayed on thee: because he trusteth in thee."*[9] In like manner, patience with others helps establish peace in our relationships and longsuffering between cultures curbs conflicts. Longsuffering prolongs love and extends enjoyments. It stretches charity and perpetuates peace.

    Patience is not mindless, militaristic waiting. Detached, apathetic deferment is not patience; even if it avoids anxiety and rush. When we are patient, our sense of anticipation or urgency is not necessarily nullified. Isaiah wrote, *"And **I will wait upon the LORD**, that hideth his face from the house of Jacob, and **I will look for him**."*[10] Being patient is more than waiting in a line at an amusement park. It is not idleness, but decisiveness. Patience is built on a foundation of focus. Thus, longsuffering is not aimless delay, rather purposeful pause.

    The depth of our patience is only as deep as our love for God. It is when we succumb to our own prerogatives that patience fails. We are patient with God and others because we love them. Because of Father's everlasting love, He is *"longsuffering to us-ward, not willing that any should perish, but that all should come to repentance."*[11] Enduring patience must be anchored with purpose. For this reason, patience has no association with apathy because it is an expression of love. Love must be patient. Were it not, love would be nothing more than a hormonal, high-school infatuation. Without longsuffering, faith is only a fling and charity is merely a tryst. Truly, longsuffering makes love everlasting.

    Time demands patience. Time is a constant; it doesn't respect individuals, status or circumstance. Time has a tyrannical hold on our lives. No amount of nail biting, pacing or finger tapping can alter the passage of time. *"Which of you by taking thought can add one cubit unto his stature?"*[12] Men have no choice but to exist through the constant *"process of time,"*[13] therefore man must become accustomed to waiting. It is the patient who have reconciled with the purpose for the process of time. They do not resent its existence, nor do they just exist as time passes. The heart of patience finds expression in ***how*** we respond to the ticking of the clock.

    The great adversary to patience is that adolescent shout – Now! Our fast-paced, contemporary lifestyle is making us too accustomed to

---

[9] Isaiah 26: 3
[10] Isaiah 8:17 – Emphasis added
[11] 2 Peter 3:9
[12] Matthew 6:27
[13] Moses 7:21

sprint work. Just as we have fast food, many expect fast faith. Some saints try to rush righteousness and even consider racing through repentance. There are no cliff notes to Christianity, and despite what society tries to sell us, character building has no short cuts. The rapid exchange of instant messages between friends fools us into expecting instant responses to our prayers. *"And Saul asked counsel of God, Shall I go down after the Philistines? Wilt thou deliver them into the hand of Israel? But he answered him not that day."*[14] As Elder Hales observed, "Too often we pray to have patience, but we want it right now!"[15]

God's course in patience is more that traffic lights and road work. Frustrating travels merely represent the busy work of patience and prepare us for the graduate classes of spiritual, personal, and social longsuffering. These are the three primary areas which we must learn to be longsuffering. In spiritual patience we learn a relationship with God that trusts His timing and interventions. We must develop an ability to be patient in the complex social relationships we have. As the great commandment in the law first focuses on God and the second on others, our interactions with others greatly reveals our capacity to be longsuffering. Finally, we must have personal patience in order to obtain inner peace and harmony. This loving longsuffering towards our-self produces the appropriate perspective of our own imperfections.

Having patience with God begins with a love for Him and is built upon trust in His plan of salvation. When we are patient, we have faith in God's plans; which includes God's global goals and specific programs. Man can suffer and endure many things and do so with honor, and when we have a cause connected to our suffering, neither earth nor hell can deter one's determination. Those who are patient have learned to see the program of life as an expression of God's love. A pious patience trusts the tutelage in trauma and believes the word which says, *"There hath no temptation taken you but such as is common to man: but God is faithful, who will not suffer you to be tempted above that ye are able; but will with the temptation also make a way to escape, that ye may be able to bear it."*[16]

Enduring patience is grounded in perspective; a perspective that finds purpose in every moment, including periods of pain. Those who are longsuffering with the Lord, lean on the belief that their specific problems in life are purposefully placed. These are they who trust that the both the timing and intensity of their trials are instructive and intentional. When we

---

[14] 1 Samuel 14:37
[15] Robert D. Hales. Waiting upon the Lord: Thy Will Be Done. *Ensign*. November 11
[16] 1 Corinthians 10:13

have such a faith in the situational spheres which God has placed us, we are granted a peculiar calm and confidence throughout our afflictions. Such a faith allows us to trust that time, tribulation and temptation are tools for the Lord's teaching.

Longsuffering resists the idea that life is planless coincidence – a random chaotic construct. Patience is empowered by a hope that God's foreknowledge has orchestrated sequences of a person's life. Patience is a faith that God has planted intentions into our precise challenges. Because of this belief the patient put off the persuasion of pleasure for higher purposes. In contrast, when we feel that our particular set of problems has no purpose we swiftly surrender to impatience. After all, why should we wait if there is no rationale to postpone our appetites? Why continue to suffer or endure difficulties without a cause? If there is no divine objective, why should anyone delay lust, impulse or whim?

Time is not the panacea for all of our problems, for time alone will not heal wounds. By combining contemplation with time, the patient replaces apprehensive pacing with the calm composure contained in hope. The patient ponder before protesting the bitter cups in life. They reflect on, instead of resent hard or even tragic circumstances. They will meditate rather than murmur over the monotony of life. They deal with life's dissonance believing that "Nothing is really routine."[17]

Since patience emerges from love, hope and faith, there are serious implications behind impatience. A person's impatience may suggest that God is uncaring, that He is omnipotent but uninterested in the affairs of the individual. The impatient will grow weary of waiting because they can no longer see the divine design in delay. It is understandable why our world is increasing in anxiety, for without hope in God's plan of salvation we succumb to counting time on mortal clocks.

In some cases, our impatience implies a belief that God has forfeited his rule to randomness. Impatience may suggest that perhaps our life events were unaccounted for, unforeseen, or unimportant. Perhaps the impatient insinuate that God's management skills are lacking, that maybe He isn't capable of handling it all. Though one may not perceive or believe in God's works, though they may not comprehend their destiny or see the stretch of the straight and narrow road in its entirety, this does not alter the truth that *"A man's heart deviseth his way: but the LORD directeth his steps."*[18]

Inspiration and discernment require patience. The patient are

---

[17] Neal A. Maxwell. The Pathway of Discipleship. *Ensign.* September 1998
[18] Proverbs 16:9

pensive, reflective, and reverential. Unswayed by chemical cognitions or hormonal rationales their analysis stays centered on the Spirit; this enables events to be placed in their proper perspective. In order to escape emotional prejudice and limbic bias, we must learn to wait upon the Lord. *"As the eyes of servants look unto the hand of their masters, and as the eyes of a maiden unto the hand of her mistress; so our eyes wait upon the Lord our God, until that he have mercy upon us."*[19]

    Longsuffering helps us remove the muffling noises of murmuring. It is only after these inward grumblings are silenced that the soft sounds of the Spirit are able to surface. As it pertains to our petitions, we see that the impatient are prone to the mistake of uttering un-pondered prayers. *"Behold, you have not understood; you have supposed that I would give it unto you, when you took no thought save it was to ask me."*[20] Too often the pace of our prayers is set at a sprint. We open our eyes and come off our knees even as we are saying amen. Though circumstances strongly influence the type of prayer we utter, concerning our personal prayers, it is no secret that one of the best ways to add real intent is to simply add time. When we take the time to reflect before and after our prayers, the Spirit will call to us from the megaphone of our memories. Reverently reviewing our past and present experiences opens our hears to receiving revelation. Similarly, it is only when we are longsuffering that we can the voice of God sounding **in** our suffering.

    Nevertheless, saints were not sent here to solely solidify their own salvation. No, the saints of the latter-days are commissioned to rescue those who are lost and struggling. Therefore, the work of salvation will require tremendous amounts of compassion to steer our patience within our interpersonal relationships.

    Though patience with God is largely dependent upon faith in God's works, social patience is primarily predicated on compassion. Those who are patient with their fellow-man are peacemakers. As a peacemaker, we *"eschew evil, and do good,"* we *"seek peace, and ensue it."*[21] Peacemakers have that most essential patience which allows human beings the space learn and grow. They look past the inadequacies of those around them *"with all lowliness and meekness, with longsuffering, forbearing one another in love."*[22]

    "Now we exhort you, brethren, warn them that are unruly, comfort the feebleminded, support the weak, **be patient toward all men***. See that none render*

---

[19] Psalms 123:2
[20] D&C 9:8
[21] 1 Peter 3:11 – "Let him eschew evil, and do good, let him seek peace, and ensue it."
[22] Ephesians 4:2

*evil for evil unto any man; but ever follow that which is good, both among yourselves, and to all men."*²³ How quick some are to pounce on other people's imperfections! Not only this, but there are those who launch full scaled retaliations over unintentional mistakes. Impulsivity in all its forms must be tempered with contemplation. Written on the heart of the longsuffering is the word which says, *"Whether one member suffer, all the members suffer with it."*²⁴ Thus, a peacemaker comforts before offering counsel, they do not forget to first suffer with their fellow man before offering solutions.

When offended, a peacemaker's decisions are stilled by compassion. They forego judgment till it is given to them by the Spirit of God. They are not *"hasty in thy spirit to be angry: for anger resteth in the bosom of fools."* Peacemakers wait patiently to hear the perspectives and opinions of others, knowing that *"he that answereth a matter before he heareth it, it is folly and shame unto him."*²⁵

For peacemakers, listening is preliminary to instruction, awareness precedes reproof and understanding takes place before judgment. Before passing judgment, the peacemaker will wait until they find the image of God in their enemy and upon finding it will love them. Only after love is obtained can divine justice be dealt. In their exchanges with all men, including their enemies, the patient seek the *"Spirit of truth"* that they might *"understand one another,"* that both may be *"edified and rejoice together."*²⁶

When we are in the presence of a patient man, we feel peace. Oh then what peace we will feel to return to the presence of "the *God of patience."*²⁷ Heavenly Father is tranquil amidst turmoil, steady during recalcitrance, and calm amidst chaos. He has a composure that instills a cooling confidence that extinguishes worry.

Great comfort is found in our Father's fortitude. It is a peace that is given *"not as the world giveth."*²⁸ In the serenity of His Spirit all anxieties are stilled, and His holy demeanor steadies every concern. Upon returning to the touch of His sacred countenance our hearts will fully comprehend the words, *"Be still and know that I am God."*²⁹ It is here we will come understand the *"perfect work"* of patience. Then as you are *"clasped in the arms of Jesus,"*³⁰

---

[23] 1 Thessalonians 5:14, 15
[24] 1 Corinthians 12:26
[25] Proverbs 18:13
[26] D&C 50:22
[27] Romans 15:5 – "Now the God of patience and consolation grant you to be likeminded one toward another"
[28] John 14:27
[29] Psalms 46:10 see also D&C 101:16
[30] Mormon 5:11

you shall know at last what it means to be *"perfect and entire, wanting nothing."*[31]

Most often we think of patience as a chronic reaction; however, patience must also be programed into our acute responses. All of the natural man's unrighteous reactions must be subdued by patience. Has turning the other cheek become a reflex response? Some *"Bless them that curse you,"*[32] but do so insincerely. Sycophantically blessing an enemy still computes as a curse. Do you do good to them that hate you so you can feel better than them? Do you turn the other cheek with a smirk?

How much are you in control of your actions? Jesus taught, *"In your patience possess ye your souls."*[33] In order to reach our potential we must have full command of our souls; a task that can only be completed with longsuffering. If a soul is only had in patience, then anger is a most malignant vice. A loss of patience is a surrender of the soul. Anger forsakes the powers of free will by yielding *"unto the power of Satan."*[34] The frightening reality is this, just as we can be *"instruments in the hands of God,"*[35] we can fall victim to the awful antithesis of this teaching. Just as one can be *"directed by the Spirit"*[36] of God, one may also *"become subjected to the spirit of the devil,"* insomuch that *"the devil hath all power over* [them.]*"*[37]

As an instrument of God, it is *"given you in the very hour, yea, in the very moment, what ye shall say."*[38] In like manner those who become instruments of Satan have malevolent language placed in their minds. This can be observed in the roaring tantrums of the angry, who dissolve peace with torrents of hastefully hateful words. Those who *"have taken the Holy Spirit for their guide"*[39] can be *"led by the Spirit"*[40] and *"carried away in the Spirit."*[41] On the other hand, those led by the devil's influence quickly get carried away by violent and vicious behaviors. Sadly, we all have at some point observed the berserk of anger. We have seen it swiftly steal away logic and replace reason with raucous. We have watched as the angry get "carried away" in a caustic craze which vacates every ounce of virtue. The angry no longer

---

[31] James 1:4 – "But let patience have her perfect work, that ye may be perfect and entire, wanting nothing."
[32] Luke 6:28
[33] Luke 21:19
[34] 3 Nephi 7:5 – "and all this iniquity had come upon the people because they did yield themselves unto the power of Satan."
[35] Mosiah 27:36 – "And thus they were instruments in the hands of God in bringing many to the knowledge of the truth, yea, to the knowledge of their Redeemer."
[36] D&C 42:13
[37] Alma 34:35 – Original: you
[38] D&C 100:6
[39] D&C 45:57
[40] Romans 8:14 – "For as many as are led by the Spirit of God, they are the sons of God.
[41] 1 Nephi 14:30

appear to be themselves; the soul and self we knew is hollow, and filling the void is a maniacal spirit of satanic savagery.

Therefore, do not *"yield ye your members as* **instruments of unrighteousness** *unto sin: but yield yourselves unto God, as those that are alive from the dead, and your members as instruments of righteousness unto God."*[42] Sin is dramatic. Would you pluck out your right eye if it hindered your salvation? Many cannot even help keep computerized games out of a chapel more or less cast the metaphorical limb from their body.[43]

Anger should have no place in our hearts. It is a leash worn by fools. With anger Satan enlists mortal emissaries to do his bidding. *"Can ye be angry, and not sin? let not the sun go down upon your wrath."*[44] Heed the words of Christ who taught, *"But I say unto you, That whosoever is angry with his brother shall be in danger of the judgment ... therefore if thou bring thy gift to the altar, and there rememberest that thy brother hath ought against thee; Leave there thy gift before the altar, and go thy way; first be reconciled to thy brother, and then come and offer thy gift."*[45]

Just as the disciple of Christ must be patience with other human beings, they must also be patient with the only human being they really and truly know – themselves. Life and the gospel prod us with sharp expectations, and we will not find peace until we mediate the paradox of perfection. Christ taught, *"Be ye therefore perfect, even as your Father which is in heaven is perfect."* However, mortality denies us this achievement. Ideals of completeness, wholeness and perfection seem impossible for man's fallible frame. We need the patience to allow ourselves time to change and grow; for one will only find inner peace by living a life loving longsuffering towards themselves.

"And now, Israel, what doth the Lord thy God require of thee?"[46] *"Every man shall give as he is able, according to the blessing of the* LORD *thy God which he hath given thee."*[47] *"And he that is able, let him return it ... and he that is not, of him it is not required."*[48] *"For we know that it is by grace that we are saved, after all we can do."*[49] *"This is good and acceptable in the sight of God our Saviour."*[50]

---

[42] Romans 6:13 – Emphasis added
[43] Mark 9:47 – "And if thine eye offend thee, pluck it out: it is better for thee to enter into the kingdom of God with one eye, than having two eyes to be cast into hell fire."
[44] JST Ephesians 4:26
[45] Matthew 5:24
[46] Deuteronomy 10:12 – "what doth the Lord they God require of thee, but to fear the Lord thy God, to walk in all his ways, and to love him, and to serve the Lord thy God with all thy heart and with all thy soul." see also Micah 6:8
[47] Deuteronomy 16:17
[48] D&C 60:11
[49] 2 Nephi 25:23

Therefore may it be said of us, as it was said of the woman at Bethany, "*She hath done what she could.*"[51] Then, after we 'cast in all that we have, even all our living,'[52] and "*offer* [our] *whole souls as an offering unto him;*"[53] which includes all that we are – imperfections included. Then "*the peace of God, which passeth all understanding, shall keep your hearts and minds through Christ Jesus.*"[54]

Have faith in the Lord, for "*The LORD is longsuffering, and of great mercy, forgiving iniquity and transgression.*"[55] He knew that you would falter. He knew that you would sin. God knows your soul, your intents, and your desires. He understands that "*the spirit indeed is willing, but the flesh is weak.*"[56] As it was for the Messiah, we do not receive "*the fullness at the first, but* [receive] *grace for grace.*"[57] Repentance is a patient process. Re-patterning thought processes, habits, and personalities requires great perseverance. The "*mighty change*"[58] of heart rarely comes in an instant.

Repentance is a constant process and sometimes the speed of our heart out-runs the strides of our legs. Sometimes the secondary and subsequent mighty change of conduct takes months if not years. This does not suggest that you should "*procrastinate the day of* your *repentance,*" but that you should "*press forward, feasting upon the word of Christ and endure to the end.*"[59] And we will have to press forward; sometimes aggressively, for godliness requires grit and a fierce resolve. Repentance has never been a passive process. It takes focused faith and conscious courage.

"*Remember all the way which the LORD thy God led thee these forty years in the wilderness, to humble thee, and to prove thee, to know what was in thine heart, whether thou wouldest keep his commandments or no.*"[60] Repentance and change takes time. Like the children of Israel's journey to the holy land, the path of repentance will first take us through the wilderness. Your sanctification will not be completed with the wave of a magic wand. In your efforts to repent psychological strategies may be useful tools, but know that they cannot

---

[50] 1 Timothy 2:3
[51] Mark 14:8 – "She hath done what she could: she is come aforehand to anoint my body to the burying."
[52] Mark 12:44
[53] Omni 1:26 – Original: your
[54] Philippians 4:7
[55] Numbers 14:18
[56] Matthew 26:41 see also Mark 14:38
[57] D&C 93:12 – "And I, John, saw that he received not of the fullness at the first, but received grace for grace"
[58] Alma 5:14 – "Have ye experienced this mighty change in your hearts."
[59] 2 Nephi 31:20
[60] Deuteronomy 8:2

substitute for the slow but strategically sojourn through the furnace of affliction. Ultimately, your sanctification will be completed by the Holy Spirit,[61] not self-help.

May Heavenly Father, the *"God of peace,"*[62] give you the *"peace of conscience"*[63] that comes from being perfect in Christ. Though in this *"corruptible"*[64] state one only obtains a *"portion of the celestial glory."* Yet if you *"deny yourselves of all ungodliness, and love God with all your might, mind and strength, then is his grace sufficient for you, that by his grace ye may be perfect in Christ."*[65] *"Most gladly therefore will I rather glory in my infirmities, that the power of Christ may rest upon me."*[66] *"Therefore render to* [God] *all that you have and are"*[67] that you may find yourself *"approved of God."*[68]

Every virtue will be placed under sanctifying stress. Thus every godly attribute will need nourishment from patience if they are to endure the process of time. But time is only part of the test men are called to endure. Perseverance is a companion to patience. Where patience conveys longsuffering through time, perseverance expresses longsuffering through affliction. Those who are longsuffering are constant through the uncomfortable flow of time. They persevere through all of life's seasons, including: fear, fatigue, dullness, solitude, pain, wealth and praise.

Patience and longsuffering are made perfect in the crucible of suffering. *"Knowing this, that the trying of your faith worketh patience."*[69] Pain parts the veil; *"For our light affliction, which is but for a moment, worketh for us a far more exceeding and eternal weight of glory."*[70] *"Behold, I have refined thee, but not with silver, I have chosen thee in the furnace of affliction."*[71] In this furnace we will face tremendous temperatures and terrifying heat; but this is not all, the test of faith will try us not only in terms of intensity, but also in relation to time. Thus we cannot be weekend worshipers who have *"not root"* in themselves

---

[61] See 3 Nephi 27:20 – "Repent, all ye ends of the earth and come unto me and be baptized in my name, that ye may be sanctified by the reception of the Holy Ghost, that ye may stand spotless before me at the last day."
[62] Romans 15:33 – "Now the God of peace be with you all. Amen."
[63] Mosiah 4:3
[64] 1 Corinthians 15:53 – "For this corruptible must put on incorruption, and this mortal must put on immortality."
[65] Moroni 10:32 – "Yea come unto Christ, and be perfected in him, and deny yourselves of all ungodliness"
[66] 2 Corinthians 12:9
[67] Mosiah 2:34
[68] JST Genesis 14:27 – "And thus, having been approved of God, he was ordained an high priest after the order of the covenant which God made with Enoch."
[69] James 1:3
[70] 2 Corinthians 4:17
[71] Isaiah 48:10

"but dureth for a while: for when tribulation or persecution ariseth because of the word, by and by he is offended."[72] Our commitment to Christ must become consistent, for we will be tried over and over again till the content of our covenants is cemented into our character.

"If ye continue in my word, then are ye my disciples indeed."[73] Any principle, no matter how lofty, is deprived of if it is not persisted in. *"Be not weary in well doing."*[74] Be not weary in love, for it is *"To them who by patient continuance in well doing seek for glory and honour and immortality, eternal life."*[75] Perseverance is necessary to obtaining Eternal life. *"Wherefore, if ye shall press forward, feasting upon the word of Christ, and endure to the end, behold, thus saith the Father: Ye shall have eternal life."*[76] One cannot retire from righteousness. There is no 401k contained in the covenant *"to serve him until you are dead."* Sharp staccato acts of service will not be enough. Your charity must be reliable and your goodness dependable, for Father's righteousness is resilient and His patience predictable.

The tongue can tell no greater tragedy than a loss of perseverance. The values of charity, faith, service, hope, meekness or any godly attribute is only worth as much as our ability to endure in each of these. Virtues are empowered by patience and it is perseverance which gives them permanence. The true mortal tragedy is for a man to live honorably the majority of his days, only to compromise covenants and give up toward the end of his life. *"Therefore we ought to give the more earnest heed to the things which we have heard, lest at any time we should let them slip."*[77] The loss of perseverance corrodes righteousness. It decays commitments, and ruins virtue. If we are unable to persevere, so much of our achievement can be undone. Take heed therefore, *"Lest haply after he hath laid the foundation, and is not able to finish it, all that behold it begin to mock him, Saying, This man began to build, and was not able to finish."*[78]

"And again, we saw the terrestrial world, and behold and lo, these are they who are of the terrestrial, whose glory differs from that of the church of the Firstborn ... These are they who receive of his glory, but not of his fulness ... These are they who are not valiant in the testimony of Jesus; wherefore they obtain not the crown over the kingdom of our God."[79] The valiant are tenacious. They do not relinquish

---

[72] Matthew 13:21
[73] John 8:31
[74] 2 Thessalonians 3:13
[75] Romans 2:7
[76] 2 Nephi 31:20
[77] Hebrews 2:1
[78] Luke 14:29,30
[79] D&C 76:71

their covenants because of trials. They do not surrender to selfishness because of suffering, they do not quit on being kind because of provocation. The valiant practice a 'durable discipleship' which perseveres through every shape of circumstance.

"*Man is born unto trouble, as the sparks fly upward.*"[80] God examines the integrity of the valiant to see if virtue will resist sloth, exhaustion, despair, self-doubt, fear and pain. It is not enough to cast Satan out from our midst in a single spectacle of righteousness. He must be cast out again and again, he must be denied over and over, till one's spirit is toned with truth. Because trials, dilemmas and temptations are so pervasive, perhaps it is appropriate to define humanity in part, in terms of the universal struggle.

To be human is to struggle. The life of man is a struggle. Opposition is real. At times it is brutally real. And the struggle does not stop. "*What are these which are arrayed in white robes? And whence came they? ... These are they which came out of great tribulation.*"[81] This "*great tribulation*" will 'prove us herewith, to see if we will do all things whatsoever the Lord our God shall command us.'[82] In order to accomplish this, the disciple of Christ must persevere past the initial naïve attempts to claim victory. Perseverance must continue propelling us even after bravery breaks. We must continue to press forward after genuine attempts repeatedly fail. The valiant do not retreat after defeat. The valiant never let their determination fade because of failure.

The valiant persevere and continue to fight, day in and day out through the blaze of the sun and the barren chill of night – they never stop, they never yield. We are told to "*Fight the good fight of faith,*"[83] and wars are not won in one day. The battle for Eternal life will not be decided after the firing of a single cannon, there will be ups and downs. Some days you will hold the enemies forces back. Other days you may suffer defeat. Though time may torment your hopes, do not let it deter you from giving the righteous response, "*Rejoice not against me, O mine enemy;* **when I fall, I shall arise**; *when I sit in darkness, the LORD shall be a light unto me.*"[84]

"*Remember my servant Oliver Granger; behold, verily I say unto him that his name shall be had in sacred remembrance from generation to generation, forever and ever,*

---

[80] Job 5:7
[81] Revelation 7:13,14 – "and have washed their robes, and made them white in the blood of the lamb."
[82] Abraham 3:25 – "And we will prove them herewith, to see if they will do all things whatsoever the Lord their God shall command them"
[83] 1 Timothy 6:12 – "Fight the good fight of faith, lay hold on eternal life, whereunto thou art also called"
[84] Micah 7:8 – Emphasis added

saith the Lord. Therefore, let him contend earnestly for the redemption of the First Presidency of my Church, saith the Lord; and **when he falls he shall rise again, for his sacrifice shall be more sacred unto me than his increase,** *saith the Lord.*"[85]

Whatever *"thorn in the flesh"*[86] is given to buffet us, we must never concede. We must never let hope, courage, or charity become a casualty in this conflict. Like the children of Israel who spent 40 years in the wilderness, or the saints who spent 40 years building a sacred temple, we must arise from recurring failures and press forward. Your soul's development, like the construction of God's temple will encounter some unpredictable and perturbing bumps along the way. So, if the sandstone foundation you have painfully struggled to build for five whole years is later found to be cracked and unsuitable, rise again and begin laying a foundation of quartz.

Perhaps man's greatest endowment is his capacity to endure. In mortality we may not be able to reach the end point of the *"way of holiness."*[87] We may not see virtue and truth emerge victorious while clothed in corruptible clay. However, all man has one thing in common. We can all press forward. We can all persevere on whatever portion of the path that now lies before us. We can endure to the next horizon, and like Oliver Granger, if we fall, we can rise again and again, onward till eternity if necessary, till the straight narrow path takes us beyond the vistas of Eternity, past the infinity of time to the throne of God where *"To him that overcometh will I grant to sit with me in my throne, even as I also overcame, and am set down with my Father in his throne."*[88]

Regardless of whatever weaknesses you may have, perseverance is within your capacity. Whatever problems, limitations or obstacles you face, you can keep moving forward. It is within your power to *"press toward the mark for the prize of the high calling of God in Christ Jesus,"*[89] and whether or not you complete the Christian curriculum in mortality, you can at least square your shoulders, face the struggles of life head on, and die with a sword in your hand. We may not be able to determine our talents, but we can choose to struggle for success. Never stop fighting. Never give up, and

---

[85] D&C 117:12,13 – Emphasis added
[86] 2 Corinthians 12:7 – "And lest I should be exalted above measure through the abundance of the revelations, there was given to me a thorn in the flesh, the messenger of Satan to buffet me, lest I should be exalted above measure."
[87] Isaiah 35:8 – "And an highway shall be there, and a way, and it shall be called the way of holiness; the unclean shall not pass over it."
[88] Revelation 3:21
[89] Philippians 3:14

never stop struggling. Jesus our Lord *"resisted unto blood, striving against sin."*[90] He is our exemplar, and it is He who *"proveth you, to know whether ye love the Lord your God with all your heart and with all your soul."*[91] Yes, your accomplishments will witness the desires of your heart; but do not doubt that the internal and external struggles you endure are an equivalent testament to your desires.

To use the timeless words of Winston Churchill, "We have before us an ordeal of the most grievous kind. We have before us many, many long months of struggle and of suffering. You ask what is our policy? I will say: It is to wage war, by sea, land and air, with all our might and with all our strength that God can give us: … That is our policy. You ask what is our aim? I can answer in one word: Victory – victory at all costs, victory in spite of all terror; victory, however long and hard the road may be."[92]

"H*e that shall endure unto the end, the same shall be saved."*[93] To what end we are called to endure I do not know. But take heart, for of the few canonical words we can specifically ascribe to our Heavenly Father, it is written, *"Wherefore, if ye shall press forward, feasting upon the word of Christ, and endure to the end, behold, thus saith the Father: Ye shall have eternal life."*[94] Page after page, horizons turn over in the book of life. I do not pretend to know that *"end"* which God has in store for your life. What is sure; is that we can all persevere and take that next step along the straight and narrow. To move forward and persevere regardless of your allotment in life is the one thing we all have absolute control over. Perhaps then, the outcome of the war is not as important as the fight itself. The ultimate victory of the valiant is to be able to exclaim, *"I have fought a good fight, I have finished my course, I have kept the faith."*[95]

---

[90] Hebrews 12:4
[91] Deuteronomy 13:3
[92] Winston Churchill. *Churchill, the Life Triumphant.* American Heritage Publishing Co. 196 p. 90
[93] Matthew 24:13
[94] 2 Nephi 31:20
[95] 2 Timothy 4:7

Justice

"O the greatness and the justice of our God!"[1] God is love, but without the principle of justice love cannot manifest. *"For whom the Lord loveth he chasteneth, and scourgeth every son whom he receiveth."*[2] Justice is the crucial counterbalancing quality of love that completes the *"eternal round"*[3] of the Lord's course. Truly, justice is a weighty principle in order to offset the combined mass of charity, mercy, compassion and kindness. The delicate equilibrium of godly virtues depends on justice; which anchors love in morality, fixes charity upon the foundation of truth, and fastens affections with ethic.

The challenge of maintaining the balance between the Christ-like qualities necessitates that justice be applied in its appropriate proportion. Today, as in most of mankind's history, we see perversions of the principle of justice. Severe consequences follow individuals and nations who perceive and practice justice disproportionately. If misunderstood, the virtue of justice may mutate into vengeance or enmity. Some even manipulate justice in order to subvert the law and excuse evil. In like manner, there are those who misuse mercy in ways that mocks justice. By denying justice, those with an overly merciful mentality may inadvertently maim truth, morality and righteousness. Those who erroneously eliminate justice allow love to be all grace at the cost of glory and godliness.

Justice need not always be associated with shrewdness. The valor in this virtue is not in vindication; but rather in its implementation of impartial charity. The just distribute measures according to equity, honesty, and fairness. Justice therefore, is much more than judgment, punishment, or recompense. Though each of these concepts reflect an aspect of justice, they do not contain the whole of justice themselves. They are simply accessories stemming from the core of justice. But what is this core? This central attitude of justice is illustrated in the character of Joseph, the husband of Mary and the designated earthly father for Jesus. Just as Mary

---

[1] 2 Nephi 9:17
[2] Hebrews 12:6
[3] See Alma 37:12 – "… his paths are straight, and his course is one eternal round."

was a chosen vessel, one 'highly favoured and blessed among women,'[4] we can rightfully assume that similar commendations are deserved of Joseph. Yet, what *"separated"*[5] Joseph from other souls? What traits did he possess that made him the selected candidate for such a significant role?

Unfortunately, very little is said in the scriptures about Joseph and even less commentary is made directly about his character. Though scarce, there is one verse in particular that mentions the manner of man he was; it states, *"Then Joseph her husband,* **being a just man***, and not willing to make her a publick example, was minded to put her away privily."*[6] What is it that makes a man just?

In the verse above, the Greek word for just is *dikaios*,[7] which means *to be just, equitable or righteous. Dikiaos* comes from the word *dike* [8] which means *right or that which is right*. Thus, to be just is to do that which is right; or to use the phrase of another scripture, the just are they who "**loveth that which is right** *before me, saith the Lord."*[9] Though the concept of doing what is right seems simple, the application of this simple virtue is as difficult an objective as any could imagine. It may be the very central feature of the test of life itself.

Whereas wisdom contains the didactic or academic discernment of good and evil, justice is more concerned with the clinical execution of wisdom in righteousness. Thus, justice is primarily a pragmatic principle. Every decision of moral merit passes through this virtue. Before any conscious action is given life, the seeds of justice can be initially identified in that internal, spiritual sensation that sifts right from wrong. For this reason, justice is closely associated with the light of Christ, *"which* **[light]** *is in all things, which giveth* **life** *to all things, which is the* **law** *by which all things are governed, even the power of God who sitteth upon his throne."*[10] A **light** of justice issues from the government of God giving man his moral **life**. The **laws** of justice enable agency and abide in man as the distinguishing taste for divine truth.

---

[4] Luke 1:28 – "And the angel… said, Hail, thou that art highly favoured, the Lord is with thee: blessed art thou among women."
[5] See Romans 1:1 – "Paul, a servant of Jesus Christ, called to be an apostle, separated unto the gospel of God"
[6] Matthew 1:19 – Emphasis added
[7] Greek Strong's Dictionary # 1342 –(dik'-ah-yos)– Righteous, just, equitable, one who does that which is right.
[8] Greek Strong's Dictionary #1349 –(dee-kay) which means right or what is right.
[9] D&C 124:15 – Emphasis added – "And again, verily I say unto you, blessed is my servant Hyrum Smith; for I, the Lord, love him because of the integrity of his heart, and because he loveth that which is right before me, saith the Lord."
[10] D&C 88:13 – Brackets and emphasis added

We can see this sense of justice influencing Alma as he grappled with a difficult ethical challenge. Describing Alma's inner struggle the record states, *"And now the spirit of Alma was again troubled; and he went and inquired of the Lord what he should do concerning this matter, for **he feared that he should do wrong in the sight of God**."*[11] This fear of the Lord, or more specifically, this 'fear to do wrong' is a manifestation of justice. The light of Christ residing in all men will communicate to us through this sense, and together these forces combine to compose man's internal compass – that enlightening conscience which directing us towards righteousness, equity and truth.

If we aspire to be just, we will have to learn ***how*** to correctly keep Christ's admonition to *"judge righteous judgment."*[12] *"Ye shall do no unrighteousness in judgment: thou shalt not respect the person of the poor, nor honour the person of the mighty: but in righteousness shalt thou judge thy neighbour."*[13] There is no prejudice in justice. It does not allow any partiality, narcissism, nepotism or propaganda. Those who *"judge righteous judgment"* heed the counsel given to Samuel, *"But the LORD said unto Samuel, Look not on his countenance, or on the height of his stature; because I have refused him: for the LORD seeth not as man seeth; for man looketh on the outward appearance, but the LORD looketh on the heart."*[14]

Our sense of justice resides deeper than the flesh's philosophy of fairness. Because the just see not 'as man seeth,' being just requires the revelatory involvement of God's Spirit. Without the inspiration provided by the Holy Spirit, which is a Spirit of perfect love; judgment fails to penetrate past the outward appearance. For example, many who judge according to their own sight succumb to misguided Mosaic morality, a mentality manifesting in a belief that because you hurt me, I am justified in returning hurt to you. Juvenile judgments such as these are made out of anger, not love. They are immature attempts to rationalize revenge. *"Ye have heard that it hath been said, An eye for an eye, and a tooth for a tooth: But I say unto you, That ye resist not evil: but whosoever shall smite thee on thy right cheek, turn to him the other also."*[15]

We must never mistake vengeance as justice. *"Dearly beloved, avenge*

---

[11] Mosiah 26:13 – Emphasis added
[12] JST Matthew 7:1-2 – "Now these are the words which Jesus taught his disciples that they should say unto the people. Judge not unrighteously, that ye be not judged; but judge righteous judgment."
[13] Leviticus 19:15
[14] 1 Samuel 16:17
[15] Matthew 5:38,39 – See Deuteronomy 19:21 – "And thine eye shall not pity; but life shall go for life, eye for eye, tooth for tooth, hand for hand, foot for foot."

not yourselves ... for it is written, Vengeance is mine, I will repay, saith the Lord."[16] Man's impatience produces much injustice; his impulse for immediate compensation is merciless. If you feel as though you have been wronged, *"ye ought to say in your hearts – let God judge between me and thee, and reward thee according to thy deeds."*[17]

Retribution will be given in the Lord's *"due time;"*[18] it is not for men to seize the throne of God by hastening the Day of Judgment. Social estrangement, rude retorts, pettiness and all other forms of caustic comebacks generally distribute justice injuriously and prematurely. In contrast, the just live with a faith in the Lord of the Harvest who said, *"whatsoever a man soweth, that shall he also reap. For he that soweth to his flesh shall of the flesh reap corruption; but he that soweth to the Spirit shall of the Spirit reap life everlasting."*[19]

Patience is such a crucial component of justice. *"Say not thou, I will recompense evil: but wait on the Lord."*[20] If we desire to be just, we must learn how to wait. The just will wait upon the Lord even while their heart cries *"with a loud voice, saying, How long, O Lord, holy and true, dost thou not judge and avenge our blood on them that dwell on the earth."*[21] There may even be times when unspeakable crimes are committed; yet the just being 'constrained by the Spirit' will *"suffer that they may do this ... that the judgments of which* [God] *shall exercise upon them in his wrath may be just."*[22] How dare mere mortal magistrates think to take the control of allocating consequences from the Great King of the Cosmos!

The just not only wait for the Lord to avenge evil, they also are long-suffering towards claiming the rewards of righteousness, *"Knowing that whatsoever good thing any man doeth, the same shall he receive of the Lord, whether he be bond or free."*[23] So it is according to *"the restoration of God,"*[24] **"For that which ye do send out shall return unto you again."**[25] *"And now behold, is the meaning of the word restoration to take a thing of a natural state and place it in an*

---

[16] Romans 12:19
[17] D&C 64:11
[18] See D&C 43:29 – "For in mine own due time will I come upon the earth in judgment, and my people shall be redeemed and reign with me on earth."
[19] Galatians 6:7,8
[20] Proverbs 20:22 – "Say not thou, I will recompense evil; but wait on the Lord and he shall save thee."
[21] Revelation 6:10
[22] Alma 14:11 – Brackets added
[23] Ephesians 6:8
[24] Alma 42:28 – "If he has desired to do evil, and has not repented in his days, behold, evil shall be done unto him according to the restoration of God."
[25] Alma 41:15 – Emphasis Added

unnatural state, or to place it in a state opposite to its nature? ... this is not the case; but the meaning of the word restoration is to bring back again evil for evil, or carnal for carnal, or devilish for devilish – good for that which is good; righteous for that which is righteous; just for that which is just; merciful for that which is merciful."[26] "*Therefore let us not be weary in well doing; for in due season we shall reap, if we faint not."*[27]

As disciples strive to 'look on the heart as the Lord looketh,' they must be careful not to be blinded by their own light. A great challenge for Christ's followers is to retain sympathy for those who struggle to overcome seemingly easy imperfections. *"Who is it that has corrupted my vineyard? ... Is it not the loftiness of thy vineyard – have not the branches thereof overcome the roots which are good? And because the branches have overcome the roots thereof, behold they grew faster than the strength of the roots, taking strength unto themselves. Behold, I say, is not this the cause that the trees of thy vineyard have become corrupted?"*[28]

The process of approaching perfection naturally makes one more acutely alert to how sins manifest. This improved consciousness of sins and mistakes is one of the initial and necessary stages of repentance. However, by improving an awareness of our own sins, we concurrently cause ourselves to catch those same distasteful traits in others. In this way the 'loftiness of the branches' may inadvertently squeeze out the strength of those struggling 'roots,' who are still learning and developing righteous habits.

Virtuosity unbuffered by humility and compassion distorts judgment. Righteous judgment always maintains meekness towards the mortal condition. It always contextualizes within the circumstances of the individual. A humble judge never loses touch with the inherent humanity of others. If we hope to be "*perfect, even as* [our] *Father which is in heaven is perfect,*"[29] our proportion of perfection must conserve sentiments towards the subjectivity in a person's difficulties. When the just measure circumstances, they do so with weights of compassion and patience for other people's imperfections.

God is approachable not repelling. As opposed to God's genuine goodness, there are those who conceal sin beneath masks of morality. Such are they "*Which say, Stand by thyself, come not near to me for I am holier than thou.*"[30] In contrast, God's virtue is vibrantly inviting. Saints establishing Zion must learn the balance between abhorring sin and embracing sinners.

---

[26] Alma 41:12, 13
[27] Galatians 6:9
[28] Jacob 5:47,48
[29] Matthew 5:48 – Originally: your
[30] Isaiah 65:5

If we are not watchful, we may fall like that ancient generation of believers who *"began to be lifted up in the pride of their eyes ... and they began to persecute those that did not believe according to their own will and pleasure."*[31]

The just abhor evil, but not at the price of abusing other's agency. Bullying bigotry and forceful coercion are not instruments of justice which refuses *"to infringe upon the rights and liberties of others."* In like manner, the just *"do not believe that human law has a right to interfere in prescribing rules of worship to bind the consciences of men, nor dictate forms for public or private devotion; that the civil magistrate should restrain crime, but never control conscience; should punish guilt, but **never suppress the freedom of the soul**."*[32]

Even though the self-righteous are quick to utter disgust against sinners, they cannot keep pace with sinners accusing good men to be self-righteous. Since darkness cringes at the appearance of light it is easier for the wicked to insult and tear down the good in others, than it is for them to come to terms with their own transgressions. Instead of elevating their own standards, the wicked find it easier to soothe their conscience by sinking others down to their level. Maybe this is one reason why the devil *"seeketh that all men might be miserable like unto himself."*[33] As the leading proponent of this timeless trap, perhaps some part of Hell clings to belief that justification can come with numbers.

When correction is given, even if it seems unwarranted, it is undoubtedly to our benefit to give a critic's intentions the benefit of the doubt. One should not assume ego behind every rebuke, for counsel does not necessarily connote conceit. Admonition is not automatically arrogance, nor is instruction always evidence of condescension. *"Woe unto them that call evil good, and good evil; that put darkness for light, and light for darkness; that put bitter for sweet, and sweet for bitter."* Woe unto them who *"*[condemn] *the righteous because of their righteousness."*[34] As you make your daily judgments, know that denying unrighteousness is not an indication of grandiosity, sharing advice is not always smug, nor is preaching a predictable indicator of pride.

Philosophizing, theorizing and debate are dead devices so long as they fail to bring judgment in some form of a somatic decision. The weight of justice standing amidst love's other qualities is illustrated in the initial pre-mortal conflict between Lucifer and the Father. The record states,

---

[31] Alma 4:8
[32] D&C 134:4 – Emphasis added
[33] 2 Nephi 2:27
[34] Helaman 7:5 – Brackets added – Originally: condemning

"*Wherefore ... Satan rebelled against me, and sought to destroy the agency of man.*"[35] What clever tactic could possibly be employed so as to destroy an eternal divine spirit's power of choice?

By what method could one uproot the godly seed of free will from an individual? The veil silences these memories. Nevertheless, our understanding of this cataclysmic issue is crucial, for Satan's objectives may be more fixed than we realize. He too may be the same yesterday, today and forever. Satan who "*drew the third part of the starts of heaven,*"[36] has not ceased his despicable slander today. His tactics and agendas have not changed. And so we ponder, in what ways does Satan continue his work to destroy our agency today? Though there are few details written about the "*war in heaven,*"[37] we can see Satan displaying his seductive schemes on a daily basis.

Satan, "*the enemy of all righteousness*"[38] utilizes two main strategies to steal man's agency. Most of us are aware of the first device, which is an upfront assault on our autonomy. Here, through means of addiction, oppression, dictatorship, manipulation, and slavery "*the devil* [grasps mankind] *with his everlasting chains.*"[39] These methods are recognizable in the familiar premise that Satan works to take away man's agency by forcing our actions. However, tyrannical forces may restrict action and compel one to making certain decisions, but these can only corral not control our reactions. These methods limit freedom and free will, but they do not destroy it.

It is written that Satan said "*send me, I will be thy son, and I will redeem all mankind, that one soul shall not be lost.*"[40] Some have supposed this sinister assertion is a proposition to force people to be and act good. Yet it is difficult to imagine that something so conspicuously diabolical would deceive spirits dwelling in the presence of the Holy Father. Also a campaign could not have run on a platform of force and control because these methods fail to fully eliminate man's agency.

If coercion could not guarantee 'that one soul shall not be lost,' what is the alternative? Seeing that agency could not be ruined by oppression, Satan perhaps devised a more devilish scheme, one with a superiorly destructive outcome. Here we see the topic of justice present itself as the premiere issue divided Satan from God.

---

[35] Moses 4:3 –
[36] Revelation 12:4
[37] Revelation 12:7 – "And there was war in heaven: Michael and his angels fought against the dragon; and the dragon fought and his angels"
[38] See Moroni 9:6
[39] 2 Nephi 28:19 – Brackets added – Originally: grasps them
[40] Moses 4:1

Men do not frequently free fall down to Hell. No, the path into the fiery pit is typically a passive and pampered promenade. As we observe Satan slyly and slowly stripping men of their divinity, we wonder if Lucifer's plight to perdition was equally as subtle. Perhaps this *"son of the morning"* [41] was not initially the malicious demon consumed by enmity, hatred and wrath that he is now. Since ferocious fascism fails to finish off autonomy, what if justice were corrupted in the opposite direction? Could compassion and mercy be construed to become that pernicious weapon employed to eradicate the *"agency of man?"* [42]

The Apostle Paul gives us hints toward the meaning of the cryptic scripture, *"Satan ... sought to destroy the agency of man,"* [43] stating, *"where no law is, there is no transgression."* [44] The Prophet Alma further expounded on this idea saying,

> *"Now, repentance could not come unto men except there were a punishment ... which also was eternal as the life of the soul should be ... Now, how could a man repent except he should sin? How could he sin if there was no law? How could there be a law save there was a punishment? Now, if there was no law given – if a man murdered he should die – would he be afraid he would die if he should murder? And also, if there was no law given against sin men would not be afraid to sin. And if there was no law given, if men sinned what could justice do, or mercy either, for they would have no claim upon the creature?"* [45]

Could it be that excessive compassion crushes choice? Mercy may not only rob justice, but it may also rob righteousness, morality, and virtue. At first glance the notion that 'all mankind will be redeemed, that one soul shall not be lost,' seems harmless. The sound of this gospel is treacherously delightful, its taste deceitfully sweet and its feel deceptively snug.

Though men may still act and react to that which acts upon him, without the moral construct of justice establishing laws backed by punishments, there may be circumstantial choices but no **moral agency**. If there isn't a system of morality completed with consequence, then there is no real moral agency. All choices equaling the same result and leading to

---

[41] Isaiah 14:12 – "How are thou fallen from heaven, O Lucifer, son of the morning! Art thou cut down to the ground, which did weaken the nations!"
[42] D&C 93:31 – "Behold, here is the agency of man, and here is the condemnation of man; because that which was from the beginning is plainly manifest unto them and they receive not the light."
[43] Moses 4:3
[44] Romans 4:15
[45] Alma 42:16-23

the same destination, makes the actual act of choosing nothing more than an illusion. *"And if ye shall say there is no law, ye shall also say there is no sin. If ye shall say there is no sin, ye shall also say there is no righteousness. And if there be no righteousness there be no happiness. And if there be no righteousness nor happiness there be no punishment nor misery. And if these things are not there is no God … wherefore, all things must have vanished away."*[46] Therefore beware of those selling mercy without justice, because real and divine love must contain both parts.

"Do ye suppose that mercy can rob justice? I say unto you, Nay; not one whit. If so God would cease to be God."[47] When consequences are rendered inert by mercy, man cannot chose between good and evil, because there is no evil or good to choose from. How could man 'become as God,' *"to know good and evil,"*[48] if there is no good or evil to select between? As paradoxical as it appears, absolute freedom from consequences utterly destroys freedom of choice. Such is why *"it must needs be, that there is an opposition in all things. If not so … righteousness could not be brought to pass, neither wickedness, neither holiness nor misery, neither good nor bad. Wherefore all things must needs be a compound in one … having no life neither death, nor corruption nor incorruption, happiness nor misery, neither sense nor insensibility."*[49] Without law, justice, and judgment, the balance between virtues is lost; *"God would cease to be God"*[50] and all things would become a compound in one – a conglomerate collection of chaos.

This war of 'principalities and powers,'[51] wages on today. More often, with compassion than oppression, and with mercy than malice does *"the devil cheateth* [men's] *souls, and leadeth them away carefully down to hell."*[52] Hiding inside the superficial slogan that 'all we need is love' is the devilish desire to undo justice. The Prophet Nephi uncloaks this damnable doctrine saying, *"and behold others* [Satan] *flattereth away, and telleth them there is no hell."*[53] Of course, saying that there is no Hell is a little too strong to take in at first, so instead the Devil spoon feeds us bite sized portions of declaring 'I'm saved, I'm saved.'

How nice it must be to squeeze this inanimate plush, teddy-bear

---

[46] 2 Nephi 2:13
[47] Alma 42:25
[48] Genesis 3:22 – "And the Lord God said, Behold, the man is become as one of us, to know good and evil"
[49] 2 Nephi 2:11
[50] See Alma 42 – "Now the work of justice could not be destroyed; if so, God would cease to be God."
[51] See Ephesians 6:12 – "For we wrestle not against flesh and blood, but against principalities, against powers, against the rulers of the darkness of this world, against spiritual wickedness in high places."
[52] 2 Nephi 28:21 – Originally: their
[53] 2 Nephi 28:22 – Brackets added

deity which soothingly testifies, *"that all mankind should be saved at the last day, and that they need not fear nor tremble, but that they might lift up their heads and rejoice; for the Lord had created all men, and had also redeemed all men; and, in the end, all men should have eternal life."*[54] But disciples mustn't let this inconspicuous con mitigate morality. Nor should it make men justify their crimes saying, *"Eat, drink, and be merry; nevertheless, fear God–he will justify in committing a little sin; yea, lie a little, take the advantage of one because of his words, dig a pit for thy neighbor; there is no harm in this; and do all these things, for tomorrow we die, and if it so be that we are guilty, God will beat us with a few stripes, and at last we shall be saved in the kingdom of God."*[55] This profane gospel is not exclusively spoken to lawless atheists, nor is solely sold over the counters of confused Christians; this hellacious teaching is insidiously offered to Christ's saints just as it is marketed to heretics.

Sin is more than an innocent difference of opinion. Prideful disobedience arrogantly asserts itself onto the throne of the Almighty. Those who would rebel against God's government, presume to usurp the presiding reign of God and rule in His stead. The scriptures say, *"That which breaketh a law, and abideth not by law, but seeketh to become a law unto itself, and willeth to abide in sin, and altogether abideth in sin, cannot be sanctified by law, neither by mercy, justice, nor judgment. Therefore, they must remain filthy still."*[56] Beware lest Satan beguile you to softly slight accountability, for if he is successful it will not be long till every preference becomes permissible.

Perhaps the most practical topic pertaining to justice is that of judging. Passing judgment is no small issue since Christ taught, *"Judge not, that ye be not judged."*[57] Nevertheless, this plain prohibition becomes very problematic when we try to unravel what it means to judge. How can we successfully heed the warning to 'judge not,' without a concrete definition of what it means to judge another person?

The problem related to the word *judge*, is that the word covers everything from innocent decisions to everlasting condemnation. Also, we cannot resolve this riddle by avoiding all forms of judgment because Christ also taught, *"Judge not unrighteously ... but judge righteous judgment."*[58] The partial paradox here is plain to see – somehow we must *"judge righteous judgment"* whilst *"judging not."* As we look past this supposed contradiction, we arrive back to that simple task to distinguish between unrighteous and

---

[54] Alma 1:4
[55] 2 Nephi 28:8
[56] D&C 88:35
[57] Matthew 7:1
[58] John 7:24 – Judge not according to the appearance, but judge righteous judgment."

righteous forms of judgment.

What does it mean to judge? Judgment is most commonly descriptive of act of making choices. Both our current terminology and the scriptures use the word judgment synonymously with decision. Such is the case when Peter said, "*Whether it be right in the sight of God to hearken unto you more than unto God, judge ye.*"[59] Judgment occurs when one consciously activates their agency. Every action and choice we make is a judgment of some sort. Within a standard morning a person will judge it better to go to work than to slough out. They judge one meal for breakfast to be preferable or healthier than another. They judge whether to brush their teeth, arrive on time, say morning prayers, drive the speed limit and so on. Whether a choice is of moral stature or mortal necessity, as long as we are alive we "*judgeth all things.*"[60]

Another type of judgment takes place within the context of naming and labeling. We can label these judgments – discernment. With judgments of discernment, we classify our surroundings. We categorize and distinguish objects, people, and thoughts in order to give them an identity. Names do need not to be negative in order to be considered judgments.

To look at another human being and say, 'this is good person' is to label or judge that person to be good. In like manner, we may judge a stranger to be kind or scary. We may see them as helpful, smart, strange, trustworthy, or as scoundrels. Whatever final description we acknowledge is a judgment. Notably, this form of judgment considerably influences the way we interact with things and people. Though some discernments are neutral, there are those that cross over into the moral plane. Ultimately, with this type of judgment we sift right from wrong, good from evil and discern between the two.

Aside from the softer forms of judgment – decision and discernment – judgment can also connote a complete and conclusive condemnation. The best example embodying the essence of condemnation is the last judgment, the day when "*all nations and tongues shall stand before God, to be judged of their works, whether they be good or whether they be evil.*"[61] It is the totality of the final judgment that makes it one of condemnation as opposed to one of examination. This form of judgment seems a suitable context for James's words, *"There is one lawgiver, who is able to save and destroy:*

---

[59] Acts 4:19 – See also Ether 5:6 – "And now, if I have no authority for these things, judge ye"
[60] 1 Corinthians 2:15 – Greek word used for judge is anakrino – means to judge, examine, investigate or discern.
[61] 3 Nephi 26:4

who art thou that judgest another?" [62]

The full spectrum of judgment, from choice to condemnation is seen in the Greek language of the New Testament. The scripture to *"judge not"* is a translation of the Greek word *krino*.[63] In most cases *krino* is rightfully translated *to decide, distinguish or choose*; whereas the most common word translated as *condemn* is *katakrino*.[64] For example, *katakrino* is used by Christ when spoke to the woman taken in adultery, *"Hath no man condemned thee? She said, No man Lord. And Jesus said unto her, Neither do I condemn thee: go, and sin no more."*[65] Though *katakrino* is the preferred term for conveying condemnation, there are a few instances where *krino* is used to denote condemnation. For example *krino* is used instead of *katakrino* in the scripture, *"For God sent not his Son into the world to condemn the world; but that the world through him might be saved."*[66]

If *katakrino* had been the word used in the directive to *"judge not,"* all these semantical problems could have been avoided. Instead, we are left to decipher the meaning of the word *judge* from the word *krino*; which again means – to decide, distinguish or choose, but in some cases is rendered as condemn. However, if the standard definition of *krino* is interpreted in Christ's admonition to *"judge not,"* there is no sensible way to reconcile it with the conflicting statement to *"judge righteous judgment."* Not only this, but it is both absurd and impossible to think that we could abstain from all judgments of choice, decision, or examination. To do so would contradict the purpose of our entire existence.

Even placing discernment into the meaning of 'judging not' renders the verse a scriptural contradiction; for we have been sent to this earth to distinguish right from wrong and good from the evil.[67] In order to *"choose liberty and eternal life through the great Mediator of all men,"*[68] we have to spiritually and cognitively pass judgments that separate the light from the dark.

Since the lighter forms of judgment are unsuitable semantical

---

[62] James 4:12
[63] Greek Strong's Dictionary #2919 –(Kree'-no)– Related to the term Krisis (#2920 – Kree'-sis) which means to investigate, to distinguish or separate. Krisis is translated as judgment, condemnation, damnation & accusation.
[64] Greek Strong's Dictionary #2632 –(kat-ak-ree'-no) build from the works kata- which can mean distribution or intensity, and krino which is defined above. Katakrino means to damn, condemn or pass sentence.
[65] John 8:10,11 – Emphasis added
[66] John 3:17 – Emphasis added
[67] See Moses 6:55,56 – "and they taste the bitter, that they may know to prize the good. And it is given unto them to know good and evil; wherefore they are agents unto themselves, and I have given unto you another law and commandment."
[68] 2 Nephi 2:27 – "they are free to choose liberty & eternal life … or to choose captivity & death"

categories for the declaration to 'judge not, that ye be not judged,' we ironically judge that this verse is warning us not to condemn others. The most descriptive and worrisome feature of condemnation is its permanence. Mortality makes men malleable. It allows people to change their disposition and make continual corrections to their character. It is imperative to believe that any person has the potential for complete transformation. Seeing that we are dependent on the doctrine of perpetual progression, why would we ever place a rigid stamp on someone's person?

Squeezing an eternal judgment into a mortal timeframe decrepitly deforms the practice of justice. In order for one to continue to breathe, they must let go of the first breath. Similarly, those who hold on to past judgments will surely suffocate. Our judgments must always leave space for forgiveness. They must always reserve room for repentance. A justice which closes itself off to the variable of repentance creates a condemnation which inhibits others, and brings condemnation to ourselves. Therefore, *"Judge not, and ye shall not be judged: condemn not, and ye shall not be condemned."*[69]

Carnal condemnations tend to be quick. Likewise they are uncompassionate and outright unkind. Be careful then, for if your measurement of men is recklessly inconsiderate, then this *"measure ye mete, it shall be measured unto you again."*[70] Though correcting others doesn't automatically imply that we are condemning them, we should regard the directive to *"judge righteous judgment,"* with the same caution we would show towards radioactive materials. When it is our role to be a judge on earth, we should exhort with humility, counsel with kindness and reprove with empathy.

Unfortunately, the familiar childhood rhyme is untrue: though sticks and stones certainly break bones, hurtful words can cause as much chronic and troublesome trauma than literal weapons. Unrighteous judgments can crush a person's spirit, as "the stroke of the whip maketh marks in the flesh ... the stroke of the tongue breaketh the bones."[71] As we try to be cognizant of these cautions, we should apply the wisdom of F. Enzio Buche who said, "Never judge anyone. When you accept this, you will be freed. In the case of your own children or subordinates, where you have the responsibility to judge, help them to become their own judges."[72]

When it is your lot to speak what would be considered harsh truth,

---

[69] Luke 6:37
[70] Matt 7:2
[71] Ecclesiasticus 28:17
[72] Busche, F. Enzio. "Unleashing the Dormant Spirit." from a BYU Devotional May 14, 1996

'speak the truth in love.'[73] When counsel is necessary; hold fast to the word which says, "*Reproving betimes with sharpness, when moved upon by the Holy Ghost; and then showing forth afterwards an increase of love toward him whom thou hast reproved, lest he esteem thee to be his enemy.*"[74] In life you will have to judge and make judgments. Every day you will analyze, discern and decide. These choices can categorize and judge our own self and the people around us. Therefore, in order to judge righteous judgment, one should check and recheck their intentions before speaking any reprimand. If you are not positive that your judgment is centered in love, the admonition should be withheld. A judgment unmotivated by love should always be deferred. This is also true in regards to our relationship with ourself. We must insure we have a motivation of self-love guiding all feelings of guilt and self-consciousness.

Remember that God's "*justice could not be destroyed; if so, God would cease to be God.*"[75] Such is why "*thou art not excusable in thy transgression,*"[76] for the Lord "*cannot look upon sin with the least degree of allowance.*"[77] Therefore, "*Deny the justice of God no more. Do not endeavor to excuse yourself in the least point because of your sins, by denying the justice of God; but … let the justice of God, and his mercy, and his longsuffering have full sway in your heart; and let it bring you down to the dust in humility.*"[78] "*See that you are merciful unto your brethren; deal justly, judge righteously, and do good continually; and if ye do all these things then shall ye receive your reward; yea, ye shall have mercy restored unto you again; ye shall have justice restored unto you again; ye shall have a righteous judgment restored unto you again; and ye shall have good rewarded unto you again.*"[79]

---

[73] See Ephesians 4:15 – "But speaking the truth in love, may grow up into him all things, which is the head, even Christ:"
[74] D&C 121:43
[75] Alma 42:13
[76] D&C 24:2
[77] D&C 1:31
[78] Alma 42:30
[79] Alma 41:14

Wisdom

Wisdom is the balance of virtue. "*The LORD possessed* [Wisdom] *in the beginning of his way, before his works of old.* [*Wisdom*] *was set up from everlasting, from the beginning, or ever the earth was ... Before the mountains were settled, before the hills was* [Wisdom] *brought forth.*"[1] Wisdom is not contained in a word. Though we use words to communicate wisdom, true wisdom transcends the tongue.

"*We speak the wisdom of God in a mystery, even the hidden wisdom, which God ordained before the world unto our glory.*"[2] God is the source of wisdom. His subtle secrets are sent in the whisperings of His Spirit. Therefore, submission to God is the center of wisdom. "*The fear of the LORD is the beginning of wisdom: and the knowledge of the holy is understanding.*"[3] But it is hard to hear the Spirit over the sound of our own voice. Ego and uncontrolled desire disrupt our reception of God's counsel. To see with wisdom one must discard their own disposition; for biases become barriers to the Spirit and must be expelled to free our views.

Pride will wear a soul out chasing praise. Lust is insatiable and will never be content. In contrast the wise are fed with forbearance. They are nurtured with temperance. God 'enriches all things;'[4] He is always giving, yet never feels empty. To be truly free, we must cut the strings of selfishness which strangle our spirits. Then after gluttony is gone and lust eliminated, we are fit to be an instrument of God. The Spirit of God will then move upon you and He will give you words, He will give you wisdom, He will give you love.

Herein is wisdom: "*the light of Christ ... Which light proceedeth forth from the presence of God to fill the immensity of space – The light which is in all things, which giveth life to all things, which is the law by which all things are governed.*"[5] God has placed us an internal law within our souls to guide us. This law, which is the light of Christ, brings us an understanding of how to govern all things in life. Life is set in motion; seasons and situations are ever changing. So long as one's heart is set on the things of this world, it will be in commotion – it will never rest; for "*there is no peace, saith the LORD unto the wicked.*"[6]

---

[1] Proverbs 8:22,23,25
[2] 1 Corinthians 2:7
[3] Proverbs 9:10
[4] See 1 Corinthians 1:5
[5] D&C 88:7,12,13
[6] Isaiah 48:22

Therefore, let *"the solemnities of eternity rest upon your minds"*[7] and *"the peace of God, which passeth all understanding, shall keep your hearts and minds through Christ Jesus."*[8]

The principle of love is built from an assortment of paradoxes. Virtues are held in place by counter-balancing virtues. When this balance is lost, virtue can become vice. Wisdom maintains the balance between the virtues. It upholds justice with mercy. It builds confidence from the foundation of humility and completes kindness with correction. *"For it must needs be, that there is an opposition in all things. If not so ... righteousness could not be brought to pass, neither wickedness, neither holiness nor misery, neither good nor bad. Wherefore, all things must needs be a compound in one; wherefore, if it should be one body it must needs remain as dead, having no life neither death, nor corruption nor incorruption, happiness nor misery, neither sense nor insensibility."*[9] No virtue is strong enough to stand alone. Godliness finds perfection in the interplay between all the righteous principles, which are ultimately *"complete in him, which is the head of all principality and power."*[10]

The pattern observed in paradoxical principles is similar to the seasons of the earth. Our planet spins cycles of death and rebirth, loss and life, want and gain, decay and growth, progress and decline. *"And again, verily I say unto you, he hath given a law unto all things, by which they move in their times and their seasons"*[11] *"And he changeth the times and the seasons: he removeth kings, and setteth up kings: he giveth wisdom unto the wise, and knowledge to them that know understanding."*[12]

"To everything there is a season, and a time to every purpose under the heaven: A time to be born, and a time to die; a time to plant, and a time to pluck up that which is planted; A time to kill, and a time to heal; a time to break down, and a time to build up; A time to cast away stones, and a time to gather stones together; A time to get, and a time to lose; a time to keep, and a time to cast away; A time to love and a time to hate; a time of war, and a time of peace."[13] In wisdom we find the balance.

Similarly there is a time to be gentle and a time to be firm, a time to teach and a time to encourage, a time to praise and a time to preach. There is a time for compassion and a time for correction; a time for compliment and a time to critique, a time to hold on and a time to let go, a time to distribute and a time to retain. *"A time to rend, and a time to sew; a time to keep*

---

[7] D&C 43:34
[8] Philippians 4:7
[9] 2 Nephi 2:11
[10] Colossians 2:10
[11] D&C 88:42
[12] Daniel 2:21
[13] Excerpts from Ecclesiastes 3:1-8

silence, and a time to speak."[14] Wisdom is the balance.

There is a time for seriousness and a time for silliness; a time to be stoic and a time to smile, *"a time to embrace, and a time to refrain from embracing,"*[15] *"A time to weep, and a time to laugh; a time to mourn, and a time to dance;"*[16] *"If thou art merry, praise the Lord with singing, with music, with dancing, and with a prayer of praise and thanksgiving. If thou art sorrowful, call on the Lord thy God with supplication, that your souls may be joyful."*[17] There is a time to be spritely and a time to be sober; a time to be meek and a time to be militant, there is a time to stand up and stand your ground as well as a time to stand down. There is a time to flee and a time to fight. God has all wisdom; in Him we find the balance.

There is a time to ponder and a time to prepare; a time for reflection and a time for action, a time to work and a time to relax. There is a time for mercy and a time for justice; a time to rush and a time to pause, a time to be reserved and a time to be rash. There is a time for reason and a time for passion, a time for curiosity and a time for caution, a time for prudence and a time to be impulsive. God grant you the wisdom to know the balance.

Man exhibits such a vast expanse of behaviors. A paradoxical mixture of emotions stirs our souls and is completely tossed into turmoil by time. Is all aggression evil? Is submissiveness cowardly or is saintly? So many of the feelings inside mankind are not inherently evil; rather, they are untempered traits of Deity. *"To everything there is a season, and a time to every purpose under the heaven."* The situational 'seasons' form the scales which God uses to measure man's motivations. Wisdom keeps the poise amidst paradoxical principles. It establishes an equilibrium between all the Godly attributes. Wisdom is to know the balance of virtues; it is to know the *"times and their seasons."*[18] Oh then, how much more vile are lies and vengeance, for there is never a season for man to manifest such evil.

We should not understate the value of wisdom; for it is written, *"wisdom is better than rubies; and all the things that may be desired are not to be compared to it."*[19] Despite the widespread utility of wisdom, most people settle for comprehending it superficially. For many, wisdom resides in a museum where it can be appreciated but not purchased. It is observed but

---

[14] Ecclesiastes 3:7
[15] Ecclesiastes 3:5
[16] Ecclesiastes 3:4
[17] D&C 136:28,29
[18] D&C 88:44 – "And they give light to each other in their times and in their seasons, in their minutes, in their hours, in their days, in their weeks, in their months, in their years"
[19] Proverbs 8:11

not owned; studied in books but not assimilated. If we truly desire this gift, we must know that true wisdom is not cerebral understanding, it is choice, obedience and action.

An important precept of wisdom is to see that many of life's decisions do not really matter since they have no eternal significance. Wise men have labeled these choices – decisions of preference, because they are of no moral consequence. The final words of the Prophet Ether express this wisdom. He says, "*Whether the Lord will that I be translated, or that I suffer the will of the Lord in the flesh,* **it mattereth not***, if it so be that I am saved in the kingdom of God.*"[20] When weighed against salvation and eternity's infinite spread, many of our daily choices rightfully appear trivial. This doesn't imply that these types of decisions are not pressing or difficult, for when they are presented to us, they can feel tremendously heavy. Yet there are times when whether you decide to go "*to the north or to the south, to the east or to the west,* **it mattereth not***, for ye cannot go amiss.*"[21]

Within the boundaries of His commandments, God gives our preferences plenty of wiggle room. Some may wonder where they should go to college, what field of work they should pursue, who they should befriend, date or help. Though these examples appear extremely significant, so long as the choice does not interfere with our progress toward salvation, the course we choose may not matter at all. Yes, there are exceptions to this principle. God can and does overturn this rule to give us special directives regarding seemingly mundane decisions. However, it requires great wisdom to recognize those occasions when the Lord guides us saying, "*And it mattereth not unto me, after a little, if it so be that they fill their mission, whether they go by water or by land; let this be as it is made known unto them according to their judgments hereafter.*"[22]

Throughout the scriptures, the topic of wisdom frequently asserts itself into the topic of correction. Though the common cure to correction is humility, because mankind struggles with this matter so much, it is given additional emphasis through the principle of wisdom.

The book of Proverbs addresses how we receive counsel multiple times with statements such as, "*fools despise wisdom and instruction,*"[23] "*Reprove not a scorner, lest he hate thee: rebuke a wise man, and he will love thee. Give instruction to a wise man, and he will be yet wiser: teach a just man, and he will increase in*

---

[20] Ether 15:34 – Emphasis added
[21] D&C 80:3 – Emphasis added – "Wherefore go ye and preach my gospel, whether to the north or to the south, to the east or to the west, it mattereth not, for ye cannot go amiss."
[22] D&C 61:22
[23] Proverbs 1:7

learning,"[24] "*take fast hold of instruction; let her not go: keep her; for she is thy life,*"[25] "*open rebuke is better than secret love.*"[26]

Sociality inescapably leads to fierce collisions of cultural and personal perspectives. When opinions crash into one another at such deadly speeds, wisdom diffuses rather than detonates potentially explosive situations. If we hope to avoid these conflicts, we will need to overcome the adolescent whine which shouts in recalcitrance – 'you can't tell me what to do.' Similarly, we will have to eradicate the heinous howl of 'it is my life; I can do whatever I want.' Together these abhorrent attitudes constitute the essence of foolishness. This mindset of impish immaturity is neither cute nor innocent; instead, it is a gross indication of damning pride. "*The way of a fool is right in his own eyes: but he that hearkeneth unto counsel is wise.*"[27]

Just as we are to receive counsel, we are also expected to give appropriate counsel. As it is often our duty "*to warn, expound, exhort, and teach,*"[28] we should be able "*also to admonish one another.*"[29] Withholding needed correction can come at great consequence to individuals and societies. We all need to have the humility to discuss our individual and collective weaknesses, if we want any hope of improving them. Even though all correction may not be correct, we must develop the meekness to give all instruction sincere consideration. As the proverb states, "*A wise man will hear, and will increase learning; and a man of understanding shall attain unto wise counsels.*"[30] Rather than making reproof a rock of offense, the wise climb up correction as a ladder of learning. For the wise, critique becomes the weight bearing boulder for climbing to new and greater heights.

Plain truths are preferable to hidden lies – especially secret resentments. Still, offering advice is an extremely delicate issue, for whenever one gives advice there can be an underlying assumption that their understanding or judgment is correct or better. Because of this underlying assumption it is easy to manipulate all reproofs to appear prideful. When giving advice we should strive to bridle our biases and impulsive and reflexive chastisements. Counsel should be the result of well pondered compassion. When correction is to be given, let it be given with the

---

[24] Proverbs 9:8,9
[25] Proverbs 4:13
[26] Proverbs 27:5
[27] Proverbs 12:15
[28] D&C 20:59 – "They are, however, to warn, expound, exhort, and teach, and invite all to come unto Christ."
[29] Romans 15:14 – "that ye also are full of goodness, filled with all knowledge, able also to admonish one another."
[30] Proverbs 1:5

approval of the Spirit of God.

Another prominent theme pertaining to wisdom is the definition of wisdom itself. A useful definition of wisdom is found in the instructive truism that, 'wisdom is the correct application of knowledge.' Wisdom is much more than just knowing a lot of facts and information. The domain of applying knowledge is the world of action. Thus, wisdom is ultimately about making the right choices and actions.

In its fullness, wisdom calculates the summation of truth, which includes every 'sphere of truth.'[31] Divine wisdom can discern every proper application of truth pertaining to every possible scenario. Because wisdom covers such an immense scope of circumstance and morality, only an omniscient mind could manage such a task. As we attempt to maneuver through a world of choices, it is not possible for man with his limitations to account for every scenario, variable, perspective and person.

Maintaining the balance of virtues weighs in on our individual and phenomenological climate. The breadth of wisdom is so vast that it isn't feasible to cover every wise practical decision. Since a fullness of wisdom can only be wielded with omniscience, what can we realistically do with this principle? We cannot tediously compose an encyclopedia of the do's and don'ts of decision. However, we are given some instructional guidelines to help us correctly apply the limited knowledge that we have.

In order to obtain wisdom, one must be securely grounded in truth – the *"knowledge of things as they are, and as they were, and as they are to come."*[32] Yet, our own subjectivity distorts our perception of truth. Our mind and heart can and often betray us. Rational thinking and logic are successful instruments for certain situations, but they are not infallible. Sometimes our own intelligence can be the vice that frustrates wisdom. Not only this, but our emotions commonly mislead us. The capricious hormonal winds of the human heart are ever blowing storms of contradictions of oscillating certainties. Passion has its place as well as rational thinking, but where is wisdom amidst these opposing voices? As long as biases of mind or heart blur our vision we will not 'see things as they really are,' instead we will see things only as they appear to us. So how do we escape this dilemma?

The only cure for self-contaminating subjectivity is the power of the Holy Spirit. *"Let him that is ignorant learn wisdom by humbling himself and calling upon the Lord his God, that his eyes may be opened that he may see, and his ears opened that he may hear."* [33] Though the enormity of wisdom escapes us, we

---

[31] D&C 93:30 – "All truth is independent in that sphere in which God has placed it"
[32] D&C 93:24
[33] D&C 136:32

can access omniscience through the all-knowing mind of the Holy Ghost. Truth transcends our senses. It transcends our intelligence. It transcends our emotions and partiality. Were it not for the undefiled vantage point provided by God's Spirit, we would never be able to escape the quandary created by our mortal limitation. With God's power we are capable of overcoming our mortal tunnel vision. Then with inspiring touch of the Spirit, we peak into the infinity of Eternal truths. All truth and wisdom are predicated on the revelation of the Holy Spirit. For this reason, it is abundantly emphasized that the *"fear of the Lord is the beginning of wisdom."*[34]

Creeping into Christianity is a curious trend to depict the third member of the Godhead as some sort of deviant deity. Some speak of the Holy Ghost as an insubordinate Spirit; one who thrives off granting exceptions to the spiritual laws established by the Eternal Father. This portrait of a rebellious divinity who emerges from the dark alleys of the Celestial Kingdom, wearing dark shades and a leather jacket, selling us special immunities needs to be refined. Somewhere along the way the word may have been lost in translation that said, the *"Father, Son, and Holy Ghost are one God, infinite and eternal, without end."*[35]

If you *"withdraw yourselves from the Spirit of the Lord, that it may have no place in you,"* it will not be able *"to guide you in wisdom's paths that ye may be blessed, prospered, and preserved."*[36] As the medium between man and God, the Spirit is our main access point to the Divine and His will. Through the Holy Ghost we are given direct access to God's omniscient mind. Nevertheless, the supreme intelligence of the Father, Son, and the Holy Ghost are not solely responsible for wisdom. The wisdom of the Eternal Godhead is the result of their endless love.

The scales of wisdom are upheld by love. We find wisdom when our actions are motivated by love. It is love that perfects the balance of justice and mercy. When love guides our actions humility and self-confidence are practiced in their proper proportions. When there is love, all service is completed in *"wisdom and order."* God's love brings every virtue and attribute of the divine nature in symmetrical harmony with one another. Though we may not have perfect knowledge, wisdom, or love, if we are filled with God's Spirit, we may through this association access and exude God's eternal perfection.

Discernment is rarely an easy task. The scriptures recognize that choices can be extremely difficult stating, *"you cannot always judge the righteous,*

---

[34] Psalms 11:10 and Proverbs 9:10
[35] D&C 20:28
[36] Mosiah 2:36

or as you cannot always tell the wicked from the righteous."³⁷ Even after great efforts, sometimes the path ahead is still not clear-cut. Times will certainly come when we are backed into a corner and constrained to discern between subtle shades of righteousness. Within the sphere of our circumstances, we will be required to practice and develop our own capacity for wisdom. We will find God during these times? We will at the very least strive to bring our minds single to the glory of God? What will you do if the challenge changes from separating light from darkness to selecting light from light? How will you decide between friendship and faith, mercy or justice, compassion or correction? How will you prepare every good and needful thing amidst paradox, irony and uncertainty?

Of all the paradoxical principles, we are most familiar with the conflict between justice and mercy. In real life, most of us have graduated from the days of deciding between justice and vengeance and cruelty. More often our lot is to determine whether justice or mercy is the will of the Lord. Life has been designed to intentionally test our ability to manage the mixture of moral principles. Somehow we must learn to balance all the divine dichotomous traits. We must work to create the equilibrium between those pious principles that are oppositely fixed.

For example, how should one correctly respond to a child who has been caught cheating? What measure of mercy and justice should this situation be treated with? The was each specific situation is set up has the potential to sour seemingly good gifts. This can be observed in the story of Job. After Job's devastating afflictions, his friends mistakenly chose chastisement over charity. They chose correction over compassion. During this period of grief, it was told to Job, "*Behold, happy is the man whom God correcteth: therefore despise not thou the chastening of the Almighty.*"³⁸ To what normally could be considered true and useful counsel, Job responded, "*To him that is afflicted pity should be shewed from his friend.*"³⁹ Sometimes failing to find the proper balance of principles makes virtue appear villainous. Therefore, "*See that all these things are done in wisdom and order.*"⁴⁰

When individuals or societies improperly emphasize certain principles, they run into serious problems. Such decisions are not necessarily diabolical, just unwise. However, if learning how to balance our

---

[37] D&C 10:37 – "But as you cannot always judge the righteous, or as you cannot always tell the wicked from the righteous, therefore I say unto you, hold your peace until I shall see fit to make all things known un the world concerning the matter."
[38] Job 5:17
[39] Job 6:14
[40] Mosiah 4:27

morals was insignificant, God might have left these experiences out of our mortal tutelage. Thus, reconciling these conundrums is as much a part of our Christian training as determining good from evil. Part of life's test is to discover balance, harmony, and order; for we must *"see that all these things are done in wisdom and order; for it is not requisite that a man should run faster than he has strength."*[41]

When we speak of balance, this does not suggest that all virtue should be utilized in equal proportions. Should confrontation be held in the same esteem as peacemaking? Humanity proves over and over again that it is unwilling to control its temper. Man strays from wisdom's path by practicing war when he should be instituting peace. The scales of wisdom esteem peacemaking greater than war. Yet it will wage war, when it is necessary. Culturally, cries for justice are sounding louder and more frequent. Yet no one thinks it strange that talk of justice is hushed as we approach the reckoning of our lives. Our civilization is getting swallowed by floods of litigation. Demands for an eye of reparation, and a tooth of compensation are utterly crushing the virtue of mercy. If we have any hope of finding *"wisdom and order,"* the work of mercy must increase.

The scales of wisdom continue to need tilting toward being kind and complimentary more than correction and rebuke. How much more is our world in need of prudence than brashness, of service than self-preservation, of gentleness than toughness? Most would do well to focus on becoming more flexible than firm. In our lives the emphasis should slant towards giving more than receiving, on listening more than talking, sharing more than stashing and service more than entertainment. The world needs less rush, fewer toys, and much less noise. We need more space for silence, pondering, connection and love.

"Let all things be done decently and in order."[42] Be compassionate, but do not smother, cherish but do not choke, serve not spoil. Be faithful without *"looking beyond the mark,"*[43] be *"as wise as serpents, and harmless as doves."*[44] The order in wisdom is honest but not harsh. It is tactful but not deceitful. It is firm but not crushing. Strive therefore to be direct without being demeaning, advise without insult, punish without pulverizing, and govern without ruling. If we are wise, we will be smart but not superior, pensive but not complacent, relaxed but not uncaring, and patient not placid. When there is wisdom there is love without lust, passion without

---

[41] Mosiah 4:27
[42] 1 Corinthians 14:40
[43] Jacob 4:14
[44] Matthew 10:16

obsession, and zeal without impulsivity.

"*Be not righteous over much; neither make thyself over wise: why shouldest thou destroy thyself.*"[45] One must learn how to stand in the spot light as well as play the part of a prop. So too we should be selfless but not ascetic, meek not masochistic, flexible not spineless, bold but not overbearing, gentle not fearful, confident not arrogant and capable not cocky. According to the wisdom of the Spirit we are to be humble but not fragile, courageous but not careless, sober but not austere, cautious not catatonic, and prudent without being prudish. The balance of wisdom is hopeful without naivety, focused without fanaticism, self-assured but not self-oriented and assertive without being pushy or selfish.

"*Finally, brethren, whatsoever things are true, whatsoever things are honest, whatsoever things are just, whatsoever things are pure, whatsoever things are lovely, whatsoever things are of good report; if there be any virtue, and if there be any praise, think on these things.*"[46] Do not allow ill will to linger. Always be ready to repent for the unbending will always be broken. To "*ascend into the hill of the Lord*"[47] one must first abase themselves in servitude. Enlarge your soul in love, "*For though I be free from all men, yet have I made myself servant unto all, that I might gain the more.*"[48]

"*Where is the wise? Where is the scribe? Where is the disputer of this world? Hath not God made foolish the wisdom of this world.*"[49] Here is wisdom – "*as ye would that men should do to you, do ye also to them likewise.*"[50] Do no harm to any man; for it is the meek who "*shall inherit the earth, and shall delight themselves in the abundance of peace.*"[51] The weak shall overcome the mighty for "*the loftiness of man shall be bowed down, and the haughtiness of men shall be made low.*"[52] Magnify your spirit by denying the flesh and you will find the freedom of obedience. "*Let us hear the conclusion of the whole matter: Fear God, and keep his commandments: for this is the whole duty of man.*"[53] "*O be wise; what can I say more?*"[54]

---

[45] Ecclesiastes 7:16
[46] Philippians 4:8
[47] Psalms 24:3 – "Who shall ascend into the hill of the Lord? Or who shall stand in his holy place?"
[48] 1 Corinthians 9:19
[49] 1 Corinthians 1:20
[50] Luke 6:31
[51] Psalms 37:11
[52] Isaiah 2:17 – "and the Lord alone shall be exalted in that day."
[53] Eccl 12:13
[54] Jacob 6:12

Honor

 The stands are vacant. There are no glaring eyes goading your actions. You are free. Free from the faces of the watchful sentinels sitting in the judgment seat. Here in these secluded segments of the Lord's vineyard, the disciple is called to labor. In this silent isolation of conscience, life's greatest battles unfold. Truth, morality, conflict and opposition make themselves known. Who will emerge victories and claim the glory and honor offered to them?

 There on the stranded field where no heralds shout his coming, the disciple provides his discreet devotion. There are none to applaud his piety. His acts will not be featured in tomorrow's headlines. His goodness will not be discussed in the morning news, nor will his sacrifice be celebrated in a prime time special. Though no praising parade sings his accomplishments, his willingness does not wane; nor does his loyalty slacken. He gives out of duty, and his duty is his pleasure. This is the disciple who walks with honor, who is "*worthy of the God who hath called him unto his kingdom and glory.*"[1]

 There was a time when a man's word was worth something, when people would say they'd do something and it would be done. "*When thou vowest a vow unto God, defer not to pay it; for he hath no pleasure in fools: pay that which thou hast vowed.*"[2] Society's standards have shifted. Acclaim is now given to schemes designed to escape obligation. Victimhood is considered virtue. The bidding for constant concessions for consecration has become so loud that talked of honor and integrity has been muted. There was a time when, "*a good name* [was] *rather to be chosen than great riches.*"[3] Today

---

[1] 1 Thessalonians 2:12 – "That ye would walk worthy of God, who hath called you unto his kingdom and glory."
[2] Ecclesiastes 5:4
[3] Proverbs 22:1 – Brackets added – Original: "A good name is rather to be chosen than great riches"

civilization's sense of duty has succumbed to a seductive side of sloth; one masquerading under a banner of freedom. However, this corrupt concept of freedom is nothing more than chaos coated in a candy shell. Without duty men lack direction. Without integrity men have no spine. Without responsibility men have no anchor, and without honor men have no merit.

What is integrity and honor? It is being true to your word. It is doing what you say you will do. Honor encompasses the valiant attributes of duty, honesty, respect, responsibility, reverence, and integrity. Honor generates glory – that presence of palpable righteousness, that tangible goodness felt in a person's presence. It is that tactile aura of power, respect and love. Though a man might obtain a lofty position, though he rules a vast empire where word of his accolades spreads from border to border, without God and love these honors are a sham – a fake, fictitious delusion.

Unfortunately, our world is more concerned with merit badges than real merit. It puts its trust in titles before truth. A person with real honor cannot be distinguished by an extravagant display of medals, certificates or trophies. Men may administer or make up merits to commend themselves for a variety of accomplishments; yet, we are mistaken if we think these trinkets will gleam against the glory of the wise, who "*shall shine as the brightness of the firmament; and they that turn many to righteousness as the stars for ever and ever.*"[4]

It is insufficient to only understand glory and honor cognitively and conceptually. Their distinct characteristics are meant to be felt. There are times when we enter the presence of people who exude glory's glow. On those occasions our spirit's sense a wholesome warmth and recognizes it as a radiating ray from the heavenly firmament. Honor speaks of God and Heaven, but glory feels like God and Heaven. Every man is endowed with a self-evident sense of honor. This component of consciences is sealed into our souls. We can observe this innate nobility working within us. It is the compelling consciousness that convinces us that indescribable significance is interlaced in our individual storyline. Though the implications of this sense are immeasurably profound, this feeling is not often an overwhelmingly momentous impression. Instead, it is soft. It is a whisper which infuses momentary memes of meaning into what superficially seems like a menial existence.

Honor generates a pure form of pride, not one of an entrapping ego, but rather a confidence created by commendations and acceptance from the Eternal Father. Man has been given an endowment of honor. We

---

[4] Daniel 12:3

all have a portion of Father's light, glory, and power placed within us – the noble birthright, a celestial essence, the unshakeable undertone of a supernal potential that accompanies those of God's progeny. Our choices either develop or deteriorate this sense of honor. We will have to choose whether to hide from these feelings or harness them. Nevertheless, regardless of the choice we make, the feeling was still assuredly there.

Where does mankind's endued nobility come from? A man's sense of honor is discovered in the immortal identity. It originates from the proclamation of the Holy Spirit saying *"we are the offspring of God!"*[5] The sense of honor is more than just comprehending who you are. It is feeling who you are. It is the spiritual feeling *"That ye may become the sons of God; that when he shall appear we shall be like him, for we shall see him as he is; that we may have this hope; that we may be purified even as he is pure."*[6]

Honor is innate in man and is therefore no respecter of persons, position, or wealth. Integrity exists in people of every social and circumstantial stratum, and such is well for understanding our true identity is a formidable shield against the adversary. We observe this doctrinal defense, reading *"And it came to pass that Moses looked upon Satan and said: Who art thou? For Behold I am a son of God, in the similitude of his Only Begotten; and where is thy glory, that I should worship thee?"*[7] Knowing yourself, your true self is paramount to protecting yourself from temptations. However, in order to fully activate this safe guard, we must understand all the implications of our eternal lineage.

True we are children of God, and *"if children, then heirs: heirs of God, and joint-heirs with Christ; if so be that we suffer with him, that we may be also glorified together."*[8] The budding possibilities of your immortal spirit include not only an exaltation in eternity, but also a magnanimity in mortality. Nonetheless, this magnificent potential must be kept in check by meekness lest pride overtake us as it did Satan, who said in his heart, *"I will ascend into heaven, I will exalt my throne above the stars of God: I will sit also upon the mount of the congregation, in the sides of the north: I will ascend above the heights of the clouds, I will be like the Most High."*[9]

Your divine nature and celestial legacy should not be the cause of arrogance or self-aggrandizement. Instead, it should instill a special ambition and self-respect. Remember also that you are deserving of an

---

[5] Acts 17:29
[6] Moroni 7:48
[7] Moses 1:13
[8] Romans 8:17
[9] See also 2 Nephi 24:14

added measure of repute; for you, who once dwelt with God are a child of promise!

Many of this current generation once stood in the midst of God and He who is like unto to Him. You of the 'chosen generation and royal priesthood'[10] were declared by the mouth of God to be *"noble and great,"*[11] a 'ruler' of righteousness. This is your identity and such is your royal responsibility. Therefore, we have considerable reason to 'hold fast to our integrity and live perfect and upright before man.'[12]

Yet, the revelation of mankind's identity is not exclusively relevant in how we see our own self. The beauty of integrity emanates from all the honorable peoples of the earth. It is a glow of goodness shining in souls all around us. Once we comprehend the holy heritage of mankind, we can detect dignity in the mundane, benevolence in the benign, prestige in the strange, and even see glory in an unglamorous face.

Our Eternal Father greatly desires to give us glory, whereas Satan is fixed on bringing us shame. Though honor is poorly portrayed by words, we can better understand honor by holding it against its loathsome antithesis – shame. Shame is the opposite of honor. It is that irksome smog that obscures a person's confidence. This foul feeling is one of the most universally distasteful sensations known to the soul. We all share memories of shame and recognize this most poignant, repulsive feeling.

Whether in a glare, a word, or regret – how such thoughts swiftly sink us! They storm the skies with thick pitch; one that clouds our hopes and dirties our dreams. Shame, that putrid muck, latches onto a heart where it feeds off of joy. Shame robs men of courage. It destroys faith and extinguishes hope. Our first reaction to shame is to run, but it doesn't leave us. We hide, but find no refuge – and though the selfsame body stands before us – a light has gone out, *"Thou art filled with shame for glory."*[13]

Over time, shame decays the sense of divinity bound to the soul and spoils man's sublime potentials. Shame is majesty soured. The once celestial spirit is now a corrupted core, a malodorous cadaver which is perpetually perturbed by rancid remorse. *"Take ye the spoil of silver, take the spoil of gold: for there is none end of the store and glory out of all the pleasant furniture.*

---

[10] See 1 Peter 2:9 – But ye are a chosen generation, a royal priesthood, an holy nation, a peculiar people"
[11] Abraham 3:22 See also D&C 138:55 – "I observed that they were also among the noble and great ones who were chosen in the beginning to be rulers in the Church of God."
[12] See Job 2:3 – "Hast thou considered my servant Job…a perfect and an upright man, one that feareth God, and escheweth evil? And he still holdeth fast his integrity, although thou movedst me against him, to destroy him"
[13] Habakkuk 2:16

She is empty, and void, and waste*: and the heart melteth, and the knees smite together ... and the faces of them all gather blackness."*[14] Misery is the fruit of shame. The devil, *"that shameful thing,"*[15] *"seeketh that all men might be miserable like unto himself."*[16] Lucifer cannot clothe us *"with robes of righteousness, with palms in our hands, and crowns of glory upon heads;"*[17] he can only shroud us with disgrace.

Integrity is a cohort to honor; these are complimentary concepts grown of the same root. Integrity rounds out all the virtues. It finishes them with a quality of completeness. Being tied to integrity, the man of honor, who 'partakes of the glories which God has revealed,'[18] carries with him a feeling of fulness. This fullness comes from the confirmation committed by the Holy Spirit, one which endues a feeling of acceptance and completeness. Thus, it is the disciples with integrity who are blessed with the assurance that they are 'complete in Christ.'[19] Men of integrity are those of uncompromising confidence; whose convictions have championed the moral test. Men of honor having an immovable faith; being purified in the furnace of affliction they stand resolute against every corrosive accusation. The honorable are brilliant lights shining in a world filled with wandering souls. Their inspiration has a tangible quality which bolsters the morale of others, and infuses a fortitude and fealty towards truth.

A disciple of honor is an invigorating reverie of *"the things which God has prepared for them that love him,"* even that which *"eye hath not seen, nor ear heard, neither have entered into the heart of man."*[20] Though mortality only allows us to feel a fraction of the fullness we find with the Father, there is no greater feeling than to obtain the calming contentment of being *"perfect in Christ."* Such is why, *"if by the grace of God ye are perfect in Christ, ye can in nowise deny the power of God."*[21]

Integrity brings the disciple to make and keep the covenant, *"I shall keep thy law; yea, I shall observe it with my whole heart."*[22] Because integrity is

---

[14] Nahum 2:9, 10 – Emphasis added
[15] Jeremiah 11:13 – The shameful thing refers to the idolatrous graven image of Baal, whose founder is the Devil. See BD: Baal – "The Prophets call Baal the Shame."
[16] 2 Nephi 2:27
[17] D&C 109:76
[18] See D&C 66:2 – "blessed are you for receiving mine everlasting covenant, even the fulness of my gospel, sent forth unto the children of men, that they might have life and be made partakers of the glories which are to be revealed in the last days"
[19] See Colossians 2:10 – "And ye are complete in him, which is the head of all principality and power:"
[20] 1 Corinthians 2:9 – See also Isaiah 64:4
[21] See Moroni 10:32 – "Yea, come unto Christ, and be perfected in him, and deny yourselves of all ungodliness"
[22] Psalms 119:10

integral in receiving Eternal life, Satan taunts us to forfeit this treasure, teasing, *"all that a man hath will he give for his life."*[23] The day will come where you too will have to face this philosophy.

Amidst life's conflicting values we will one day learn that the price of honor is more than body or blood – it is the whole soul. The cost of the crown is consecration. Therefore, honor and integrity is giving God your "everything" and not holding anything back. There is no prestige in partial piety. Divided disciples who *"keep back part"*[24] not only *"desire to know the truth in part,"*[25] but they are limited to *"enjoy that which they are willing to receive, because they were not willing to enjoy that which they might have received."*[26]

The formula is simple. In order to receive 'all that the Father hath,'[27] we have to give God all that we have. Consecration is not about hitting a quantifiable sacrificial quota, there are no clever tax cuts or loopholes to pure religion. One cannot cheat their way into becoming charitable. The way of truth is seen in the Savior's teaching, *"And there came a certain poor widow, and she threw two mites, which make a farthing. And [Jesus] called unto him his disciples, and saith unto them, Verily I say unto you, That this poor widow hath cast more in, than all they which have cast into the treasury: For all they did cast in of their abundance; but she of her want did* **cast in all that she had, even all her living.**"[28]

Incomplete loyalty cannot fulfill our religious obligations. Even those who give genuinely and generously may still secretly be keeping back part. Though they show no lack in philanthropy, they may still 'lack something yet.' And *"there came one running, and kneeled to [Jesus], and asked him, Good Master, what shall I do that I may inherit eternal life?"*[29] *"And he said unto him … if thou wilt enter into life, keep the commandments …The young man saith unto him, All these things have I kept from my youth: what lack I yet?"*[30] *"Then Jesus beholding him loved him, and said unto him, One thing thou lackest:"*[31] **"If thou wilt be perfect"**[32] *"go thy way, sell whatsoever thou hast, and give to the poor, and thou shalt have treasure in heaven: and come, take up the cross, and follow me."*[33]

---

[23] Job 2:4
[24] Acts 5:3 – See whole story of Ananias and Sapphira found in Acts 5:1-5
[25] D&C 49:2
[26] D&C 88:32
[27] See D&C 84:38 – "And he that receiveth my Father receiveth my Father's kingdom, therefore all that my Father hath shall be given unto him."
[28] Mark 12:42-44 – Emphasis and brackets added – Originally: he
[29] Mark 10:17 – Brackets added – Originally: him
[30] Matthew 19:17,20
[31] Mark 10:21
[32] Matthew 19:21 – Emphasis added
[33] Mark 10:21

Have you decided to grant yourself some form of diplomatic immunity to certain doctrines and commandments? Though there are unique occasions allowing concession of law, we must be skeptically wary lest we mistake the deceptive spirit of extenuating circumstance to be the Spirit of God. A practice of conditional Christianity is an unacceptable sacrifice. As it was said of Solomon and David of old, it is *"evil in the sight of the LORD"* if we go *"not fully after the LORD."*[34] Disciples with integrity have full fealty to the Father. They live their religion in a way that conquers the exceptions and excuses in inconvenience and circumstance.

If we wish to retain our honor, we must defeat today's detestable resurgence of a selling of indulgences. These modern indulgences bypass the priestly consultations practiced of old and mitigate immorality within one's own self. Instead of 'working out their salvation with fear and trembling,'[35] many barter badness for acts of benevolence. Being heroically righteous in some areas, some followers of Christ behave as if they have acquired an exemption to select transgressions. These intentionally hold fast to a keepsake of sin, hiding it underneath a wealth good works. But more devious than the concealment of their corruptions is their tolerant taste for it. Such are they who seek refuge from the scathing sun of a strenuous day underneath the *"mists of darkness,"* instead of the *"cloud of the Lord."*[36] Those hoping to fully follow the Father must even be willing to sacrifice their favorite sins.

In like manner there are laissez-faire followers of Christ who work to domesticate their deity. They ride atop a tamed god and place a bit in his mouth to ensure that he won't run off in an embarrassing direction. This god is best kept bridled lest he get out of hand and requires something new, untimely or difficult. With reins of righteous-relativism, these steer gospel principles to their preference, practicing the relaxed religion. And so they ride along the 'wide and broad'[37] way, free from responsibility, free from oaths and duty. But we must not listen to the Spirit as one listens to the radio: staying put so long as our favorite tune is playing, but when a distasteful song plays, simply change the station or switch it off. This tepid type of discipleship no longer feels the *"burning fire shut up in* [their] *bones,"*[38]

---

[34] 1 Kings 11:6
[35] See Philippians 2:12 – "as ye have always obeyed, not as in my presence only, but now much more in my absence, work out your own salvation with fear and trembling."
[36] See Exodus 40:38 – "For the cloud of the Lord was upon the tabernacle by day, and fir was on it by night, in the sight of all the house of Israel, throughout all their journeys."
[37] See Matthew 7:13 – "Enter ye in at the strait gate: for wide is the gate and broad is the way, that leadeth to destruction, and many there be which go in thereat"
[38] Jeremiah 20:9

and *"then because thou art lukewarm, and neither cold nor hot,* [God] *will spue thee out of* [His] *mouth."*[39]

Some manifest split loyalty or 'keep back part' by choosing to be pop-culture Christians. These prefer to practice an un-tucked obedience; who suppose that they have become spiritually savvy by sleekly sliding in worldliness into their worship. For such, being a click of cool Christians is much preferred to being a *"peculiar people."*[40] Here a different tone of pride is manifest than that of the ancient. Instead of 'making their phylacteries broad,' they make them colorful, stylish and hip. But all is done for the selfsame purpose – *"all their works they do for to be seen of men."*[41] Instead of enlarging the borders of their garments, they decrease the fabric of their garments;' they want their religiosity both revealing and fitted. Such deviants takes the tools the Master Tailor into their own hands; therewith they trim God's standards to their own comfort and contest.

Though these persons desire to be seen, they do not desire to appear righteous. These persons wish to exhibit their individuality. Their practice of religious rite is used as a podium to display their uniqueness. Those who make themselves a spiritual spectacle should consider that it is difficult to simultaneously stand out secularly and *"fall down at the feet of Jesus."*[42] One cannot carry the cares of the world and expect to have strength left to carry the cross of discipleship.

Oddly, pageantry disciples often store a secret hope that others will stereotype them. Seeing others seemingly judge them gives them their desired thrill. It is as if such suppose that the fashionable faith is excused when others 'judge' them. Expecting 'harsh, prudish saints' which notice their theatrical demonstrations to judge them, these pardon their own sins by saying that those judging them are no better than they. Ultimately, those practicing popular piety are incompletely committed; they limit themselves to being cardholders of an ecclesiastical click, instead of fellow-citizens *"of the household of God."*[43]

Those without integrity appear visibly virtuous but are silently vain. They are publicly kind but privately carnal; outwardly spiritual, but inwardly

---

[39] Revelation 3:16 – Brackets added – Originally: I
[40] See Deuteronomy 14:2 – "For thou art an holy people unto the Lord thy God, and the Lord hath chosen thee to be a peculiar people unto himself, above all the nations that are upon the earth."
[41] Matthew 23:5 – "they make broad their phylacteries, and enlarge the borders of their garments"
[42] See 3: Nephi 11:17 – "And they did fall down at the feet of Jesus, and did worship him."
[43] Ephesians 2:19 – "Now therefore ye are no more strangers and foreigners, but fellow citizens with the saints, and of the household of God."

worldly. Some valiantly avoid sin while secretly supporting sin. Though they personally resist wickedness, they keep back part by aiding wicked corporations or evil ideals. They refuse unrighteousness but do not denounce indecency. In fact, they finance these fiendish factions. They abstain from immoral gospels but are the capitol of corrupt companies. Integrity rejects the dissonant sound of condemning coarse practices while clutching significant stocks in crooked creeds.

Similar dissonance is noted in those who are doctrinally intelligent, but untrustworthy in matters of duty. Likewise, there those that are spiritually eloquent but lame in living gospel standards. Christ's church needs more disciples and fewer groupies. He needs more servants than scriptorians, more builders of the kingdom than bloggers of the kingdom. Those who are honorable keep their understanding of doctrine proportionate to their dedication to doctrine.

Anecdotal discipleship which lacks current conviction is also inadequate. The facebook faith which has never fought on the frontlines of conviction falls short. Similarly, there are saints who prefer rumor to rigors, conjecture to covenants, and allegations to allegiance. Christian discipleship is meant to be a conduct not a dialogue, a sacrifice instead of a discussion. As Neal A. Maxwell observed, "Still others find it easier to bend their knees than their minds. Exciting exploration is preferred to plodding implementation; speculation seems more fun than consecration, and so is trying to soften the hard doctrines instead of submitting to them. Worse still, by not obeying, these few members lack real knowing. (See John 7:17.) Lacking real knowing, they cannot defend their faith and may become critics instead of defenders!"[44] If we hope to be *"valiant in the testimony of Jesus,"*[45] we cannot conceal our convictions. We cannot be covert Christians.

Some intemperate fools have supposed they could purchase honor with wealth. *"And when Simon saw that through laying on of the apostles' hands the Holy Ghost was given, he offered them money, Saying Give me also this power, that on whomsoever I lay hands, he may receive the Holy Ghost. But Peter said unto him, Thy money perish with thee, because thou hast thought that the gift of God may be purchased with money."*[46] One cannot buy honor from Heaven, for *"no man taketh this*

---

[44] Neal A. Maxwell. "Settle This in Your Hearts." *Ensign*. November 1992. 65
[45] See D&C 76:79 – Vs. 78,79 – "Wherefore, they are bodies terrestrial, and not bodies celestial, and differ in glory as the moon differs from the sun. These are they who are not valiant in the testimony of Jesus; wherefore they obtain not the crown over the kingdom of our God."
[46] Acts 8:18-20

honour unto himself," "*It is* [the] *Father that honoureth.*"⁴⁷

True honor is not something received by pulling mythical weaponry from brute boulders. Nor is it something that is acquired after winning a majority vote from an electoral college. Occupation itself is not an endowment of honor. "*Better is a poor and a wise child than an old and foolish king, who will no more be admonished.*"⁴⁸ A prideful President is worse off than a honest blue-collar worker. There can be as much honor in disposing garbage as there is in governing a country so long as the job is done with an intent to serve others and God. The "*glory of Zion*"⁴⁹ cannot be bargained for with any earth object, for character is the currency in the eternal economy. The prize of prominence can only be purchased with purity.

Having the poise of purity, integrity emits a definite and discernible aura of light. An ambient presence of respect is the emblem of integrity; thus the honest man always carries his honor with him. His concern and care for others is ever on display. His fidelity is not flaunted; but being brightly beneficent, the honorable are quick to extend commendations for other's accomplishments. Christ taught, "*If any man serve me, let him follow me; and where I am, there shall also my servant be: if any man serve me, him will my Father honour.*"⁵⁰ Therefore, serve others and God will honor you, grow you and give you glories and joys unmeasurable.

God honors the diligent servant; He showers the humble with His Spirit and rewards those who deny themselves with a crown. In contrast, the world honors those who build themselves up. It pays no regard to Christ's words, "*Whosoever of you will be the cheifest, shall be servant of all.*"⁵¹ Men and women with real honor are also the most willing to honor others. They do not hoard ovations or recognition. The honorable freely share esteem with those around them. They do not only associate with the select and elite, rather they actively seek out those of a shrunken status to lift them. Here we learn of the captivating charisma of integrity: we feel an ennobling and ascending force lifting us in their presence, company and speech.

The allure of integrity's illuminating majesty has attracted both good and evil. "*For, behold, the devil was before Adam, for he rebelled against me,*

---

[47] John 8:54 – "Jesus answered, If I honour myself, my honour is nothing: it is my Father that honoureth me"
[48] Ecclesiastes 4:13
[49] D&C 124:60 – "and let it be a delightful habitation for man, and a resting-place for the weary traveler, that he may contemplate the glory of Zion, and the glory of this, the cornerstone thereof"
[50] John 12:26
[51] Mark 10:44

saying, Give me thine honor, which is my power."[52] From the beginning it was Heavenly Father's prerogative to give His children honor, but Satan lusted after glory. He unwholesomely 'aspired for honors' paying no heed to *"this one lesson—That the rights of the priesthood are inseparably connected with the powers of heaven, and that the powers of heaven cannot be controlled nor handled only upon the principles of righteousness."*[53]

Satan misunderstood the system God designed. The glory Satan sought could not be handed over like some material gift. Glory and honor can only be acquired through opposition, trial and strain. Therefore, God's plan of salvation requires that *"people must be tried in all things, that they may be prepared to receive the glory that I have for them,"*[54] for *"He that keepeth his commandments receiveth truth and light, until he is glorified in truth and knoweth all things."*[55] Therefore *"ye shall bind yourselves to act in all holiness before me – That is inasmuch as ye do this, glory shall be added to the kingdom which ye have received. Inasmuch as ye do it not, it shall be taken, even that which ye have received."*[56] Let us then, *"by patient continuance in well doing seek for glory and honour and immortality, eternal life."*[57]

One of the ways we transmit and receive honor is in the form of respect. Though respect may be imitated by tyranny, it is only found in freedom. Fear is fear, not respect. Likewise, pre-eminence and intimidation do not sow sincere reverence. Each of these may mimic a certain shade of reverence, but unlike true respect, they are not enduring. In order to have any effect, fear, intimidation, and pre-eminence must be constantly monitored. These instruments cover an extremely limited scope, because their power only operates inside a person's immediate presence. As soon as a supposed follower leaves their small sphere of influence, the esteem promptly turns into insult and courtesy to mockery. True respect comes through love, for there is no pre-eminence in love. Love generates unity and equity. Love creates willing obedience and zealous adoration. With love there are no borders baring a person's respect.

Have we as saints of the Most High God given *"unto the Lord the glory due unto his name?"* Is your Sabbath worship more about filling up your time or filling up your soul? Come *"bring an offering, and come before him:*

---

[52] D&C 29: 36
[53] D&C 121:35,36 – "Because their hearts are set so much upon the things of this world, and aspire to the honors of men, that they do not learn this one lesson---That the rights of the priesthood are inseparably connected with the powers of heaven"
[54] D&C 136:31
[55] D&C 93:28
[56] D&C 43:9,10
[57] Romans 2:7

worship the Lord in the beauty of holiness."[58] Reverence toward the Father needs to be more than suffering through sacrament services while sucking on electronic pacifiers. Today even adults can be seen pouting over worship. Some begrudgingly go to church with the same grimaces children make over their chores. Not only this, but the tribute offered to the Eternal God is on the verge of being offensively paltry. How could a disciple think it is sufficient to sprinkle God with praise for a few hours a week and then leave with no expectation of making any critical changes in their life?

Integrity is more than applying the breaks to avoid an encounter with the heavenly highway patrol. "*Verily I say men should be anxiously engaged in a good cause, and do many things of their own free will, and bring to pass much righteousness.*"[59] Similarly we should be "*zealously affected always in a good thing, and not only when I am present with you.*"[60] The man of integrity gives graciously without any ovation. He works quite good even when there is no camera, spotlight, or entourage.

Every extrinsic material motivation may someday be removed in order to ensure that our devotion is not conditional upon rewards or recognition. This is the only way that we can obtain the enduring Christian character required for a celestial climate. Because of the destiny awaiting us in eternity, man must "develop his own resources so that he can act independently and yet humbly … we must learn to be righteous in the dark."[61]

Integrity cannot be contrived. Its rich luminous glow is wholesome and warm because it is genuine. Thus honesty is the fundamental ingredient to integrity. Most simply we understand honesty as being truthful. We also understand honesty through its associating antonyms of lying and deception. Most of the time we think of lying as an initial statement or act. We picture a liar as a person who makes an untruthful statement or fake commitment right from the start. The liar says they will do something when they really had no intention of completing the task. This basic type of lying is a lot easier to conquer compared to the other forms of dishonesty.

For many the most clinically significant form of lying is the belated lie. This subtler type of dishonesty comes after the original promise is made. What makes this matter intriguing is that the initial commitment

---

[58] 1 Chronicles 16:29
[59] D&C 58:27
[60] Galatians 4:18
[61] Young, Brigham. A citation from "Brigham Young's Office Journal, 28 January 1857." *Ensign.* October, 1984

may have been completely sincere. Yet somewhere down the road standards loosen and a compromise is made. Then for whatever reason, a person either betrays their pledge, or feels that their former pledge should no longer be binding. This type of dishonesty dangerously opposes integrity and honor.

Well, the clever lawyer speedily devises a simple solution to this problem. Since we cannot foretell future circumstances, why not circumvent these lies by discontinuing commitments all-together. Slick as this strategy may appear, one cannot be honest by being noncommittal. True, they may dodge dishonesty, but their neutrality neutralizes integrity. An evasive individual who avoids binding himself with his word is living a vague life. Tactful ambiguity is yet another attack against integrity. Integrity is not just being true to our word. It is also being able to give our word. A life without responsibility will be a life without honor, respect and glory.

Honesty isn't only a principle of speech, but of personality. The consequence of being honest in word and deed is an enlarging of responsibility and accountability. *"Woe unto them that seek deep to hide their counsel from the Lord, and their works are in the dark, and they say, Who seeth us? And who knoweth us?"*[62] Concealing our sins will not cause shame to depart; there isn't a spot on this planet where one can hide from the demon of disgrace. Those who bury guilt are never free from it. They constantly tote the torture of entombed regrets. In contrast, the honest do not run from disgrace, rather they confront and accept in order to overcome it. They 'bear the iniquity of their priesthood,' which means that they will 'bear any guilt incurred in failure to bear the full responsibility thereof.'[63]

Time and tears alone cannot cover our regrets; contrition cannot be complete without confession. Though integrity despises dishonor, it will nevertheless suffer shame if such is the price for reconciliation. We must accept the reality and responsibility of our sins before the 'cover' of Christ's atonement can reach our regrets. Yet, this feat can only be done by exposing and presenting our errors to the Father, not burying them.

Ultimately integrity is giving everything that you have and are. It is "[presenting] *your bodies a living sacrifice, holy, acceptable unto God,*"[64] holding

---

[62] Isaiah 29:15
[63] See Numbers 18:1 footnote 1A – "thou and thy sons with thee shall bear the iniquity of your priesthood."
[64] Romans 12:1 – Brackets added – "I beseech you therefore, brethren, by the mercies of God, that ye present your bodies a living sacrifice, holy, acceptable unto God, which is your reasonable service."

nothing back. Decency alone does not cut it, especially since God knows you are *"noble and great."*[65] In order to receive *"the honour that cometh from God only,"*[66] we will have to 'retain our integrity'[67] and pronounce as did Job, *"Though he slay me, yet will I trust in him."*[68]

Because life is a test, everyone will face the limits of their devotion. As part of this test, the devil will come before each of us and present us a most enticing offer. Lucifer, that cunning con artist haggles for honor in moral markets. Just as Satan spoke to the Messiah, he will say to you, *"All this power will I give thee, and the glory of them: for that is delivered unto me; and to whomsoever I will I give it. If thou therefore wilt worship me, all shall be thine."*[69] Satan's final attempt to steal man's godliness is expressed in the verse, *"What shall a man give in exchange for his soul?"*[70] Straightforwardly Satan says to us all – Name your price!

Satan does not need to offer men palaces when 'pottage' will suffice. Judas, who exchanged Christ for a pathetic sum of 30 pieces of silver, was neither the first nor last person to gamble worldly stocks against the spiritual economy. Concerning the finance of faith, Christ counsels us, *"Lay not up for yourselves treasures upon earth, where moth and rust doth corrupt, and where thieves break through and steal: But lay up for yourselves treasures in heaven, where neither moth nor rust doth corrupt."*[71] Nevertheless, despite this admonition many *"sell themselves for naught"*[72] by investing in sinful practices.

Which *"of my creditors is it to whom I have sold you? Behold, for your iniquities have ye sold yourselves."*[73] *"Bread and pottage of lentiles"* seems a lofty sum compared to the current rates spirits are selling for. Today we find ourselves trapped in a moral market where mischievous merchants barter for men's beliefs. All about us the dealers shout, auctioning a temper for a covenant. Across the street we see a large gathering of men lined up, waiting to deal in integrity for entertainments. Nearby is a pack of peddlers selling impatience at the price of sacred promises, while shopkeepers market their jokes in exchange for kindness. As the trade of virtue for

---

[65] Abraham 3:22
[66] John 5:44 – "How can ye believe, which receive honour one of another, and seek not the honour that cometh from God only?"
[67] Job 2:9 – "Then said his wife unto him, Dost thou still retain thine integrity? Curse God, and die."
[68] Job 13:15
[69] Luke 4:6,7
[70] Mark 8:35-37
[71] Matthew 6:19,20
[72] 2 Nephi 26:10 – "they sell themselves for naught; for, for the reward of their pride and their foolishness they shall reap destruction"
[73] Isaiah 50:1

reputation continues, we see some men straightway sell their soul for a tantrum.

Though *"the worth of souls is great,"*[74] people trade away their soul, which is appraised as *"precious;"*[75] they "[change] *their glory for that which doth not profit."*[76] But *"what shall it profit a man, if he shall gain the whole world, and lose his own soul?"*[77] The ultimate test of honor weighs whether we will have the world or integrity. *"For whosoever will save his life shall lose it; but whosoever shall lose his life for my sake and the gospel's the same shall save it."* In matters great and small, mundane and dramatic, we must be true to our word and declare, *"till I die I will not remove mine integrity from me. My righteousness I hold fast, and will not let it go."*[78]

Glory be to God who never let go of His integrity. In a life that constantly called for perfection, He never became 'weary of well doing.'[79] There was never a moment when Christ held back benevolence. He did not 'keep back any part' of His perfection, but *"poured out his soul unto death."*[80] There is no lie in Jesus' love. He bears no secret grudge for bearing *"the sins of the world."*[81] His service is sincere and not used for self-gain or aggrandizement.

When others would have traded their purity for prestige, Jesus chose righteousness instead of riches. He was offered kingdoms for His covenants, thrones for His vows and dominions for His word, but He would not sell His loyalty, nor tarnish His name, which name is the *"only name which shall be given under heaven, whereby salvation shall come unto the children of men."*[82] Jesus did not use His holiness to grant Himself immunity to the principles of the gospel. He did not accept any exceptions when offered the bitter cup. Not once did Jesus 'justify himself in committing a little sin,' instead he *"glorified the father in taking upon* [himself] *the sins of the world."*[83] *"Worthy is the Lamb that was slain to receive power, and riches, and wisdom, and strength, and honour, and glory, and blessing."*[84] *"Let the beauty of the* LORD *our God*

---

[74] D&C 18:10 – Remember the worth of souls is great in the sight of God"
[75] See Alma 39:17 – "I say unto you, is not a soul at this time as precious unto God as a soul will be at the time of his coming?"
[76] Jeremiah 2:11 – Brackets added – Originally: changed
[77] Mark 8:36
[78] Job 27:6,7
[79] 2 Thessalonians 3:13 – "But ye, brethren, be not weary in well doing."
[80] Isaiah 53:12 – Also Mosiah 14:12
[81] D&C 76:41 – "he came into the world, even Jesus, to be crucified for the world, and to bear the sins of the world, and to sanctify the world, and to cleanse it from all unrighteousness"
[82] Moses 6:52
[83] 3 Nephi 11:11 – Brackets added – Originally: me
[84] Revelation 5:12

be upon us,"[85] for *"then shall the righteous shine forth as the sun in the kingdom of their Father,"*[86] and *"Thine eyes shall see the king in his beauty."*[87]

"Behold the man!"[88] who in a negligible garden demonstrated celestial nobility; who before a dozing audience carried the accountability of an infinite atonement. His crowd slumbered while the dignity of a Deity was on display. Christ did not run from the responsibility of His role to redeem all men. While others would have condoned complaints for enduring a crooked verdict, a scourging and a cross, Jesus kept Himself perfect and consecrated Himself to the will of the Father. Amidst consuming suffering Jesus did not soften His stance against sin. He did not succumb to His extreme extenuating circumstances.

"Now unto the King eternal, immortal, invisible, the only wise God, be honour and glory for ever and ever."[89] The humiliation of His crucifixion is replaced by the glory of His resurrection. The shame of His scourging is supplanted by His eminence and sovereignty in the universe. The embarrassment of the cross is swallowed up in the seraph's song, *"Allelulia; Salvation, and glory, and honour, and power, unto the Lord our God."*[90]

---

[85] Psalms 90:17
[86] Matthew 13:43
[87] Isaiah 33:17
[88] John 19:5 – "Then came Jesus forth, wearing the crown of thorns, and the purple robe"
[89] 1 Timothy 1:17
[90] Revelation 19:1

The Gifts of the Spirit

God is waiting! From the formation of man, when life was first breathed into bodies of flesh and blood, 'the Gods have been watching those things which they had ordered until they obeyed.'[1] It is a patient process surveying swells of civilizations; watching as empires are born and broken in recurrent ripples of revolutions and renaissances. Silently embalmed in the tomb of time are stories of tragedy and valor as numerous as the specks of dirt burying their authors.

Where among the dwelling place of worms lie the crumbled bones of those who kept the obedience ordered by the Holy Ones? Who among the hordes of man combing the earth can comprehend the destiny coded in the immortal soul? Few have considered what God intends to make from such clumps of carnal clay.

God is waiting! The *"deep sleep"*[2] of the saints has lasted long enough. There is an anticipatory anxiety stirring in the heavens as angels await the awakening of *"the noble and great ones."*[3] Celestial courts are muffled by an overtone of cherubic chatter as congregations clamor over the news of a *"chosen generation."*[4] Inquisitive seraphs 'stoop' over a canopy of hovering clouds 'desiring to look into'[5] the souls sent to prepare the way of the Messiah. It is a tickled chill hustling inside huddles of spirits contemplating the signs, seasons and covenants spoken by the Prophets. The world in which you now live, a seemingly oblivious orb lost in the

---

[1] Abraham 4:18 – Original: "And the Gods watched those things which they had ordered until they obeyed."
[2] Alma 5:7 – "Behold, he changed their hearts; yea, he awakened them out of a deep sleep, and they awoke unto God."
[3] Abraham 3:23 – "Now the Lord had shown unto me, Abraham, the intelligences that were organized before the world was; and among all these there were many of the noble and great ones"
[4] 1 Peter 2:9 – "ye are a chosen generation…that ye should shew forth the praises of him who hath called you"
[5] 1 Peter 1:12 – "but unto us they did minister the things, which are now reported unto you…which things the angels desire to look into."– Greek Strong's Dictionary #3879: word for 'look' is parakupto which is translated: "to bend beside, i.e. lean over (so as to peer within): - look, stoop down."

infinity of space has captured the attention of all the hosts of Heaven – for at last the days of prophesy have come.

God is searching! "*Beneath the glance of his all-searching eye,*"[6] "*God looked down from Heaven upon the children of men, to see if there were any that did understand, that did seek God.*"[7] It is fascinating that a being of infinite knowledge finds our current human affairs worthy of His focus. "*What is man, that thou art mindful of him?*"[8] Mankind itself has mocked his own station and like Prince Hamlet declares with doubt and sarcasm, "What a piece of work is a man! How noble in reason, how infinite in faculty! In form and moving how express and admirable! In action how like an Angel! In apprehension how like a god!"[9] Is there at least one man among God's countless creations who can speak these words with conviction? Who will call upon God and "*access with confidence*"[10] the promises of His covenant? The heavens have waited long enough! Who among the children of men 'understands' and will 'seek' the Omnipotent God, for it is written, "*ye shall seek me, and find me,* **when** *ye shall search for me with all your heart.*"[11]

Yet, 'for what cause do you bow your knees unto the Father of our Lord Jesus Christ?'[12] Do you beg for that which comes of the ground or supplicate God for spiritual substance? Since His "*divine power hath given unto us all things that pertain unto life and godliness,*"[13] do we specifically ask the Father for godly things? Far too many people are confused about the produce of prayer. It is as if they have come looking to buy groceries from a jeweler.

We have been plainly instructed to set our "*affection on things above, not on things on the earth,*"[14] yet how often do we honestly seek heavenly gifts? In like manner we are told, "*care not for the body, neither the life of the body; but care for the soul, and for the life of the soul.*"[15] Notwithstanding this counsel, how many of us spend the premium of our prayers wishing for worldly things?

---

[6] Mosiah 27:31 – "and they shall quake, and tremble, and shrink beneath the glance of his all searching eye."
[7] Psalms 53:2 – vs.3: "Everyone of them is gone back...there is none that doeth good...4: they have not called upon God."
[8] Hebrews 2:6 – Vs 7: "Thou madest him a little lower than the angels; thou crownedst him with glory and honour"
[9] Shakespeare, William. Hamlet, Act 2 Scene 2, p 40. Leipzid Bernh Taughnitz Jun. 1843
[10] Ephesians 3:12 – Vs 11: "Jesus our Lord: 12: In whom we have boldness and access with confidence by the faith of him"
[11] Jeremiah 29:13 – Emphasis added
[12] See Ephesians 3:14 – "For this cause I bow my knee unto the Father of our Lord Jesus Christ"
[13] 2 Peter 1:3
[14] Colossians 3:2 – "Set your affection on things above, not on things on the earth."
[15] D&C 101:37

It is a serious problem when supplications start sounding like letters to Santa. God should not be reduced to the role of a red suited, global, philanthropist whose mission is to spoil the earth with delightful presents.

Not only do we need to start asking for spiritual things, we also need to improve our gratitude for them. Though we exclaim, *"Blessed be the God and Father of our Lord Jesus Christ, who hath blessed us with all spiritual blessings in heavenly places in Christ,"*[16] we fill our prayers with the puff and fluff of temporal concerns. When was the last time you praised God for your spiritual gifts? We are quick to give gratitude for the food on our tables, the house over our head, for clothes, work, schooling, travel … etc. But are we giving at least equal attention to the shelter of the scriptures with its protective roof of revelation? Do you ask with regularity for the daily *"bread of adversity and the water of affliction"*[17] to nourish and strengthen your charity?

Prayer can be so much more than a pep-talk. By accessing prayer's full potential people can reshape their perceptions and perfect their conduct. The most common problem in acquiring spiritual gifts is that we simply are not asking. In this regard, Christ could chide us with the same words He spoke to His Apostles, *"Hitherto have ye asked nothing in my name: ask, and ye shall receive."*[18] Reading this verse sometimes feels life a plea. It is as if God is saying please! Please start asking me for blessings. Father so eagerly desires to bless us. He wants to give us power, strength, help, and a variety of spiritual blessings. However, His movements are restricted because we are not asking.

Among the current generation of disciples, some have never even thought to ask directly for a gift of the Spirit. Though we have not 'denied the gifts of God,'[19] our "[zeal] *of spiritual gifts"*[20] has not exactly been exemplary. Perhaps if men were as passionate about Heaven's blessings as they are for earthy possessions, comforts or entertainment, we might have already *"come in the unity of the faith, and of the knowledge of the Son of God, unto a perfect man, unto the measure of the stature of the fullness of Christ."*[21]

It is no secret that the Father is primarily preoccupied with spiritual realities as it is written, *"all things unto me are spiritual, and not at any time have I*

---

[16] Ephesians 1:3
[17] Isaiah 30:20
[18] John 16:24
[19] See Moroni 10:8 – "I exhort you, my brethren, that ye deny not the gifts of God, for they are many"
[20] 1 Corinthians 14:12 – "forasmuch as ye are zealous of spiritual gifts, seek that ye may excel to the edifying of the church."
[21] Ephesians 4:12

given unto you a law which was temporal."[22] Sadly, the prevailing trend of our day tends to concern itself more with homework than humility; it worries more about status than sacrifice, food than devotion, and travels instead of virtues. In your conversations with God, have you been guilty of focusing on the things that expire over the things that are eternal?

"Lay not up for yourselves treasures upon earth, where moth and rust doth corrupt, ... But lay up yourselves treasures in heaven, where neither moth nor rust doth corrupt ..."[23] If we are to access our divine nature, we must no longer remain ignorant of spiritual gifts in our prayers.[24] God has said to seek *"earnestly the best gifts;"*[25] thus we need to start today to earnestly and specifically seek the gifts of the Spirit.

Greater effort can be made so that *"we look not at the things which are seen, but at the things which are not seen: for the things which are seen are temporal; but the things which are not seen are eternal."*[26] However, only part of the solution is to start asking for spiritual gifts. Unsurprisingly, 'earnestly seeking the best gifts' requires more than a simple shout out. Inquiry is only the first step. Do you pursue God's blessings in a hard-fought hunt, or do you shrink the size of your search to your own sofa? The 'powers of heaven' are not administered through happenstance, they are obtained by conscious and consistent sacrifice and focus.

We must always be ready to pay the price of our prayers. The outcome rests on us, for God *"will order all things for your good, as fast as ye are able to receive them."*[27] Do you make payments of pennies expecting to receive a prize of pearls? Are your expectations like those of a child who on Christmas Eve merely goes to sleep expecting a room full of gifts in the morning? Whether it is the result of naïvety or entitlement, false expectations are immature impediments to our appeals.

After we have taken the time, thought, and preparation to petition God for spiritual gifts, what is our next step? *"Now, as you have asked, behold, I say unto you, keep my commandments, and seek to bring forth and establish the cause of Zion."*[28] The key point is to realize that after 'we have asked,' we need to start acting, or more specifically we need to start serving. Revelations,

---

[22] D&C 29:31
[23] See Matthew 6:19,20
[24] See 1 Corinthians 12:1 – "Now concerning spiritual gifts, brethren, I would not have you ignorant."
[25] D&C 46:8 – "that ye may not be deceived seek ye earnestly the best gifts, always remembering for what they are given"
[26] 2 Corinthians 4:18
[27] D&C 111:11
[28] D&C 11:6 also 12:6 and 6:6

powers and answers will come to us more often while we are on our knees serving, than on our knees groveling.

Truman G. Madsen illustrated this principle while re-telling a story about Brigham Young, "Brother Brigham Young was hung up on a sandbar crossing a river on the plains. His companion, troubled, said, 'Let's pray,' Brigham replied, 'Pray? I prayed this morning. Let's get out and push,' There is a time for total concentration in prayer and a time for answering prayer with your own muscles."[29]

That we might 'push' in the right direction, here are a few additional principles worth consideration. When seeking the gifts of the Spirit it is essential for us to first focus on cleansing our inner vessel. As long as we are clutching to sin, we will not have sufficient grip to grasp the gifts of God. Repentance frees our hands and heart to receive the glory of Heaven and eventually 'receive all that the Father has.'[30] As the Lord said to the Prophet Joseph, *"repent of that which thou hast done which is contrary to the commandment which I gave you ... Except thou do this, thou shalt be delivered up and become as other men, and have no more gift."*[31] When prayers go unanswered, some accuse 'God for not drawing near unto them,' yet all the while they are the ones not 'drawing near unto the Lord.'[32] Proximity does have its place in prayer though, for the closer we come toward the Father, the easier it is to hear His voice and take hold of His hand.

One of the ways we can draw nearer to the Lord is to utilize the full power of the fast. *"Is not this the fast that I have chosen? To loose the bands of wickedness, to undo the heavy burdens, and to let the oppressed go free, and that ye break every yoke ... Then shalt thou call, and the LORD shall answer; thou shalt cry, and he shall say, Here I am."*[33] The ritualistic fashion of the fast should not overshadow its important function; that is finding response to our prayers and freeing our divine nature from the shackles of sin. In order for this to happen, fasting needs to be more about focus than food. It needs to be more about supplication than starvation.

Fasting should not just begin and end with prayer. The entire process itself should be the prayer. Imagine halting your life, pausing every project, putting your routines on standby and stopping every selfish habit so that you can commit a single day to focus on a specific spiritual

---

[29] Truman G. Madsen. "Souls Aflame" From a BYU devotional given November 8, 1983
[30] See D&C 84:38 – "And he that receiveth my Father receiveth my Father's kingdom; therefore all that my Father hath shall be given unto him."
[31] D&C 3:10,11
[32] See D&C 88:63 – "Draw near unto me and I will draw near unto you; seek me diligently and ye shall find me; ask and ye shall receive; knock, and it shall be opened unto you."
[33] Isaiah 58:7,9

objective. The day of fasting is a wrestle; it is a test. It is a day of sacrifice where every minute points to the purpose of your appeal. Through the fast we are symbolically trying to get God's attention; thus we should put at least an equal proportion of consideration into our fast that we are hoping to get in return.

After the Apostles unsuccessfully attempted to cast out evil spirits Jesus said, "*Howbeit this kind goeth not out but by prayer and fasting.*"[34] Yet, exorcism is not the only application of fasting. Bands will be loosed, habits will be broken, addictions dissolved, stubborn sins excised and gifts of the Spirit will be granted. This full potential of the fast will never be accessed until we improve our focus. Only then that we can confidently claim the promise, that "*thy light break forth as the morning, and thine health shall spring forth speedily: and thy righteousness shall go before thee; the glory of the LORD shall be thy rearward.*"[35]

Fasting is not the only way to capture heaven's attention. There are additional resources one can utilize to give their pleas a second look. Ironically, one of the most powerful methods God has given to man is largely unused. Therefore prepare yourself to 'receive counsel that it may be shown unto you **the keys whereby [you] may ask and receive**, *and be crowned with the same blessing, and glory, and honor, and priesthood, and gifts of the priesthood.*"[36] To whom should a person seek, when they desire a blessing from God? If God were physically next door, you would have no need to retreat to a secluded closet to make your request. Why would you text your petitions or crawl into a dark cave to make your communion if God were literally in "*your midst?*"[37]

If receiving a blessing from God were your greatest desire, to what lengths would you go to obtain it? "*Again, the kingdom of heaven is like unto a merchant man, seeking goodly pearls: Who, when he had found one pearl of great price, went and sold all that he had, and bought it.*"[38] When you feel such urgency – **how** do you go about making your appeal? Whom did Abraham seek for when he was "*desiring also to be one who possessed great knowledge, and to be a greater follower of righteousness, and to possess a greater knowledge, and to be a father of many nations, a prince of peace, and desiring to receive instructions?*"[39]

In Abraham's case, he specifically searched for someone with the

---

[34] Matthew 17:21
[35] Isaiah 58:8
[36] D&C 124:95
[37] D&C 50:44 – "Wherefore, I am in your midst and I am the good shepherd, and the stone of Israel"
[38] Matthew 10:45,46
[39] Abraham 1:2

rights to administer blessings in behalf of God. His journey was to find one holding the authority and privileges of the Holy Priesthood. Abraham understood that through this authority the Almighty God 'would lay His hand upon him by the hand of His servant.'[40] It should not be surprising that Abraham was looking for a Priesthood authority to grant him the blessings he desired, for *"The Melchizedek Priesthood holds the right of presidency, and has power and authority ... in all ages of the world,* **to administer in in spiritual things.**"[41] But what are the *"spiritual things"* which fall under the jurisdiction of the Order of the Priesthood? The spiritual blessings administered by the Priesthood are not limited to ordinance work. There are diverse ways the Priesthood serves and blesses humanity.

"Is any sick among you? Let him call for the elders of the church; and let them pray over him, anointing him with oil in the name of the Lord."[42] According to the rights and powers of the Priesthood, man may administer blessings in the name of the Messiah. It is a strange thing to consider that the infinite power which shaped *"worlds without number"*[43] abides within common men living in communities across the earth. But what are we doing with this ultimate power in the universe? For some it is a sniffle, others a cough, perhaps it is the beginning of a new semester or the start of a sport season. How much divine power is expended on superficial sickness and chicken pox problems? Not that there is anything sinister in seeking God for relief from physics tests, illnesses or any of the challenges of life. However, we must avoid omitting the weightier matters of the spirit? When was the last time you petitioned God through His Priesthood concerning the sicknesses which afflict the soul?

Spending so much attention on temporal troubles almost seems like a waste of divine power, especially when we consider the extent that undiagnosed diseases of the spirit run around untreated. Are not the maladies of the immortal soul far more mischievous and serious than the sicknesses of the flesh? *"And it shall come to pass in that day, that his burden shall be taken away from off thy shoulder, and his yoke from off thy neck, and the yoke shall be destroyed because of the anointing."*[44] If iniquity presents the greatest eternal threat to man, could not the emblematic anointing of Christ be used to break the bonds of sin imprisoning struggling spirits?

---

[40] See D&C 36:2 – "And I will lay my hand upon you by the hand of my servant Sidney Rigdon"
[41] D&C 107:8 – Emphasis added
[42] James 5:14
[43] Moses 1:33 – "And worlds without number have I created; and I also created them for mine own purpose"
[44] Isaiah 10:27

If the Higher Priesthood was meant to attend to *"spiritual things,"* the prerogative of Priesthood power should be to anoint against the sickness of sin. Why not entreat God through His ordained servants to treat the plague of pride, infectious impatience, or septic selfishness. *"Is any sick among you?"* What of the terminally mean, chronically callous or degeneratively grumpy. In the eternal perspective a hard heart is more costly than a clogged artery, vengeance more deadly than cancer, sloth more devastating than dementia and selfishness as consequential as smoking.

We are told that in last days 'the power of the Lamb of God will descend upon the saints and arm them with righteousness and with the power of God in great glory.'[45] And though we cry to the heavens, *"Awake, awake,* **put on strength, O arm of the Lord:** *awake, as in the ancient days;"*[46] God often responds, *"Awake, awake;* **put on thy strength, O Zion;** *put on thy beautiful garments, O Jerusalem; the holy city."*[47] How ironic that in the same hour we plead to God to manifest His might, we are met with a retort to stir ourselves out of our own slumber.

Still, what is *"meant by the command in Isaiah ... which saith: Put on strength, O Zion?"* We are told Isaiah *"had reference to those whom God should call in the last days, who should hold the power of priesthood to bring again Zion, and the redemption of Israel; and to put on her strength is to put on the authority of the priesthood."*[48] The Priesthood is the strength of Zion. There is more potential power in the Priesthood than we now realize. The day will come when men shall see the full extent of this gift. In that day man will shake heaven and earth with righteousness.

Like Abraham, our own quest for greater knowledge and righteousness may lead us toward one capable of acting in God's authority. If we are to put on the strength of the Lord, we will have to 'put on,' or access the power of the Priesthood. When was the last time you sought a blessing from the Priesthood to receive an answer to a question, or sought God through the Priesthood for a spiritual gift? *"And this greater priesthood administereth the gospel and holdeth the key of the mysteries of the kingdom, even the key of the knowledge of God."*[49] The gift of the Holy Ghost contains within it all the powers, blessings and gifts of heaven; yet in many cases we unlock these endowments with the keys of the holy Priesthood. The Priesthood contains the rights for distributing spiritual things; it holds the key of the

---

[45] 1 Nephi 14:14
[46] Isaiah 51:9 and 2 Nephi 8:9
[47] Isaiah 52:1 and 2 Nephi 9:1
[48] D&C 113:7,8
[49] D&C 84:19

mysteries of the kingdom and the key of the knowledge of God. Thus, there may be no better way to equip the armor of God than by the power of the Priesthood.

Remember that *"the powers of heaven cannot be controlled nor handled only upon the principles of righteousness."*[50] Satan seeks to spoil the administration of spiritual gifts. He works on men's hearts to ruin their intentions and tempts us to *"ask amiss, that* [we] *may consume it upon* [our] *lusts;"*[51] thus we ask and receive not. Remember *"these gifts come from God, for the benefit of the children of God."*[52]

The gifts of the Spirit are not simply given to empower a person, but to strengthen societies. This program is not one of self-help. On the contrary, it is designed to stop helping yourself and start helping others. We can approach God and partake of His power only when our intent is pure; when our motive is to build God's kingdom and strengthen others. In the pursuit of spiritual gifts, we *"must have no other object in view"* but to glorify God. We must not be influenced by any other motive than that of building His kingdom, 'otherwise we cannot get them.'[53]

As it pertains to the gifts of the Spirit, we should remember the following principle lest we make a malignant misconception. The administration of the gifts of the Spirit does not always come as an acute, adrenal, explosive endowment. Sometimes God slowly enlightens and enriches us over the course of months or years. The quickening of our capabilities may come upon us just as fast as they may go. Some gifts are given to operate in us permanently, whereas others are distributed for a single situation. Also, when one is given a gift, this shouldn't imply that it has been given in its entirety. In most cases gifts are only given to us *"in part."* *"For we know in part, and we prophesy in part. But when that which is perfect is come, then that which is in part shall be done away."*[54]

Spiritual endowments often come in the form of a seed. They are bestowed as an inner potential or talent. Some gifts are dormant. They are awaiting for us to nourish and cultivate them to their full potential.

---

[50] D&C 121:36
[51] James 4:3 – Brackets added – "Ye ask, and receive not, because ye ask amiss, that ye may consume it upon your lusts."
[52] D&C 46:9
[53] See JSH 1:46 – Brackets added "I must have no other object in view in getting the plates but to glorify God…otherwise I could not get them."
[54] 1 Corinthians 13:10 – See also D&C 88:29-31 – "Ye who are quickened by a portion of the celestial glory shall then receive of the same, even a fulness. And they who are quickened by a portion of the celestial glory shall then receive of the same, even a fulness. And they who are quickened by a portion of the telestial glory shall then receive of the same, even a fulness."

Therefore, temper your expectations and know that the type of gift as well as **how** the gift is distributed will be according to God's holy will.

What are the gifts of the Spirit? It may not be necessary or possible to list all of the spiritual gifts that exist, for it has been said "Spiritual gifts are endless in number and infinite in variety. Those listed in the revealed word are simply illustrations."[55] Since God's gifts are so numerous, it is impossible for us to not be affected and blessed by them on a daily basis. We encounter these miraculous endowments in routine interactions. They are evidenced even in homely human beings. By increasing our awareness of these gifts, our feeling to glorify God grows and we begin to see the scenic show of Heaven's miracles constantly playing before us. Therefore, in the spirit of an analysis once made by Marvin J. Ashton – "Let us review some of these less conspicuous gifts."[56]

It *"is given to some to speak with tongues," "And again, to another all kinds of tongues."*[57] We are familiar with those scriptures recording miraculous episodes where individuals were quickened with an ability to speak new languages. Many have witnessed these abrupt endowments of speech – periods where foreign words and ideas flow flawlessly from a person's lips. It is also accepted that the gift of tongues works by quickening a person's mind to learn new languages with greater speed. However, one should not forget that the entire essence of the gift of tongues is communication.

Miscommunications and misunderstandings are not unique to the language barriers that exist between two different dialects. Confusion is common even within the same language. With the gift of tongues we are able to transmit ideas with clarity. According to the gift of tongues, God may give us words that excel our own imagination within our native language. Thus, to some it is given a power to communicate. Such gifts may manifest as articulation or as cleverness; whereas in others it may work as a *"gift of bearing a mighty testimony."** Whatever the case may be, by the gift of tongues people are given abilities of enhanced expression, *"and thus are the secrets of* [the] *heart made manifest."*[58]

Closely related to the gift of tongues, with its power to communicate are the gifts of teaching. *"For behold, to one is given by the Spirit of God, that he may teach the word of wisdom; And to another, that he may teach the*

---

[55] Bruce R. McConkie, A New Witness for the Articles of Faith, 371
[56] Marvin J. Ashton Conference Report, Oct. 1987 – Gifts mentioned hereafter attributed to Elder Ashton are indicated with a *
[57] Moroni 10:8-16
[58] 1 Corinthians 14:25 – Brackets added – Originally: his

word of knowledge by the same Spirit."[59] It takes a trained tongue to transfer knowledge and teach wisdom. With the influence of the Spirit, great teachers organize, illustrate and speak ideas in ways that hone in on a person's degree of understanding. *"And all these gifts come from God, for the benefit of the children of God."*[60]

Another group of spiritual gifts could be classified as the gifts of perception, or to use a more scriptural title we could call them the gifts of *"discerning of spirits."* [61] Whether by sight, sound or other modalities, God blesses His children with abilities to better sense the various flavors of reality from life's vast pool of experiences. To some degree we all possess some form and portion of this gift, for eternal truth is only gained when our faculties are enhanced by the power and will of God. Just as God magnifies the ability to communicate through tongues for some, He also strengthens spiritual receptivity in others.

One form of perception is simply comprehension. This includes skills of understanding ideas and thoughts. The gift of the *"interpretation of tongues"*[62] is an example of how a person's understanding can be expanded. With this gift one is more aware of the concept, feeling and essence of an idea. Thereby one attains an understanding which captures both the mind and heart of the messenger. With the interpretation of tongues we are able to look past a person's words and see into their sentiments. Everyone has experienced this gift at some point in their lives; times when simple messages illuminate our soul with brilliant clarity; then, not only do we see and hear the message, we capture the spirit of the messenger. On these occasions we discover that communication is not a transfer of ideas like a hand off, instead it is a connection where *"he that preacheth and he that receiveth, understand one another, and both are edified and rejoice together."*[63]

Other sensory gifts include a greater receptivity to spiritual impressions. Such are they who hear the voice of God clearly and frequently. This most often doesn't come as an audible sound, rather it is a fluency of that language which speaks to the soul. People with this level of discernment are often perceptive of even the slight brushes of the Spirit. Discernment can also manifest as an ability to feel and read the presence and spirit residing in others, as well as in settings. Others may be granted a heightened receptivity to the words of the scriptures; a gift which makes

---

[59] Moroni 10:9,10
[60] D&C 46:26
[61] D&C 46:23
[62] 1 Corinthians 12:10
[63] D&C 50:22

one more vulnerable the voice of God speaking from its pages. In contrast another person may be more prone to spiritual promptings emanating from pondering instead of reading.

There so many diverse expressions of godliness and truth around us. In general, individuals are given special affinities for receiving one or many of them. Because the number of ways truth is spoken and manifest, it is not possible to discuss them all. Nevertheless, regardless of the source, the principle is the same – by the power of the Spirit we can discern insight from an exhaustive range people, places and experiences. Also, through the divine gift of discernment, it is given *"by the Holy Ghost ... to know the differences of administration"*[64] and to know the *"diversities of operations, whether they be of God."*[65]

To some it is given a gift of sight to see things which are *"not visible to the natural eye."*[66] These see the workings of God in the world, in their life and in those around them. With this vision God gives one *"power that* [they] *may behold and view ... things as they are."*[67] Seeing life through this power, reveals the light of God and godliness in others or within themselves. Some may be blessed to see or understand concepts, ideas, and thoughts with ease. Others manifest this vision with an improved ability to see how things fit together. Whereas others may be given a blessing of an enlarged memory. With a gift of discernment, one may be given a blessing of a keen mind or an ability to learn readily.

To *"others it is given to prophesy;"*[68] even *"that he may prophesy concerning all things."*[69] Though the *"testimony of Jesus is the spirit of prophecy,"*[70] foresight should not be completely excluded from this gift. Though a person may not in perfection prophesy concerning all things, they may still see in part things which *"must surely come to pass."*[71] For others, prophecy may manifest as an ability to anticipate the consequences of a choice, or to predict possible future scenarios. But remember *"all have not every gift given unto them; for there are many gifts, and to every man is given a gift by the Spirit of God. To some is given one, and to some is given another, that all may be profited thereby."*[72]

---

[64] D&C 46:15
[65] D&C 46:16
[66] Moses 6:36
[67] D&C 5:13 – "I will give them power that they may behold and view these things as they are"
[68] D&C 46:22
[69] Moroni 10:13
[70] Revelation 19:10
[71] Jacob 6:1 "this is my prophecy – that the things which this prophet Zenos spake...must surely come to pass."
[72] D&C 46:11,12

There are gifts of love and charity. All people are blessed with these gifts in some part. Commonly these gifts are seen swelling within us and reaching power peaks in particular situations. We all have had, and will have yet again moments when God 'fills us with charity;'[73] a feeling of love which nearly consumes the flesh.[74] However, to have this gift in its entirety is to be as God is, for God is love. To have charity is to love as God loves. To receive the fullness of charity is to be locked in God's embrace for all eternity. Ultimately the gift of charity is Eternal life – to be and love, as God is and loves. But charity may be distributed in subtle ways. To some is given a love which endures against hatred, to another is given a love that unifies others freely with a familial oneness.

Some are given capacities to love quickly and easily. For these it takes little to no effort to care for and love both stranger and acquaintance. Others may be blessed with an ability to feel God's love more acutely or to have a greater love for their self. To some it is given a gift of unconditional love, to another it is given a gift to love their enemies. Others may be blessed to be as Solomon; who was given a "*largeness of heart, even as the sand that is on the sea shore.*"[75] Another particularly precious gift is the gift of kindness, wherewith we are able to make others feel loved. Some spread kindness in their countenance, others in their smiles and other with their works. Kindness can be accomplished in a vast variety of ways, whether by "*speaking the truth in love,*"[76] or by considerate gestures, great and small.

Compassion is another gift of the Spirit. One way this gift manifests is an ability to see past the façades of the flesh and sense an inner struggle within in a person's soul. For some the gift of compassion manifests as a gift of being able to listen to others, to hear a sound of sadness in a person's voice, or tap into a secret cry of tribulation in a person's tone. Similarly, some are blessed with an ability to read a person's countenance and thereby find hidden pains secretly stashed behind pleasantries.

There are some who are blessed with sympathy and empathy; while to another is given a disposition to succor and respond to suffering with haste. In like manner gifts of compassion can express as a gift to 'mourn with those that mourn' or to weep over sin and suffering. Some are given

---

[73] See Moroni 8:17 – "And I am filled with charity, which is everlasting love; wherefore, all children are alike unto me"
[74] 2 Nephi 4:21 – "He hath filled me with his love, even unto the consuming of my flesh."
[75] 1 Kings 4:29
[76] See Ephesians 4:14 – "But speaking the truth in love, may grow up into him in all things, which is the head, even Christ"

the gift of a caring and tender heart and a willingness to bear other's burdens. To another it is given to bring comfort and calm to the distressed. There are those with this gift where only the shadow of their presence is needed to console one's spirit. Oh then, what sweet solace we shall find in the presence of God, He who perfectly possess this gift!

The gifts of the Spirit include gifts of selflessness and humility. To some it is given a desire or preference of the happiness of others, with an ability to regard others before regarding their self. There is a gift of being willing to sacrifice, a gift of obedience, and a gift of being a servant. To another is given a gift of non-maleficence. These are they *"in whose spirit there is no guile."*[77] There is a gift of meekness, a gift to be gentle, and a gift to speak using a still, small voice.* Others are blessed to be peacemakers. Such are they who possess the ability being agreeable* and of avoiding contention.* Some are blessed by being easy to be entreated, while others are blessed with a gift of asking for help or being prayerful. The capacity to be teachable is another gift of the Spirit. So too is being apologetic and being able to recognize and confess faults and mistakes.

Mercy is a gift of the Spirit. There is a gift to be forgiving and a gift of forgetting. Some are blessed to be able to see people as a new person. Some are given to see the light and good in others. To another it is given a gift to not bear grudges, while to another is given the gift of a trusting spirit. There are those blessed with a gift of being a confidant. These are they whose love is as it were a tangible aura, herewith others are made to feel comfortable enough to willingly confess their faults. In such cases confessions come not by interrogation, rather they are voluntarily vulnerable about their regrets, guilt and shame. Consider then the wonder of our Father's mercy; despite the shame of our past sins, He causes us not to shrink from His embrace. Though God knows the secret embarrassments of each individual, His mercy is such that we are made to feel comfortable in His holy presence.

There is a gift of being able to ponder,* a gift of reflection; introspection and analysis. To some it is given the gift of being patient and to another a gift of perseverance; an instinct to never give up. With such a prize, peoples are granted a gift to endure hardship, pain, and darkness and ultimately see tasks to their end. There is a gift to wait, to be calm, still and assured. Like other aforementioned gifts, each of these characteristics can manifest within a person themselves or they may work in an ambient way –

---

[77] Psalms 32:2--"Blessed is the man unto whom the Lord imputeth not iniquity, and in whose spirit there is no guile.

exuding through presence a spiritual power to people around them.

Some need only share their presence to empower the patience of others, therewith they strengthen comrades to hold on just a little longer. So it is with the gift of courage. It may be given to one to have courage, while another may be blessed with a gift to embolden others. According to the gift wherewith God has blessed them, these people have a presence that sends surges of strength to other's spirits. They cause freedom and confidence to course inside those in their company. With the gift of courage, we may be blessed with boldness, bravery or even a gift of exploration.

Included in the gifts of the Spirit are gifts of honor and integrity. For some it may be given to have a gift of leadership or a gift of charisma. These manifest in a variety of ways: some have a quality of making others feel bigger, stronger, and safer. When you are around these types of people, they bring you a special confidence and fill you with inspiration. Some have a way of making you want to be better, more faithful and more godly. Being clothed in the gift of glory, God may make one emanate a tactile aura of honor – one that intrigues people with a conspicuous sensation of reverence, respect or power.

Marvin J. Ashton marked that to some it is given the gift of avoiding vain repetition.* In like manner there is a gift of sincerity and a gift to pray and speak with real intent. There is a gift of honesty; and a gift to love truth and right. To some it is given to make commitments, while to another is given a gift of being loyal. Others may be blessed with a gift of candor or a gift of authenticity. Some are blessed to be valiant, zealous or to be a disciple.* Some are given a trueness to their work, and to make and keep covenants. To another it may be given a desire to seek and establish righteousness.* *"And all these gifts come from God, for the benefit of the children of God."*[78]

The sense of justice is a gift from God. This sense should not be confused with the twisted views of a vigilante. Instead, the just have a strong sense of morality, of right, wrong and fairness. There are gifts of equity, firmness and sobriety. Some may be blessed with a greater awareness of agency's consequences, while others may be given a gift to feel remorse for wrong just as it is with gifts of being accountable and responsible.

There is a gift to be joyful, to have mirth and laughter. Some are blessed with a gift to be happy, *"and to rejoice in his labour; this is the gift of*

---

[78] D&C 46:26

*God."*⁷⁹ Some are given a gift to smile, a gift of enthusiasm or a gift of optimism. To another it may be given to have a gift of gratitude which heightens the awareness of the debt they owe to God. There are those whose countenances are so bright that they radiate joy, cheer and life. By this power they bring hope and happiness to the hearts of everyone around them.

Gifts of faith can express in many ways. To *"some is given the working of miracles,"*[80] *"to another, that he may work mighty miracles."*[81] There are those who appear almost immune to the standard doubts of mortality. Such souls see outside mortal barriers and perceive grander realms of possibilities. There is also a gift of curiosity and gift of asking* or inquiry, a gift of examination and a gift of experimentation. To some it is given to have a gift of conviction; to have a deep and penetrating belief which expresses faith in action. Some are blessed with the gift of *"exceedingly great faith;"*[82] a faith that causes miracles to happen. A power to perform causation is also seen in the *"gifts of healing."*[83] *"And again, to some it is given to have faith to be healed; And to others it is given to have faith to heal."*[84]

Through the gifts that come from God, we are granted inspiration, intelligence and revelation. *"To some it is given by the Holy Ghost to know that Jesus Christ is the Son of God, and that he was crucified for the sins of the World. To others it is given to believe on their words, that they also might have eternal life if they continue faithful."*[85] Spiritual truth can be discovered in all of God's creations. Some may find that they are convinced by the testimony of the word, others by the testimony of men, and to another it may be by the testimony originating from the beauties of the earth.

We all have some experience with the gift of hope. As real as cloven tongues of fire or the rush of mighty wind,[86] God sends the invigorating breath of hope to rebuild broken hearts and cure contrite spirits. The gift of hope is not always fleeting, for some hope is infused into their personality.
The gift of hope works in one's spirit as a resilient, residual remembrance of Heaven. To others hope manifests as an unbreakably bright, bubbly nature.

---

[79] Ecclesiastes 5:19
[80] D&C 19:21
[81] Moroni 10:12
[82] Moroni 10:11 – "And to another, exceedingly great faith; and to another, the gifts of healing by the same Spirit."
[83] 1 Corinthians 12:9 – To another faith by the same Spirit; to another the gifts of healing by the same Spirit"
[84] D&C 46:19,20
[85] D&C 46:11
[86] See Acts 2: 2,3

The brightness of hope shines so strong in some that God has given to them to be lights to the world; therewith God enlivens the hopes of those around them. Some accomplish this in their words, others in their works, some in their smiles and others with their cheer.

Wisdom is a gift of the Spirit for we read that *"the Lord gave Solomon wisdom."*[87] To *"some it is given by the Spirit of God, the word of wisdom. To another it is given the word of knowledge, that all may be taught to be wise and to have knowledge."*[88] What makes one wise? Are they more in tune with the Spirit? Or are they the only ones with enough sense to follow it?

According to the gift of wisdom one may have *"the gift of offering prayer,"** or *"the gift of looking to God for guidance."** In like manner, by the Spirit some are given a gift of imagination, creativity or brilliance. To others it is given an ability to craft and make things beautiful. Nevertheless, there are many gifts, and diverse operations wherewith the Spirit manifests itself among the children of men, but *"all these gifts come from God, for the benefit of the children of God."*[89]

Godliness is all around us! As we become aware of the many gifts of the Spirit, we see past the veil into a world of wonder we once knew. So pay attention to man, they who are created in the image of God. Take notice of the divine powers displayed in humanity's expressions and accomplishments. Look closely at the love of a parent. Watch as the care for and patiently put up with an obstinate child, for therein you may catch a glimpse of the Lord's long-suffering. Take notice of the kindness, compassion and love of those close to you, for God reveals portions of His grandeur through man's divine nature. When you weep, consider the tears that fall alongside you. Look! For God is in your midst and uncovers the celestial culture in meekness, patience, humility, peace, joy, service, love, courage and faith. You are a child of God. Godliness is already a part of you – God is already a part of you. With the gift of the Holy Ghost, you have the conduit and promise of Heaven's powers. Therefore, pray to God that the Holy Spirit may awaken your divine nature.

"Awake, and arise from the dust, O Jerusalem; yea, and put on thy beautiful garments, O daughter of Zion!"[90] *"For the eyes of the LORD run to and fro throughout the whole earth to shew himself strong in the behalf of them whose heart is perfect toward him."*[91] God is searching! He is searching for those to whom He can

---

[87] 1 Kings 5:12
[88] D&C 46:17,18
[89] D&C 46:26
[90] Moroni 10:31
[91] 2 Chronicles 16:9

manifest Himself. He is searching for those whom He can show his strength in. Is your heart perfect before God? Are there any left on earth with a pure heart; who 'delight in chastity,'[92] whose 'thoughts are garnished unceasingly' with virtue? If so *"let him come,"*[93] for his *"confidence shall wax strong in the presence of God."*[94]

You are not just capable of hard things; you are capable of great and miraculous things. And though you have been reserved to come forth in these last days, you should not be reserved in your efforts to fulfill your destiny. This destiny is not an endowment and will not drag you along by a leash. Your destiny will not be obtained by talent, but by sacrifice. God, *"according as His divine power hath given unto us all things that pertain unto life and godliness ... hath called us to glory and virtue."*[95] *"Who will rise up for* [Him] *against the evildoers? ... who will stand up for* [Him] *against the workers of inquity?*[96]*" "Awake, awake again, and put on thy strength, O Zion,"*[97] *"it is high time to awake out of sleep; for now is our salvation nearer than when we believed."*[98] *"The kingdom of heaven is at hand ... Hosanna! Blessed be the name of the Most High God."*[99]

---

[92] Jacob 2:28 – "For I, the Lord God, delight in the chastity of women."
[93] Exodus 32:26 – "Moses stood...and said, Who is on the LORD's side? Let him come unto me."
[94] D&C 121:45 – "Let virtue garnish thy thoughts unceasingly; then shall thy confidence wax strong"
[95] 2 Peter 1:3 – Emphasis added
[96] Psalms 94:16 – Brackets added
[97] 3 Nephi 20:36
[98] Romans 13:11
[99] D&C 33:10

REFERENCES

All scriptural quotations are taken from the King James Version of the Holy Bible, The Book of Mormon, The Doctrine and Covenants, and The Pearl of Great Price. Published by: The Church of Jesus Christ of Latter-Day Saints Salt Lake City, Utah, U.S.A. 1989.

Hebrew and Greek dictionary references attributed to –
Strong, James. *A Concise Dictionary of the words in The Hebrew Bible; with their renderings in the Authorized English Version*. Abingdon press: Nashville 1890
Strong, James. *A Concise Dictionary of the words in The Greek Testament; with their renderings in the Authorized English Version*. Abingdon press: Nashville 1890

Godliness

1:39 – Lewis, C.S. *The Quotable Lewis*. Edited by Wayne Martindale and Jerry Root. Tyndale House Publishers Wheaton, Illinois. 1989. p246 (Original Quotation found in Lewis, *The Weight of Glory*, 1942. P18-19)
1:51 – Maxwell, Neal. "The Inexhaustible Gospel." Published in the *Ensign*. April 1993. Adapted from a speech given at BYU August 18, 1992. Retrieved from: https://www.lds.org/ensign/1993/04/the-inexhaustible-gospel?lang=eng

Love

2:2-4 – Smith, Joseph (1805-1844). "The King Follett Sermon." *Ensign*. April and May 1971.
Retrieved from: https://www.lds.org/ensign/1971/04/the-king-follett-sermon?lang=eng&query=follett+(publication %3a%22Ensign%22)
2:30 – Twain, Mark (1835-1910). Retrieved from:
http://www.quotationspage.com/quote/41949.html
Also Quoted by David Meyers *Psychology Eight Edition* (New York: Worth Publishers, 2007), p. 695

Charity

3:67 – Nelson, Russell. "The Atonement." *Ensign*. Nov. 1996. p34
Retrieved from: http://www.lds.org/ensign/1996/11/ the-atonement?lang=eng

Compassion
4:71 – Busche, F. Enzio. "Unleashing the Dormant Spirit." Remarks made during a BYU Devotional May 14, 1996.
Retrieved from: http://www.scribd.com/doc/106857314/Busche-Unleashing-the-Dormant-Spirit-1996-BYU-Dev

Mercy
5:18 – Shaw, Bernard. *Man And Superman*. Act 1. p37 New York Brentano's Publishers (1929). Retrieved from:
http://books.google.com/books?id=XPG0Oo7XANQC&printsec=frontcover&source=gbs_ge_summary_r&cad=0#v=onepage&q&f=false

Kindness
6:5 – Maxwell, Neal. "Patience." *Ensign*. Oct. 1980. p 28. Remarks were made in an address given at BYU November 11, 1979. Retrieved from:
https://www.lds.org/ensign/1980/10/patience?lang=eng

Humility
8:8 – Haight, David. "Joseph Smith, the Prophet." *Ensign*. Dec 2001. Obtained from: http://www.lds.org/ensign/2001/12/joseph-smith-the-prophet?lang=eng
8:62 – Joseph Smith, The King Follett Sermon, Published Ensign April 1971. Obtained from: https://www.lds.org/ensign/1971/04/the-king-follett-sermon?lang=eng&query=follett+(publication%3a%22Ensign%22)
8:66 – Quote attributed to George Bernard Shaw. – Obtained from:
http://thinkexist.com/quotation/most_people_do_not_pray-they_only_beg/206781.html
8:70 – Mark Twain. The Adventures of Huckleberry Finn (Tom Sawyer's Comrade). Harper and Brothers Publishers, New York and London, 1912, Chapter 31 p295

Faith
9:47 – Thomas S. Monson. "Come unto Him in Prayer and Faith." *Ensign*. March 2009

Hope
11: 8 – Sigmund Freud, *The future of an illusion*. (New York: W.W. Norton and Company, 1961) Retrieved from:

http://www.pbs.org/wgbh/questionofgod/ownwords/future2.html
11:43 – Carroll, Lewis. *Alice's Adventures in Wonderland*. (Boston: Lee and Shepard, 1869) p89,90

Joy
12:17 – Neal A. Maxwell. But For A Small Moment. From a speech given September 1, 1974
Retrieved from: http://speeches.byu.edu/?act=viewitem&id=1022
12:37 – Neal A Maxwell. The Pathway of Discipleship. *Ensign*. September 1998. From a talk given at BYU on January 4, 1998
Retrieved from: http://www.lds.org/ensign/1998/09/the-pathway-of-discipleship?lang=eng&query=neal+maxwell +pathway+discipleship

Longsuffering
13:15 – Robert D. Hales. Waiting upon the Lord: Thy Will Be Done. *Ensign*. November 11
13:17– Neal A. Maxwell. The Pathway of Discipleship. *Ensign*. September 1998
13:92 – Winston Churchill. *Churchill, the Life Triumphant*. American Heritage Publishing Co. 1965, p.90

Justice
14:72 – Busche, F. Enzio. "Unleashing the Dormant Spirit." Remarks made during a BYU Devotional May 14, 1996
Retrieved from: http://www.scribd.com/doc/106857314/Busche-Unleashing-the-Dormant-Spirit-1996-BYU-Dev

Honor
16:44 – Neal A. Maxwell. "Settle This in Your Hearts." *Ensign*. November 1992. p65
Obtained from: http://www.lds.org/ldsorg/v/index.jsp?vgnextoid=2354fccf2b7db010VgnVCM1000004d82620aRCRD&locale=0&sourceId=f00b9209df38b010VgnVCM1000004d82620a
16:61 – Young, Brigham. A citation from "Brigham Young's Office Journal, 28 January 1857." *Ensign*. October, 1984
Obtained from: http://www.lds.org/ensign/1984/10/sharing

The Gifts of the Spirit
17:9 – William Shakespeare. Hamlet. Act 2 Scene 2.(Leipzid Bernh Taughnitz Jun. 1843) p40
17:29 – Truman G. Madsen. "Souls Aflame" From a BYU devotional given November 8, 1983
17:55 – Bruce R. McConkie. A New Witness for the Articles of Faith. p371
17:56 – Marvin J. Ashton Conference Report. Oct. 1987, p23

www.ingramcontent.com/pod-product-compliance
Lightning Source LLC
LaVergne TN
LVHW041614070426
835507LV00008B/231